LATIN AMERICA

James Petras
Editor

Petras, James F1, 1957—

Latin America:
From Dependence
to Revolution

JOHN WILEY & SONS, INC. | NEW YORK LONDON SYDNEY TORONTO

Library of Congress Cataloging in Publication Data:

Petras, James F   1937-
Latin America: from dependence to revolution.

1. South America—Politics—20th century—Addresses, essays, lectures. 2. South America—Economic conditions—1918-   —Addresses, essays, lectures. 3. South America—Relations (general) with the United States—Addresses, essays, lectures. 4. United States— Relations (general) with South America—Addresses, essays, lectures. I. Title.

F2237.P47   320.9'8'003   72-13437
ISBN 0-471-68446-5
ISBN 0-471-68444-9 (pbk)

Printed in the United States of America

10-9 8 7 6 5 4 3 2 1

TO LUCIANO CRUZ
AND RODRIGO AMBROSIO,
WHO DIED BEFORE THEIR TIME

Preface

The main concern of this book is the contrasting styles of development found in Brazil and Chile in the context of a changing political environment.

During 1970 to 1971, while I was collecting documents, conducting interviews and traveling through several South American countries, I was struck by the revitalization of political life in contrast to previous visits in the middle to the late 1960s, a period of declining revolutionary movements, stable military regimes, general political depression, and economic stagnation.

Although no new social revolutions have occurred during the 1970s and, except for several countries (such as Chile and Peru), few reforms of lasting value have been consummated, there is a sense in which the oppressive and imposed "apathy" of the late 1960s is gone. In Argentina, mass general strikes are almost a monthly phenomena, the military elite is on the defensive, and traditional Argentine political life is slowly being undermined. In Uruguay the long-standing commitments to the traditional parties are wearing thin; popular discontent is finding expression through a new left-wing coalition: The Broad Front or through the Tupamaros guerrilla groups. In 1971 in Bolivia a popular assembly was organized—on the basis of elections held in the factories, mines, and fields (since then there has been a military coup that has perhaps temporarily arrested the process). Even in countries where revolutionary politics appeared to be dying, as in Columbia and Venezula, new nationalist and populist movements are emerging and redefining class and foreign relations. Countertrends also appeared in the form of the increasingly effective rule of the Brazilian military regime; its highly publicized growth patterns and its defeat of the guerrilla groups impressed many observers who were disturbed both by the rising tide of popular mobilization and the incapacity of Latin countries to sustain high rates of growth. Because of this fluid situation I came to two conclusions. The analysis and projections of the 1960s regarding Latin America's allegedly "conservative" or alternatively "revolutionary" future were being challenged in ways unforeseen by journalists and scholars. Latin America was developing a whole new set of options that did not "fit" the patterns prescribed by U.S. or Latin American social scientists. Second and more important, the "models" that were being considered were no longer Cuba or the United States—but Chile and Brazil. More and more, Latin Americans were looking at themselves and their neighbors, trying to determine which development options were most appropriate. The essays in this book examine the new trends in Latin American politics and future possibilities within circumstances that have evolved in the recent past.

In lectures and discussions in seminars, classrooms, and political meetings, students and professors have raised many of the questions that the essays deal with: How viable is the Chilean road to socialism? Can the Brazilian military overcome backwardness and develop the economy? What are the possibilities for basic changes in Argentina? What role will the United States play in Latin America in the 1970s? I owe a great deal to the students and professors in North and South America, whose intellectual curiosity, commitment to human liberation, and continuing concern for such issues and problems have put many of these questions in the forefront of scholarly concern.

Contents

James Petras | Introduction

This volume of essays is concerned with the major issues of inequality, development, dependency, and participation in several critical countries: Chile, Brazil, and Argentina, nations which today have generated the greatest amount of attention and concern among scholars, policy makers, and political activists in both South America and North America. The essays vary in their approach; close-up, empirical studies as well as broad-range, interpretative, historical essays. By combining an analysis of the present with an interpretation of the past, we can best understand the process of change and rediscovery in the area. My view of Latin America is that the multifaceted polarization emerging will eventually bring about radical structural changes and produce new alignments not only within the continent but in international politics. Polarization is occurring on several levels; on the international level between the U.S. and Latin American nationalists; on the regional level between Chile and Brazil; and on the national level between the industrial elite (and its allies among foreign investors, bankers, and landlords) and the industrial workers and peasants (and their allies among students, white collar workers, and the marginal poor). The focus of these essays is on the social forces and regimes that contribute to or oppose the process of change as well as the policies that are fashioned in pursuit of change or stability.

The polarization within Latin societies is now expressed on the national level; the choice is between the Brazilian and Chilean development approaches. The Brazilian effort embodies the notion that rapid economic development can forestall revolution and secure the position of the economic elites through the trickling down of wealth to the poor. The Chilean effort is directed at bringing about a more egalitarian society (before the constraints of the parliamentary system forestall the promised changes) as a precondition for inducing commitment to development. Regional polarization between Chilean-style socialism and Brazilian "corporatism" most clearly defines the options open to the rest of Latin America.

The options, however, are mediated through the political forces in each country. Latin American countries respond to the demands for social change and development according to their own history and social structure. For example, in Colombia the push for social change has come from populist forces led by General Pinilla. In the declining postpopulist welfare states of Argentina and Uruguay, the downward cycle of the economy has accentuated class conflict; in these countries the Brazilian and Chilean "examples" are being most seriously considered.

The rapid rise and fall of conservative and/or populist governments in Latin America, and the varied and shifting policies adopted by conservative and/or populist regimes is in part due to the lack of any broad and firm basis of social support that would be willing to sustain a serious development effort. The increasing reliance on informal and formal mechanisms of control—for example, police-training courses funded by AID—may have contributed to short-term stability but most likely have postponed the day of reckoning. The existing "legitimate" parties and leadership groups, self-selected from among the agrocomercial, financial and industrial elites, no longer have the capacity to channel demands of workers, peasants, and poor people generally. The alternative has been the heightening of political repression and police control to restrain demands.

Large-scale migration to the city, the growth of massive urban slums, and the lack of governmental services to provide bureaucratic linkages with the growing "unincorporated urban masses" have led in the past to emergence of mass national-populist movements. Populist movements have had a larger popular following than most socialist movements in Latin America. The prominent cases include ANAPO in Colombia, Peronism in Argentina, APRA and now the military regime in Peru, and Vargas and Goulart in Brazil. Even today the populist movements have great appeal among the less politicized masses in Argentina as well as in other countries in the region. Nevertheless, populist governments have been unstable coalitions of antagonistic social forces, which have led to the eventual downfall (or overthrow) of the populist caudillo. Historically, populism has not been a long-term stable alternative to traditional elite rule. The recent history of Chile and Brazil illustrate this clearly; in Chile the populist Christian Democratic government of Frei and in Brazil the populist Labor Party government of Goulart were transitory phenomena leading to a more radical socialist government in Chile and a corporatist solution in Brazil.

Along with the problem of mass political exclusion, the key issue facing Latin American intellectuals and policy makers is the problem of "dependence"—foreign control over key economic resources and Latin American reliance on foreign technology, capital, exports, and markets. Writers on this theme have distinguished between traditional and modern dependence. Traditional dependence involved direct foreign ownership of raw materials (agromineral products), commerce, and banking and was usually found in very underdeveloped, largely agricultural societies, principally in the Caribbean area. The newer forms of dependence occur largely in relatively modern urban semiindustrialized societies, such as Argentina, which have partially broken with the pattern of rural-elite domination and have developed modern industries. Despite its "modern industries," Argentina has not been able to develop an autonomous "national" pattern of development, falling victim to new forms of foreign control and dependence; foreign firms control the technology, capital, research, and, more and more, the major industries. Petras and Cook's essay on the Argentine industrial executives describes the background of the industrial elite and their attitudes toward collaboration with foreign investors—suggesting that autonomous nationalist economic development is hardly likely to develop under the auspices of the "national" bourgeoisie even in a Latin American country such as Argentina, which has the most established and entrenched industrial groups.

In past years, U.S. writers have argued for a moderate democratic approach to the problems of exclusion and underdevelopment, and the "middle sectors" were presented as the classic group capable of carrying through democratic change. The problems of economic and popular exclusion were for years thought to be problems of Latin American countries that did not possess a bourgeoisie. Nevertheless, from 1966 to 1973 Argentina was ruled by a military dictatorship which was supported by the middle class—at least initially. In the 1970s inflation, economic stagnation, and spiraling foreign debts have generated massive strikes, guerrilla activity, and political repression. Argentina has become "Latin Americanized." The political economy of social and economic regression (away from a progressive democratic welfare state toward an impoverished underdeveloped authoritarian state) has contributed to the growing support among a variety of elite groups for nondemocratic forms of participation. The failure of police state capitalism and its inability to deal adequately with key socioeconomic issues and the ambiguity among Argentine elites regarding democratic and Brazilian-type solutions are discussed in the second paper by Petras and Cook.

Prospects for change and development in Latin America appeared dim throughout most of the 1960s; the Alliance for Progress and its Latin American supporters (the self-styled "democratic left") failed to accomplish their goals, while the revolutionary left was temporarily defeated or isolated.

Nevertheless, in the 1970s Latin American countries face two radically different approaches to the problems of development and change. In Chile, the Marxist Left through free elections has won the presidency and has initiated a development program including nationalization of major foreign holdings and massive expropriation of large landed estates. On the other hand, the rightist military regime in Brazil, which seized power in 1964, has in recent years initiated a far-reaching program to promote economic development based largely on concessions to private investors, especially foreigners. The Chilean and Brazilian experiences each pose different answers to the problems of popular participation, economic development, and social change. The two essays by Petras on Chile and by Tavares and Serra on Brazil analyze the differential benefits and costs of each development strategy for different social classes. No longer is it deemed sufficient to consider growth or change as ends in themselves. The questions that the authors ask and attempt to answer is, "Change and growth for whom?" "What social forces benefit from current policies?" The U.S. government has already indicated which development strategy it approves; President Nixon has pointed to Brazil as the leader in Latin America. On the other hand, the Chilean socialist government has attracted numerous supporters throughout Latin America. The issue has been joined; the resolution will have a profound effect on all of Latin America in the 1970s.

The liberal democratic formulas have little or no appeal or following in Latin America today. Liberalism apparently does not carry weight with U.S. policymakers—despite the ritualistic lip service that is still paid to "democracy" on ceremonial occasions. Today discussion no longer revolves around the problems of dictatorship or democracy. The issues that are discussed at international conferences and in government ministries, in universities and in clandestine meetings of armed insurgents include the "marginal masses," dependency, structural change, modernization, and economic development.

The larger conditioning factor affecting the alternative development options open to Latin American nations is U.S. policy. The ability of the Latin Americans to fashion their "own" distinctive national or regional solutions depends on the policy posture adopted in the United States. The high degree of U.S. economic, political, and military involvement within Latin America means that the United States can influence and in turn will be affected by radical shifts within Latin American societies.

The two pivotal issues around which U.S.-Latin American relations have revolved are embodied in the Monroe Doctrine and economic nationalism. The case has been made that for Latin America the problem has not been one of expansion but of survival—the defense of its sovereignty, first from European and later from U.S. incursions. The Latin American response to the Monroe Doctrine has taken the form of juridical declarations of self-determination, frequently embodied in hemispheric treaties. In the twentieth century, growth of U.S. political and military power and influence throughout the hemisphere was paralleled by the penetration of the Latin American economies. Hence it was natural that Latin American nationalism would manifest itself increasingly in the economic sphere; the notion of self-determination was expanded to include national control of basic economic resources and industries. Long-term U.S. hegemony in the hemisphere codified in the Monroe Doctrine has been periodically challenged by indigenous movements intent on modifying the terms of dependence or rupturing the relationship. The linkage of U.S. policy with business interests in Latin America has led to governmental intervention and pressure on Latin American governments on behalf of U.S. corporate interests. In the last quarter of the twentieth century, the major conflict looming on the horizon involves the economic expansion of the United States and rising economic nationalism to the south.

An adequate discussion of the development options and their costs must face the problems posed by U.S. policy. The choice that Latin America developmentalists make—especially the decision to free themselves of U.S. tutelage—has costs as well as benefits. In the last section of the book, the U.S. response to economic nationalism as well as the evolution of the Monroe Doctrine are examined in some detail in order to place the development options of the Latin American nations in international perspective. It is out of the matrix of internal development efforts, external dependency, and U.S. policy decisions that the new Latin American polities will be shaped.

I am grateful to numerous colleagues and friends, in Latin America as well as in the United States, for their help and encouragement: David Baytelman, Hugo Zemelman, Ernesto Benado, Jacques Chonchol, Manuel Garreton, Anibal Quijano, Jose Nun, Guillermo Lora, Antonio Castro, Theotonio Dos Santos, Irving Horowitz, David Apter, Richard Falk, Paul Sweezy, Maurice Zeitlin and numerous other students and scholars. I would like to thank the Ford Foundation and the Social Science Research Council for the fellowships that allowed me to do field work. I would also like to thank Carl Beers for his editorial suggestions and comments.

1

Alternative Approaches
to Development:
Left and Right

1

James Petras | Political and Social Change in Chile

The process of political and social change in Chile can best be understood by discussing several dimensions which together provide an adequate account and explanation of the events that are occurring. The areas to be explored include:

1. Preconditions for sociopolitical change.
2. Factors facilitating the peaceful transition of governmental transfer from Frei to Allende.
3. The breadth of change—institutional and structural changes.
4. The depth of change—measuring changes in perception and political consciousness among radical or potential constituents of the Allende government.
5. The tempo of change—discussion of time periods in relation to the subjective and objective conditions that facilitate or block change as well systemic constraints on the transition to socialism.
6. Options, alternatives, and consequences for the future—the nature of confrontation and possible realignment of political forces.

PRECONDITIONS FOR CHANGE

Two sets of interrelated factors led to the profound changes that have occurred in Chile during the early years of the Allende government. One general category can be considered "global contextual factors"; the other can be considered "internal conditions." The former allows us to see how the world political situation impinges on political developments inside Chile; the other focuses on the more specific question of the internal social conditions and socioeconomic basis for a socialist government.

EXTERNAL FACTORS FACILITATING CHANGE

Two aspects of the external situation were favorable to change within Chile—the position of the regional hegemonic power (the United States) and the "political climate" in the South American region (the rise of regional nationalism).

In the decade following the Cuban Revolution, there was a continent-wide confrontation between the United States, with its allies among the Latin American propertied groups, and a broad assortment of revolutionary forces, backed in various degrees by the popular classes. In each country where a major revolutionary force appeared to be gaining support and preparing to take power, the United States and the native Latin American ruling classes, aided by the armed forces, intervened and prevented the victory of a popular government.

For a brief period (roughly the years 1964 to 1968), it appeared that United States hegemony was once again firmly established. Guerrillas were in retreat or decimated, popular leaders were in exile or jailed, and pro-U.S. policy makers such as Castelo Branco and then Costa e Silva in Brazil, Barrientos in Bolivia, Ongania in Argentina, Frei in Chile, Belaunde in Peru, Lleras Restrepo in Colombia, Pacheco Areco in Uruguay, Leoni in Venezuela, and Balaguer in the Dominican Republic, reigned throughout the continent.

The military-political phase of the restoration of U.S. hegemony was eminently successful, but it rested on a very fragile socioeconomic structure. Vast inequalities persisted, spawning the hostility of the poor and the alienation of the intellectuals, students, certain churchmen, and military officers. Only the active visible vanguards had been destroyed. Discontent had been repressed, not eliminated, by the counterinsurgency programs funded by the United States. And the expansion of United States capital during this period definitively displaced the national bourgeoisie: the multinational corporation proletarianized the Latin nations, increasing their dependency and awakening dormant nationalist sentiments. In general, although the United States was not heavily committed to any particular area, it had a relatively free hand in its dealings with Latin America.

This situation changed rapidly in the late 1960s. The price exacted by United States policy makers (and sectors of the Latin American ruling class) for securing their immediate interests was deemed too high by portions of the lower-middle and middle class. The countries' increased dependency was felt by sectors of the armed forces. Military governments took power in Bolivia and Peru, and nationalized U.S. enterprises. In Colombia, Argentina, Uruguay, Venezuela, and Ecuador large-scale demonstrations against the U.S. presence demanded structural reforms and nationalist policies.

Allende's victory in Chile and the mass mobilizations throughout most of Latin America are an integral part of this new nationalist upsurge—nourished by, and in turn feeding, it.

Moreover, the massive commitment of U.S. manpower and economic resources in Southeast Asia, the subsequent military and political stalemate, and the almost unanimous rejection of the war in the United States have considerably weakened U.S. capacity to manage and control political affairs in the southern hemisphere. The obsession with Southeast Asia and the growing internal malaise cut the United States off from the changing realities of Latin America. The old certainties were shattered: the certainty that Latin generals would always follow the orientation of the United States; the certainty that eliminating rural guerrillas eliminates social revolution; the certainty that security and private investment would bring about generalized prosperity; the certainty that United States loans, technical know-how, and reformist governments would always defeat the "communists" in truly free elections.

It is in this international context—where the U.S. capacity to dominate local situations in the Third World has at least temporarily been weakened, and where old policies are no longer relevant (and new policies have yet to be devised)—that a Marxist Socialist, Allende, was able to take office in Chile. With the exception of Brazil (and its satellite, Paraguay) the United States does not have a single ally in Latin America even remotely capable of mounting a serious political campaign to topple the Allende government. The only policy the United States can follow is to hope for the development of an internal subversive movement capable of providing the basis for an interventionist policy.

These circumstances helped make it possible for the Chilean Left to take over the government, but did not completely eliminate serious problems in the transfer of power.

Allende's victory surprised many people, including the U.S. Ambassador (one week before the election he assured a visiting U.S. professor that the victory of Alessandri was certain and cited private polling results), and perhaps the Left itself. *Unidad Popular* (UP)—the left-wing coalition that elected Allende is called Popular Unity—did not have a meeting place arranged or microphones set up to celebrate the victory on election night.

INTERNAL FACTORS FACILITATING CHANGE

Three sets of internal factors were linked to the deteriorating position of the external force that facilitated change: the socioeconomic conditions within Chile, the relatively high degree of class consciousness and organization, and the division among the antisocialist political forces.

The six-year term of Christian Democratic President Eduardo Frei did little to alter the basic inequalities that characterized Chilean socity. The halfway measures adopted to redistribute income and land did not greatly affect the prerogatives of the rich and at best raised expectations that were subsequently frustrated. The great concentration of economic wealth, especially in the banking, industrial, and commercial sectors, were not adversely affected by the Frei government's policies. The growth of foreign enterprise participation in the manufacturing sector may have actually contributed to heightening the distance between owners and workers. The high degree of social rigidity evidenced throughout Chilean history continued. The proportion of sons and daughters of workers and peasants having access to higher education continued to be infinitesimal. Within the several score industrial enterprises that account for over 60 percent of total output, an industrial working class was recruited, disciplined, and concentrated. Within the Chilean industrial proletariat, there were ties with the combatitive mining workers and unions. Born within a tradition of class struggle, the industrial workers turned to class solidarity and organization as the most reliable and secure method for achieving their immediate socioeconomic ends. The relatively high degree of industrialization, literacy, and social organization—combined with the continuation of a high degree of inequality and social rigidity created the conditions for the emergence of class politics—the organization of parties, elections and struggle around class alignments, allegiances and appeals.

For many years, U.S. and Latin American sociologists circulated the notion that support for Marxist socialism was largely a product of the economic backwardness and "tradionalism" of Third World countries; that modern urban industrial cities served to "moderate" the outlook and behavior of the working class—especially the better paid industrial workers. Some sociologists who accepted this view began to speak of "integrated" sectors or classes (including urban industrial workers) and "marginal" classes. The notion of a "bourgeoisified" industrial proletariat even shaped the outlook of left-wing intellectuals who began to speak of a "labor aristocracy" and to look to the peasantry as the sole basis of hope for a revolutionary transformation. The idea that the working class could combine and act as a class in favor of a socialist society against capitalist exploitation and inequality seems to have eluded scores of U.S. investigators who claim to study the lower classes in Latin America. A careful analysis of the political behavior of the Chilean working class refutes the "integration" thesis.

From its formation in 1956, the Marxist Popular Action Front (FRAP) directed its political activity toward gaining the support of the working class. In 1958, the FRAP candidate, Salvador Allende, lost by a margin of 35,000 votes out of a total of 1.3 million votes. In the 1964 elections, in a virtual two-way race, Allende gathered about 39 percent of the vote (about 45 percent of the male vote). In 1970, Allende, the candidate of the Marxist-led Popular Unity, won the election with 36.2 percent of the vote. The major base of support in all three elections was the industrial proletariat located in the modern urban-industrial centers.

As Table 1 indicates, in 1970 FRAP obtained the support of the municipalities (comunas) that had the highest concentration of industrial workers. The higher the proportion of industrial workers, the higher the ratio of votes in favor of Allende. Obviously, the experience with a Christian Democratic government did not change the workers' political loyalty; on the contrary, the voting ratio of Allende to Alessandri, and Allende to Tomic, seems to have increased. The Presidential voting results suggest that the Christian Democratic "reform" government completely failed to win over the working class, as many of its supporters both in Chile and the U.S. had hoped. The industrial workers chose to maintain their loyalty to the Marxist candidate and to reject the Christian Democratic alternative.

The Christian Democrats, proponents of a "third way" between socialism and capitalism, found little support among the class-conscious Chilean working class for their program. No doubt the links between the Christian Democrats and U.S. and Chilean businessmen weakened their ability to pass social legislation and economic reforms that would have redistributed income and increased the participation of the working class in the industrial system. This suggests that the ability of the Unidad Popular to maintain itself in

TABLE 1

Relative Indices of Votes between Allende and Frei (1964), Allende and Alessandri (1970), Allende and Tomic (1970). Masculine Votes in Nine of the most Important Cities and Towns of Chile (Percentages)

Percent of the Labor Forces in Manufacturing, Mining and Construction		City or Town	Number of Allende Votes for Each 100 Votes for Frei (1964)		Number of Allende Votes for Each 100 Votes for Allessandri (1970)		Number of Allende Votes for Each 100 Votes for Tomic (1970)	
Under 30	20	Temuco	51		78		108	
	25	Chillan	113	80[a]	175	129	225	154
	28	Valparaiso	75		135		129	
30-35	30	Vina del Mar	71		100		130	
	30	Talca	112	100	193	151	194	182
	30	Antofagasta	116		159		222	
36-40	36	Valdivia	122		173		247	
	39	Concepcion	95	117	153	208	170	204
	30	Talcahuano	134		299		196	

I   [1] All the   [a] Average.

political power will depend on its capacity to meet the demands of the industrial working class for radical anticapitalist changes in the urban industrial centers.

The non-working class municipalities continued to give their support to the Right (Alessandri) and to the Christian Democrats (see Table 2). This suggests that the political support of the non-Marxist parties (Radicals, API, Social Democrats, and MAPU) was largely irrelevant in determining the size of the vote for Allende in the urban centers.[1] The size of Allende's vote in

---

[1] In rural Chile, MAPU played an important role in mobilizing peasant support for Allende.

TABLE 2
Relative Indices of Votes between Allende and Frei (1964), Allende and Alessandri (1970), Allende and Tomic (1970). Masculine Votes in the Comunas (Municipalities) of Gran Santiago Classified by the Relative Size of its Working Class (Percentages)

Percent of the Labor Forces in Manufacturing, Mining and Construction		Commune or Municipality	Number of Allende Votes for Each 100 Votes for Frei (1964)		Number of Allende Votes for Each 100 Votes for Allessandri (1970)		Number of Allende Votes for Each 100 Votes for Tomic (1970)	
Less than 20	9	Calera de Tango	68		100		70	
	9	Lampa	89		122		117	
	13	Providencia	29	71	31	80	82	105
	16	Quilcura	79		108		152	
	19	Las Condes	42		47		103	
20-29	27	Nunoa	59	59	86	86	142	142
30-39	31	Santiago	67		94		143	
	32	San Bernardo	92		146		155	
	35	La Florida	65	80	108	134	161	162
	36	Maipu	85		153		171	
	39	Conchali	92		168		180	
40-49	43	Puente Alto	104		166		252	
	45	La Cisterna	90		164		188	
	46	Quinta Normal	96	103	168	188	191	203
	46	Renca	104		193		179	
	46	Barrancas	122		250		205	
50 or more	51	San Miguel	114	121.5	208	235	238	258
	52	La Granja	129		261		277	

the urban industrial centers was largely the result of the traditional voting behavior of the industrial proletariat. Thus the non-Marxist parties are probably overrepresented in the seats of government in relationship to their contribution to Allendes' victory. Political agreements with the non-Marxist parties, while they served to bolster the image of a "multiparty government," worked against a coherent and profound reform program that could have sustained the popular support of the government. The imbalance between the homogeneous social base of the Allende victory (largely industrial working class socialists and communists) and the politically heterogeneous character of the party leadership has caused serious problems—such as Allende's vacillation in choosing the constituency that he wishes to serve.

The second major basis of support for the Left was the mining sector, consistent supporters of Marxist political parties for several decades. Even among the highest paid sectors of the industrial proletariat (copper workers), Allende received over 2½ times the vote of Alessandri. And in the ultramodern, technologically advanced Chuquicamata mine, Allende received 106 votes for every 100 votes for Alessandri. The notion of a "workers' aristocracy" hardly serves to explain the behavior of this highly paid sector of the labor force—which may have voted for the nationalization of the mines

TABLE 3

Relative Indices of Vote between Allende and Alessandri and Allende and Tomic (1970). Masculine Votes in the Mining Centers (Percentages)

	Number of Allende Votes for Each 100 Votes for Alessandri		Number of Allende Votes for Each 100 Votes for Tomic	
Copper Mining Zones				
Chuquicamata	106		301	
Potrerillos	232	265	225	303
Sewell	406	(average)	307	
El Salvador	319		381	
Nitrate mining zones				
Iquique	194		258	
Pozo Almonte	300		289	
Lagunas	130	325	173	337
Toco	412		541	
Pedro de Valdivia	591		426	
Coal mining zone				
Coronel	640		448	
Lota	916	794	658	571
Curanilahue	827		608	

knowing that it might not improve its standard of living but, instead, serve Chilean economic development.

As Table 3 suggests, the mining workers expressed a high degree of class solidarity, rejected the nonsocialist alternatives, and voted in overwhelming numbers for the Socialist, Allende. The political implications are clear. A social basis for an extensive program of nationalization of mines clearly exists in the sectors of the labor force most intimately involved. If Allende fails to carry out his program of nationalization, it cannot be blamed on the lack of political support.

The third major support for Allende's victory was urban working class women. Most observers have mistakenly generalized about the conservative voting behavior of Chilean women without taking account of the *class differences among women*. If we take all the municipalities in greater Santiago that contain 40 percent or more industrial workers (see Table 4), we find that Allende received 119 feminine votes for every 100 for Alessandri and 147 for every 100 for Tomic.

If we consider the only two municipalities in the capital city of Santiago with an absolute majority of industrial workers (San Miguel and Granja), Allende received 130 feminine votes for every 100 for Alessandri and 203 for every 100 for Tomic.

It appears that when modern industrial capitalist economic and social relations penetrate the Chilean household and when strong working-class organizations emerge, they have the effect of breaking down the traditionalist

TABLE 4
Relative Indices of Votes between Allende and Alessandri and Allende and Tomic (1970). Female Votes in Seven Working Class Municipalities (Comunas) in Greater Santiago (Percentages)

Percent of Labor Force in Manufacturing, Mining and Construction	Municipalities (Communes)	Number of Allende Votes for Each 100 Votes for Alessandri	Number of Allende Votes for Each 100 Votes for Tomic
40 or more	Puente Alto La Cisterna Quinta Normal Penco Barrancas San Miguel Granja	119	147
50 or more	San Miguel Granja	130	203

beliefs of women, making them receptive to radical political movements. The social concentration of class-conscious workers in particular neighborhoods appears to create a radical political culture that destroys the traditional paternalistic values that have customarily influenced women voters. In other social contexts, the lower proportion of women voting for the Left is probably due to the fact that the women's vote is disproportionately influenced by such nonclass factors as the mass media.

From a theoretical viewpoint, the social situation of work in a dependent capitalist society, the experiences that the workers acquire there, the conflicts engendered, and the manner of resolving them are the central determinants of the working-class vote.

The massive support of the Socialist and Communist parties resides in the working class, and this provides, particularly when they are politically allied, a cohesive and strategically situated social base that can be mobilized for social and political struggles and change. The Christian Democrats were not able to overcome the immobilism of the social situation, mainly because its base was (and is) constituted by a heterogeneous mass of individuals with contradictory values and interests.

The radicalization of the industrial working class in Chile is largely the result of the failure of Chilean and U.S. capitalist to generate dynamic development. At the same time, the radicalized workers, through their social struggles and political power, have provided the Marxist parties with an opportunity to develop Chilean society through socialist policies and institutions.

Despite the solid support that the Left received from the economically active sectors of the lower class, without the division of the opposition a Socialist would not have been elected to the presidency. The conflicts between the antisocialist forces and the rivalry between the right-wing National Party and the Christian Democrats was instrumental in allowing Allende to gain the presidency without an absolute majority.[2] The theoretical problem that this raises can be posed in the following way. Under what conditions will an antisocialist opposition fragment, creating political divisions that allow for the coming to power of a socialist government? Basically two sets of interrelated factors can be cited to explain the division of the antisocialist forces: the policies of the Christian Democratic government of Frei (1964 to 1970) and their impact on the upper and lower classes, and, the conflicting tactical approaches adopted by the two forces in response to the Frei-induced changes.

The efforts by the Frei government to modernize but not revolutionize Chilean society generated conflict on two sides; sufficient changes occurred

[2] The possibility of a Socialist candidate winning a majority before taking office is highly unlikely given the capacity of the bourgeosie to manipulate the less politically aware among the lower class. Even after taking state power the task of creating a socialist majority is onerous.

(especially in the areas of peasant unionism, taxation, and land distribution), to antagonize propertied groups, but insufficient changes occurred to satisfy the rising expectations of the propertyless groups. Caught between the conflicting demands of his polyclass constituency, Frei alternated pacifying the needs of one at the expense of the other and ended by alienating substantial sectors of his original electoral coalition.

Two conflicting responses emerged among the antisocialist forces that had supported Frei against Allende. One approach, favored by the Right and promoted by the candidacy of Alessandri, took the line that change under Frei had gone far enough and that the time had come to "consolidate" the reforms and promote development and productivity. The second approach, embraced by the left-wing of the Christian Democratic Party (PDC) and the presidential standard bearer of that party, Radomiro Tomic, proposed extending changes to integrate the masses in the "revolutionary process."

The halfway measures of the reformist government led to further social polarization, which in turn generated political conflict among the parties of the property groups—which allowed the Left to win the elections. It was almost a year after Allende took office that the antisocialist alliance was re-formed under the leadership of the conservative wing of the Christian Democratic Party. The threat to private property interests was sufficient cause to heal the wounds of internecine warfare among the antisocialist forces.

THE TRANSITION FROM FREI TO ALLENDE: PEACEFUL CHANGE AND LATENT VIOLENCE. Following the electoral victory, Allende and the UP faced two critical problems: the successful transfer of government; and the selection of the first political measures to establish the initial image of the new government. The Chilean Left distinguishes clearly between control over the executive branch of the government and control over the productive and financial resources of the society. Obviously the former facilitates the latter.

The Christian Democratic government of Eduardo Frei did everything possible—short of provoking civil war—to avoid handing the government over to the UP. Economic reports by Minister of Economy Zaldivar describing the flight of capital were publicized by all the mass media, which stimulated panic, while inadequate measures were taken to prevent the sacking of the nation's economy. Security controls were lax, despite the overt action of right-wing terrorists. Plots and conspiracies were not detected, and the attempted kidnapping of the commander-in-chief of the Army, General Schneider, led instead to his assassination.

The Christian Democratic Party demanded and received a guarantee from the UP that all their political appointees throughout the middle and lower levels of the bureaucracy would remain; this was part of the package formally described as a Guarantee of Democratic Rights. The UP was able to surmount these obstacles during this period principally because of massive support from the working class, peasants, students, and trade unions, who stood ready to launch a civil war if the PDC or the right wing attempted to violate the constitution and customary rules of the game.

As the confidential memoranda of the International Telephone and Telegraph Company subsequently revealed, Frei wavered between joining in a CIA-inspired conspiracy to overthrow the Allende government and efforts to create economic havoc. The U.S. Ambassador Korry who was actively involved in the plotting was considerably annoyed by Frei's "weakness"—his incapacity to act decisively to block Allende taking office. What is abundently clear however is that the Frei government's lax security measures and fear-inspiring economic policies were not errors but calculated moves directed toward undermining the electoral choice. The Christian Democratic Party and their U.S. partners, especially ITT, did not willingly give up power for the sake of an abstract ideal called the "democratic tradition," but for very specific reasons. Three factors account for the relatively peaceful transfer of office: the latent threat of violence on the part of the Left, made credible by the existence of a mobilized mass; the existence of revolutionary organizations (the Movement of the Revolutionary Left—MIR), which neutralized the efforts by the Right to carry on terrorist activity mainly through intelligence work; the existence of a reformist wing in the PDC willing to recognize Allende's victory because it supported many initial nationalist democratic reforms of the Popular Unity program.

Writers and commentators have stressed the importance of the Chilean democratic tradition and the customary peaceful nature of political change, yet no explanation is given as to why these traditions and customs were maintained during this specific event (the election and assumption of government by a Marxist). In reality, of course, violent attempts were made by the right wing to block the transfer of government. More important, serious consideration was given, in discussions among the major antisocialist parties, to proposals that could have prevented Allende from taking power. What prevented these projects from taking hold was the threat of violence by the Left. Leading spokesmen of the Socialist and Communist parties openly declared that if Allende was not allowed to take office—if the democratic rules of the game were violated—a civil war would result. The Christian Democratic leaders took these warnings very seriously. Despite the inclination of the right-wing PDC to accept a deal with the right-wing National Party, they did not want to be "responsible for a civil war that could lead to unforeseen consequences," as one of the ministers in Frei's cabinet said to me after the elections. The fact that a minimal amount of open violence took place does not mean that potential violence was not an important factor in preventing the "losers" from denying the UP its victory; the mass organizations of the UP, their potential for paralyzing the economy, their availability for street combat and armed confrontation ensured that the "democratic tradition" was maintained. It was quite probable that in the absence of a mobilized mass and of the explicit threat of violence, the democratic tradition might easily have been violated.

Apart from the threat of a massive violent confrontation, the UP was aided by the support of the defeated presidential aspirant of the PDC, Radomiro Tomic. Within the PDC, pressure from the Left prevented the Party from aligning itself with the right-wing National Party in the Congress to prevent Allende's election.

The timely intelligence work of the Movement of the Revolutionary Left (MIR), which had infiltrated the right-wing terrorist groups, prevented the Right from realizing its plans of sabotage and assassination.

Both on the political and security fronts, therefore, the UP was able to neutralize and even capitalize on the problems it encountered. The abortive right-wing terror campaign, which culminated in the assassination of General Schneider, contributed to the growth of support for the UP and to the isolation of the Right. The UP gathered support from broad sectors of the lower-middle class and even of the middle class, which were repelled by the violent methods of Allende's opponents.

THE BREADTH OF SOCIOECONOMIC CHANGE: INCREMENTAL AND INSTITUTIONAL CHANGES. Two policy approaches were put into practice by the Socialist government. One set of measures was essentially short-run impact programs (to last 6 to 12 months) to elicit popular support and build electoral support. The long-term larger structural changes were directed at transforming the basic structure and organization of the Chilean economy. To measure the breadth of change it is important to consider three aspects to the Chilean process and their impact on political development: the multisectoral dimensions of the process (the agrarian, financial, and mining reforms); the equalitarian measures adopted to promote income distribution; and the advances in productivity.

During the first few weeks of the new government, each of the six political forces making up the UP struggled to maximize its share of positions in the government. These forces include the Socialist, Communist, Social Democratic, and Radical parties, the United Popular Action Movement (MAPU), and the Independent Popular Action group (API). As a result, many posts were filled rather slowly, and this delayed the programming of government activities. In addition, Allende was obligated to retain the great majority of functionaries from the Frei government. Many of these officials were at best indifferent, and in many cases hostile to the new programs and policies. Once in office, the left-wing ministers were faced with a new problem. Little prior attention had been given to the formulation of a government program; most energies had been concentrated on the electoral struggle and subsequently on securing the transfer of government.

The UP government's first task was to establish its strategic goals, and then to define immediate measures. The economic program of the new government was oriented toward the "transformation of the traditional structures of dependent capitalism, in favor of characteristics and forms which the Chilean people wish to impose."

This program, the "Chilean Road to Socialism," defines three types of property: (1) state property, deriving from the expropriation of "foreign and national monopoly enterprises, especially those connected with natural resources, banks and finance, industry, distribution, foreign commerce, and all those areas strategic to national development"; (2) the area of mixed property, in which private capital (national and foreign) participates with state capital, and is managed jointly; and (3) the areas of private property (largely small and medium firms, retail enterprises, and the like).

The second objective of the government's policy was the redistribution of income, through wage and price policies, to favor the lower half of the population. The third objective was to broaden and accelerate the agrarian reform —to break up the latifundio and increase agricultural productivity.

Having defined its general policy, the government hastened to take a number of immediate measures to affirm its authenticity as a government of the people.

ESTABLISHING A NEW IMAGE: THE FIRST MEASURES. During its first months in office, the Allende government adopted several populist measures which, while, not in themselves revolutionary, did strengthen popular feeling that the government was committed to fulfilling its promises—an important element in a country where politicians have frequently been elected on a popular program only to betray it once in office. Workers and lower-level salaried employees received a 30 percent increase in pay, while prices were frozen; a ceiling of about $1200 per month was put on public salaries; every child received a half liter of milk per day; rents were fixed at 10 percent of family income; the riot-control police were dissolved, and so forth. In the area of foreign policy, Chile quickly established diplomatic relations with China, Cuba, and East Germany, and defined a new position independent and critical of United States policy in Latin America.

But the electoral campaign and the postelection tension aroused expectations, especially among the more exploited and previously excluded sectors of the rural and urban population, who were not satisfied by the immediate achievements. To many land-hungry peasants, the period of government reorganization appeared to be a delaying action; soon land seizures began to occur, led by the Revolutionary Peasant Movement (MCR), the peasant organization of the MIR.

TRANSFORMATION ON THREE FRONTS: BANKS, LATIFUNDIOS, AND MINES. The revolutionary process in Chile, unlike the process elsewhere in Latin America, is orderly and legal. In contrast to the exaggerated revolutionary rhetoric that accompanies even moderate changes in other countries, sweeping changes in Chile have been accompanied by moderate, low-key statements, linking the changes to development needs. Both the form and language of Chilean government declarations would, in other countries, suggest a government only slightly left of center, perhaps a moderately progressive social democratic government. But in Chile, during the first six months of the new government, several measures were announced which, taken together, suggested that socialist politics underlay the Chilean process. In December, Allende, after a mass meeting, sent Congress a bill nationalizing the giant U.S. copper mines; at about the same time, the government began taking control over the major banking interests by buying up stock; and the expropriations in rural areas began to accelerate.

The UP wisely selected these three critical areas of the economy for concentrated attack. On the issue of the United States-owned mines, the Christian Democratic Party and even the Right had declared themselves in favor of nationalization; hence, the rejection of Allende's bill would result in a plebiscite which the UP would almost certainly win. Since the agrarian reform is currently being carried out under the law passed by the Christian Democrats, the conflict is minimal, especially since many of the peasant unionists seeking land are, or were, supporters of the PDC. The government's control over the banks, achieved through the purchase of stock, is completely legal, leaving the opposition few options within the established rules of the game. While increasing its economic leverage and realizing complementary socioeconomic changes (banking and credit along with agrarian reform), the UP is also dividing the ruling class and isolating some sectors, thus preventing them from acting in concert. The loss of economic resources (land, banks, and mines) will sap the political strength of the Right and its capacity to mount expensive propaganda campaigns. Finally, these three issues were those likely to elicit the broadest popular support without alienating sectors of the urban-middle and lower-middle classes, thus helping the government to consolidate popular support. By the middle of 1971, the government had taken a series of measures which, while in themselves not implying a qualitative change in social relations, definitely pointed in that direction. By June, the results suggested that major commitments had been undertaken that would significantly strengthen the noncapitalist sectors. In agriculture, banking, and mining, the government was intervening decisively, thus surrounding the last bastion of capitalism: the industrial sector.

The municipal elections of April 1971, six months after Allende took office, reflected the growing strength of the Popular government. Unlike previous municipal elections which were substantially influenced by local personalities, those of 1971 were fought out on the national level by all participants, and thus represented a national plebiscite. The electoral results showed that the Allende government had popular support. Within the UP coalition, the greatest increase went to the Socialist party, which registered a 65 percent increase over its 1967 vote; the Radical Party suffered the greatest decline, a

Chilean Municipal Election, 1971

	Number	Percent
Partido Socialista	631,939	22.89
Partido Comunista	479,206	17.36
Partido Radical	225,851	8.18
Socialista Popular	29,123	1.05
Social Democrata	38,077	1.38
Total, Unidad Popular	1,404,196	50.86
Partiod Democrata Cristiano	723,623	26.21
Partido Nacional	511,679	18.53
Democracia Radical	108,192	3.91
Democrata Nacional	13,435	0.49
Total, opposition parties	1,356,929	49.14

100 percent drop (from 16 to 8 percent of the vote). The gain achieved by Allende's SP, the most radical sector of the coalition, clearly demonstrated the growing support for socialist policies.

In a senatorial by-election in southern Chile, the Socialist Sepulveda gathered 52 percent of the votes; his closest rival was the Christian Democratic former Minister of Economy, Andres Zaldivar, with 31 percent of the votes. The opposition could no longer refer to the Popular government as representing a minority. The majority obtained by the UP and the decline of the Christian Democratic Party from 29 percent in the September 1970 elections to 26 percent in the April 1971 election substantially weakened the authority of the opposition and strengthened the government.

THE AGRARIAN TRANSFORMATION

After two years of government, the Allende government has virtually put an end to the traditional latifundio. During this period, more land was expropriated and families settled than occurred during the six years of the Frei government. During 1971, 2.5 million hectareas of land were acquired by the State for the benefit of 26,000 families. As the government accelerates the pace of expropriation, an irreversible process sets in. When the latifundio is eliminated, one of the main supports of Chilean capitalism is weakened, and a social basis of support in the countryside is created that can aid the working-class struggle in the cities. A speedy and thorough agrarian reform under the leadership of the major working-class parties can lead to a political linkage between new rural beneficiaries and the industrial workers.

The bridge between the peasantry and the working class is the trade unions. Under the protection and promotion of the Allende government, peasant unionism has grown from 104,279 in 1970 to 217,791 members by February 1972.

The major innovations both in land tenure and trade union organization have occurred in the most social explosive areas, the areas in the south—Cautin, Linares, and Nuble. The process of change is characterized by popular initiative and favorable government action, both leading to the transformation of social relations.

The overall effect of the measures taken by the UP government has been to radicalize the peasantry and to penetrate the last bastions of the traditional landowning elite in southern Chile.

Nevertheless, because of differences between the socialists who favor more rapid moves toward collective ownership and the communists who favor individual farming within cooperatives, government policy directives have not always been consistent and effective. More important, many of the large farms—some estimates run as high as 50 percent—were "privately subdivided" (distributed among the family and a few chosen peasants) by the landholders and are now below the legal limit for expropriation (80 hectareas). Thus thousands of peasants have been excluded from farms that are not within the "legal" agrarian reform because the landholder and his family are referred to now as "middle farmers." The pressure to extend the agrarian reform is leading to demands to lower the legal limit exempt from expropriation to 40 hectareas. Within the Popular Unity government the Communist party has been the major force resisting further extensions of the agrarian reform—in the name of an "alliance" between the middle and poor peasants. It also appears that many of the property-owning peasants continue to support the opposition, as does a substantial proportion of the early beneficiaries of the reform during the Frei period.

BANKING AND FINANCE: THE GRADUAL EXPROPRIATION. By the end of 1972, the UP government had taken over all but four of the leading 21 banks, and had acquired over 80 percent of bank stocks. Through control of credit, the government is promoting the development phase of the agrarian reform and the growth of state industries.

The process of expropriation of banks reveals a great deal about the style of the Chilean revolution, especially in contrast with the Cuban experience. The Allende strategy has been to initiate basic changes through existing administrative agencies, laws, and decrees, thus presenting a hostile Congress with a fait accompli. The statification of the banking system occurs with the active support of bank workers' unions, which have at critical points "occupied" banks to prevent outgoing executives from creating unnecessary problems. The expropriated bank is incorporated to the existing state financial system, and the bank employees, through their committees, become involved in the decision-making structure along with the government-appointed interventor.

Throughout Chilean history, a substantial body of legislation that lends itself to the socialization of the economy has accumulated. In the past, most of this legislation was a dead letter, consisting largely of measures taken to comply formally with electoral pledges and to provide symbolic assurance, but never seriously applied. The Popular government has taken advantage of this formal legislation; with the socialist orientation of Allende's executive team, it has substantially transformed the pattern of ownership of the banking system and is on the way to breaking the power of the financial-banking oligarchy. While this basic change is taking place, there are no large-scale "mobilizations" in the street, or long passionate speeches from the balcony of the Presidential Palace. Prior to an expropriation, at the most critical point a number of unionized bank workers may peacefully occupy the building until the government *interventor* arrives, whereupon a committee is elected to collaborate with him. The result of this "legalistic," "bureaucratic," peaceful change is to reorient credit fundamentally, and to provide the government with the resources to strengthen the social or state sector of the economy. Because one does find a great many of the same institutional agencies that have existed in Chile's past, it is easy to miss the fundamental changes that are in fact taking place within institutions, and that will increasingly redefine the nature of the Chilean economic, social, and political system.

Despite the significant advances in statifying the financial system—the private sector still controls a minority of important banking institutions and refuses to sell its stock to the government. What complicates matters even more is the fact that the opposition-led Congress refuses to pass any legislation to allow legal expropriation and, at the same time, insists that further expropriations take place through congressional action.

Barring new executive branch initiatives or a change in the political composition of the Congress, it is unlikely that full governmental control over the financial system will be brought about—leaving Chile with a "mixed," private-public financial setup.

MINING: NATIONALIZATION OF BASIC RESOURCES. The Popular Unity government expropriated all major coal, iron, and nitrate mines. In July

Profits Remitted Abroad by Large Copper Mining Corporations
(in Millions of Dollars)

Year	Amount
1964	80.2
1965	73.9
1966	122.9
1967	131.4
1968	125.7
1969	122.0
1970	72.8

Source: Panorama Economico (March 1971), p. 39.

1971, the major export producer, the giant U.S.-owned copper mines, passed into the hands of the Chilean government. The mining expropriations are to be the basis for the formation of a state-owned machine-industry complex. The foreign mining sector was a principal source of Chilean dependency and underdevelopment, largely because of the profits remitted abroad.

By nationalizing the copper mines, the government seeks to stop the decapitalization of the economy, channel copper earnings into new development projects, and create industries that will develop new copper-based products.

While most mine owners were satisfactorily compensated, the U.S. owners of the giant copper mines objected to the lack of what they considered adequate compensation. The Chilean law—passed by unanimous vote of the democratically elected opposition-controlled Congress—allowed the President to deduct "excess profits" from the amount of compensation paid to the expropriated. The Chilean President, using as his base figure the average profits of the copper companies for their worldwide operations, came to the conclusion that the U.S. companies *owed* Chile back taxes that exceeded the market value of the mines. In effect, there was to be no compensation. The U.S. government responded by cutting off most loans and lines of credit, using its influence in the "international" banking agencies to pressure further the Chilean government. The Minister of Foreign Relations, Clodomiro Almeyda, concluded extended visits to Western and Eastern European countries to expand commercial relations. Chile hopes to neutralize some of the pressures that the United States has applied as a result of the expropriation policies adopted by the government.

NATIONALIZATION OF INDUSTRY: THE SLOW MARCH. The basic program of the Popular government calls for the nationalization of "strategic monopoly industries" and of "those activities that condition the economic and social development of the country." It is estimated that 150 enterprises among 30,000 firms and workshops are monopolies to be expropriated.

Only a very small number of monopoly industrial enterprises have been nationalized. The major steel company, Compania de Acero del Pacifico, has been nationalized, and the state has bought into, and formed, mixed enterprises with a half-dozen machine and metal-working firms. The government has nationalized the cement firms Cemento Melon and Cemento Polpaico, all the major textile enterprises, and the food firms Purina and Cecinas Loewer; in May 1971, the Ford motor plant was requisitioned for having paralyzed production. The pattern of ownership varies. In the electrical, chemical, and rubber industries, the state has formed mixed enterprises with foreign capital. The reasons for mixed enterprises vary: technological necessity (need to import technology), political considerations (not wishing to alienate a particular nation), and technical and administrative reasons (lack of trained personnel to manage the enterprises). In other industrial branches such as cement, textiles, and the food industry, the state has taken complete ownership of the expropriated firms. A number of smaller firms on the verge of closing have been taken over to prevent unemployment.

Regarding the expropriation of industrial monopolies, there appear to be varying emphases among the components of the UP. The Communist party, Allende and his Cabinet, the Radical party, and the smaller groups (API and Social Democrats) seem to favor a go-slow policy on the industrial front: limit nationalizations to very special cases (at least for the time being), or form mixed enterprises and concentrate on increasing production and providing guarantees and credits to industrial enterprises to meet increased consumer demand resulting from wage increases. MAPU and many industrial workers of the CUT—mostly socialists—put great emphasis on rapidly expanding the participation and mobilization of the workers as protagonists of the process of expropriation. Perhaps the decisive factor will be the attitude and behavior of the industrialists themselves. To the extent that they fail to respond to government incentives and guarantees, they will be strengthening the arguments of the more militant sectors of the UP. By increasing production and collaborating, the industrialists may be able to postpone the day of expropriation. It is too early to predict the pattern and road that the government might follow regarding industry; the political tendencies are still very fluid. By May 1972 the Communist party and Allende apparently won out over the more militant Socialist wing of the Popular Unity government led by the former Minister of Economy, Pedro Vuskovic—the emphasis shifted from extending the social sector through further nationalizations to consolidating the existing changes and increasing production. Vuskovic was replaced by a "moderate" closer to the position of the Communist party and Allende.

ECONOMIC DEVELOPMENT UNDER ALLENDE: 1970 TO 1972. The charge was made throughout 1971 that after the U.S. managers and private investors left Chile, copper production would decline. Comparative statistics tell us a different story. Copper output from the large nationalized mines, run by Chilean technicians, reached 572,000 tons, an increase of 6 percent over the previous year. The copper industry does have problems, but the most serious issues have little to do with *socialist* politics. The major problem has been the decline in the international price of copper from 61 cents per pound during 1970 to 47 cents a pound in 1971 (for each cent decline in price, Chile loses $7 million). The decline in copper price is a major factor accounting for the decline in foreign reserves, an increasingly serious problem facing the Allende government. The decline in foreign reserves has more to do with the international market and international corporations than with efficiency of the Allende government.

Despite the *Wall Street Journal's* predictions of "industrial disaster," industrial growth is another feature of Chilean economic development under Allende. The manufacturing industry represents nearly a third of national production and *during 1971 industry increased by more than 12 percent over 1970*. This growth occurred at a time when a number (80) of industrial plants (including textiles, cement and steel) had been nationalized or intervened.

The sharpest discrepancy between the accounts in the United States news media and the actual performance of the Chilean economy is to be found in the agricultural sector. The Allende government has expropriated over 2000 landed estates—*and agricultural production increased by 6 percent in 1971* (almost double the growth rate of the Frei government). Despite the vast changes that are occurring, the great majority of the reforms are taking place in a peaceful and orderly fashion. As the production figures suggest, change is occurring with a minimum of social dislocation. Part of the success in agriculture is because the government—through the purchase of banks— controls 80 percent of the credit, which it has in part directed to the land reform beneficiaries. In addition, agricultural growth has been promoted by the establishment of a state national distribution firm to aid the peasants in the commercialization of their crops.

The construction industry has grown by 12 percent, having initiated the building of 90,000 houses, almost four times the output of the last year of the Frei government. The consumer price index rose 35 percent during 1970 (under Frei). Under Allende in 1971 it rose to 22 percent.

Some shortages have persisted under the Allende government—especially the supply of beef. Many factors have caused shortages including extensive hoarding by the rich and the middle class (some basements look like food warehouses; some freezers resemble display cases of meat markets). The government began in July 1972 to restrict the consumption pattern of the rich through rationing meat, limiting purchases of plush restaurants, and attempting to make supplies available to workers through neighborhood supply committees. Shortages have resulted from the common practice of expropriated landowners slaughtering animals—including stud bulls and pregnant cows—to cause the government and people hardships. A major reason for shortages is the increased purchasing power of the people. In 1971, beef consumption increased 15 percent, fowls 16 percent, potatoes 55 percent, onions 54 percent, condensed milk 10 percent, and so on. While wages were increased, prices and profits were frozen—as a result the salaried and wage proportion of national income has increased from 53.7 percent in 1970 to 59 percent in 1971. The economy, stimulated by government investment and the increased purchasing power of the masses, began to expand. Unemployment in Santiago declined from 8.3 percent in December 1970, a month after Allende's inauguration, to 3.8 percent in December 1971. There are already labor shortages in some provinces of the country.

The government carried out a policy of deficit financing to absorb the unused manpower and resources, to increase the purchasing power of the poor, and to broaden public investment substantially. The increase in public investment has compensated in great part for the decline in private and foreign investment. In 1972 the government gave greater emphasis to long-term investments, and belt-tightening measures were adopted.[3]

Probably the most popular measure adopted by the Allende government was his decision not to pay compensation in the course of nationalizing the copper mines. Most Chileans feel that the billions of dollars the companies have taken out of the country over the years are sufficient payment. Many Chileans feel that the United States companies, not the Chilean government, should assume payment for the $700 million debt assumed by the companies during their expansion period.

Chileans (not the United States investors) now control strategic sectors of the economy such as mining, the peasants have received 2.84 million *hectareas* of land (about 6.8 million acres) in one year, and the banks serve the public sector and small and medium entrepreneurs. More important, these changes occur with the maximum of freedom for the opposition. The antigovernment coalition of Christian Democrats and the National Party still control the majority of the mass media of the country and spend enormous amounts of time and money financing publicity campaigns to sabotage government programs; through public meetings and demonstrations, they protest the lack of "freedom."

One of the major challenges facing government development plans is its ability to limit wage and price increases while increasing productivity. This problem is exacerbated by opposition efforts to undercut this program through noninvestment in the private sector and excessive wage and salary demands in the state sector. In addition, the Left's efforts in the past mainly concern wage and salary issues and they have thus conditioned workers over the years to consider socioeconomic problems from this narrow "economist" conception.

THE DEPTH OF CHANGE: POLITICAL CONSCIOUSNESS

In discussing the degrees to which popular and elite attitudes toward the status quo and structural transformation have changed, it is important to consider a number of aspects. In what sense are voting attitudes an accurate reflection of "radicalism" or conservatism? Can one observe boh radicalism and conservatism among Chilean workers, the major supporters of the government (as discussed previously)? Is "economist" or "socialist consciousness" dominant among Chilean workers (which segments or strata?), and what are the implications for government policy? What are the costs and benefits of the political elites decision to opt for electoral as opposed to mass mobilization politics? Given an incremental-additive style of change regard-

---

[3] The growth for the first six months of 1972 was a respectable 6 percent.

ing urban classes, can this be continued indefinitely or might it be modified by new contingencies?

While it is now obvious that the Left has increased its voting strength substantially since the September presidential elections, it is altogether not clear what the changing attitudes mean in terms of Socialist politics. Through a series of open-ended interviews, a contradictory pattern seemed to emerge. While voting attitudes become more favorable toward the left-wing candidates, the concerns of the voters were the traditional bread and butter issues. Amid radicalization of political choices there was an underlying continuity of basic concerns. Chilean radicalism has grown and prospered on the basis of unfulfilled traditional demands.

ECONOMIST CONSCIOUSNESS AND SOCIALIST CONSCIOUSNESS

Among workers there is an *inverse* relationship between degree of participation and interest in participation in decision making on the one hand and level of income and status. We found that workers with the highest degree of interest in participation, interaction, and solidarity were the *pobladores* in the Campamento *Nueva Habana;* the next highest were the peasants in the Socialist and MIR peasant unions in the Nuble and Cautin area; the textile workers from ex-*Hirmas* were next highest in their interest in participation; the copper miners in El Teniente were next to last, and the miners in Chuquicamata were in last place.

	Rank Order	
Group	Participation in Leadership	Salary and Status
Pobladores "Nueva Habana"	1	5
Peasants (Nuble, Cautin)	2	4
Textile workers (Hirmas)	3	3
Copper workers (El Teniente)	4	2
Copper workers (Chuquicamata)	5	1

The inverse relationship between salary, status, and participation does not, however, explain very much—in turn *it* needs to be explained. Low income and status in themselves do not explain high levels of participation or interest in participation. If we compare the two groups "high" in participation (pobladorse and "Southern" peasants) to the groups ranked "low" in participation (the copper miners of *El Teniente* and Chuquicamata), we find some interesting differences. The low scorers in participation have been organized in trade unions for over a half-century and have engaged in a great number of strikes and "job actions" led by leftist trade union leaders. The high scorers have been organized only in the past year or two (at the most), and most of them lacked previous organized political experiences. The leaders of recently organized groups are the MIR and the left-wing of the Socialist party. Paradoxically then, it appears that the groups with the longest experience of class struggle and the longest tradition of class organization under leftist leadership are the ones least interested in participation in decision making within the nationalized firms. A closer view, however, reveals several factors that throw some light on the problem.

The newly organized squatters and peasants were led by revolutionary socialist political cadres whose vision of the process led them to constantly infuse immediate piecemeal changes with a broader perspective embracing the whole system. The older organized groups (the copper miners) were led by Socialist trade union leaders who had achieved leadership positions on the basis of their trade union skills (ability to organize strikes and negotiate substantial wage increases) rather than because of their political militancy. The copper miners' supported leftist politicians because of their ability to reinforce the demands of their trade union leaders.[4] Partly because of past experiences and partly because leftist trade unionists focused primarily on economic issues (salaries) the copper miners have developed little in the way of a radical political consciousness that would enable them to see themselves in decision-making positions instead of as mere wage workers. The newly organized workers on the other hand—from their initial organizing efforts—came into contact with the most "advanced" political groups in Chilean society: the MIR and Left Socialist political leaders whose demands went beyond statification of the economy to a Socialist program based on *workers and peasant control* as the *central* issue. The most exploited and lowest paid groups—those literally without houses, work, or land—were the major groups *not* organized by the established left-wing organizations; thus, they were available to the more revolutionary groups like the MIR and the Left-Socialists.

The better organized and paid workers were the workers who had been socialized over the years to electoral and "economist" politics; they were conditioned to think of politics as casting a ballot once every four or six years for a parliamentary representative. Once elected there was very little direct contact and discussion between the representative and the worker-voter—except insofar as a wage dispute necessitated parliamentary support. The only meetings that directly affected the copper workers under the previous private ownership system were those that discussed salary questions.

[4] Even so, conservative political leaders such as Jorge Alessandri received substantial voting support in the 1970 elections, especially in Chuquicamata, although there are no Alessandrist trade union leaders.

Hence, the only period of activity and discussion revolved around the periods of salary negotiations. As a result in the postreform period copper miners tend to identify "greater participation" with a greater share in the profits—not greater responsibility in the decisions of the enterprise.

The land squatters and peasants on the other hand *began* their activity with the expropriation of land and thus immediately faced larger questions concerning the management and administration of the whole community. There was little "prior schooling" in electoral or economist policies. The very act of expropriation of land itself was in many instances organized from below and carried out by the people themselves—thus creating a tradition of solidarity around global issues. On the other hand, the copper miners' solidarity was based on limited goals—wage demands for themselves—and they were very reluctant to participate in solidarity action with other oppressed groups if it meant a day's lost pay. The expropriation of the copper mines themselves was carried out through parliamentary action and executive negotiation. At best the copper miners voiced support for the action—and in some cases had serious reservations concerning its possible effects on their social and economic benefits.

Thus, those sectors of the working class that were *late-organized* and led by *extraparliamentary* political groups, infused by a global vision of the process, show greater interest in the democratic participatory mode of organizing the nationalized industries than do the established organized union workers led by electorally oriented trade unionists.

The key question facing the Allende government is not, as Hobsbawm[5] suggests, one of increasing the number of leftists among the lower classes (a careful analysis would show that the Left has practically exhausted its possible support among the urban and rural workers, perhaps however not among urban slum women voters); the Left *has* the support of the great majority of the productive sectors of the society—peasants, miners, industrial workers, and land squatters. The real question facing the Left is its ability to transform the *"economist"* consciousness of its supporters into socialist consciousness. If this is indeed the key issue, then the program of the Left should not concentrate on the populist redistributive measures—a la Peron—which Hobsbawm suggests as means of "increasing popular support," but should instead focus on creating institutions for workers' participation. Only through directly participating in the management of an enterprise—with all the errors and risks that may result—will the workers get the experiences that will deepen their political awareness and make them conscious of the socialist nature of the transformation. One key problem in establishing democratic workers councils in a national level, however, is the preexisting political institutions, namely the parliamentary system.

[5] Eric Hobsbawn, "Can Allende Make It," *New York Review of Books* (September 23, 1971), pp. 23–32.

ELECTORAL PARLIAMENTARY AND MASS MOBILIZATION POLITICS

The political method of the Allende government has been eminently legalistic. Largely through parliamentary institutions and administrative agencies, the government has initiated and carried through most changes. There is no doubt that the broad changes that have so far been achieved have been at very low social cost; few injuries or deaths have occurred and resistence has paled before governmental authority. The electoral-parliamentary approach therefore has at least one basic advantage over other methods: low initial costs. This, however, in turn, depended on the existence of a body of legislation and administrative practices that allowed executive initiative. And this legislative heritage was the result of a history of social struggle and organization that goes back at least 50 years.

The costs of the electoral-parliamentary approach, however, are equally high—especially from the point of view of sustaining and accelerating the momentum of change. Two interrelated consequences of reliance on top-down decision making has been popular immobility and decline in participation. Paradoxically the growing number of radical voters among the working class and peasantry have become increasingly apathetic. Measures to bring about change have been initiated by administrative leaders or have come about through the duly constituted legislative chambers—leaving to the populace the chore of voting and occasional rallies to support the government's legal standing. The Allende government's reliance on the parliamentarian style of politics results in maintenance of the elitist as opposed to a mass mobilization style of politics: changes are negotiated between opposing elites; expropriation by governmental agencies results in compensation for the displaced elite; postreform decision-making structures resemble those of the prereform period. This has resulted in the most serious deficiency from the point of view of revolutionary-socialist politics: the lack of permanent and effective political organizations that could serve as vehicles for direct mass participation in the process of change.

Lacking an institutional basis for direct mass participation, the newly introduced changes have been incremental-additive—they have benefited the masses but have not seriously encroached on the privileges of the urban upper and middle classes.

The personal privileges of the elite persist in such areas as housing, private education, private exclusive clubs, private transportation, summer homes, personal services (maids), and hoarding of scarce commodities. The future possibilities of maintaining the elite privileges and providing new programs for the masses are very dim. The Allende government faces the choice of either cutting into middle-class privileges or else sacrificing popular programs. The possibility of even short-term polyclass coalitions is not promising. As the recent university elections clearly indicate, Chile is increasingly a class-polarized society; the middle-class students and professors voting for the opposition candidate, Boeninger, while the "nonacademic" personale (many of whom are workers and secretaries) voted for the progovernment candidate, Herrera.

University Elections For Rector 1972

	Professors	Students	Nonacademic
Boeinger (Opposition)	4391	22,620	3788
Herrera (Government)	3655	17,848	3973
Pascal (MIR)	241	2,783	155
Vitale (Trotskyist)	63	460	76

Since the government has realized the nationalist-democratic reforms in its programs and has attempted to implement anticapitalist measures, it has lost the support of the middle class. The ability of the Right to capture these social forces is a result of the tempo and policies that the government adopted during the first year.

THE TEMPO OF CHANGE

From the purely quantitative aspect, numerous institutional changes were implemented or initiated during the first six months of the Allende government. Yet, "qualitative" changes—control of strategic political and economic centers of decision making—were not consumated. Let us first examine these two aspects of the process and try to relate them to overall development in Chile today.

In a general sense, during the first six months "objective conditions were ripe" for a basic transformation; the mass of voters shifted with the government—the bandwagon effect—and many were won over by the initial populist-redistributive measures. The initial responsiveness of the populace was extended even to broad sectors of the middle class that had temporarily lost its traditional ties to the "alternative pole"—the large property holding elites and their parties. The second aspect characterizing this optimal situation was the disorientation and flight of the elite. Factory owners abandoned their firms; rightist political leaders were discredited because of their ties with the assassination of the Commander-in-Chief of the Army; and the rightist political organizations lost control of the executive branch. Together these factors contributed to the disorientation of the elite—facilitating change.

The government responded by initiating reforms *and* recreating the conditions for orderly development. The government sought the restoration of the economy; as a condition for change, continuity and development were stressed. Paradoxically, the government's success in restoring the economy prevented accelerated and radical change. By creating confidence and resorting to piecemeal legal changes the government gave the property groups a chance to return, operate at full capacity, organize themselves, and influence broad segments of the petty bourgeoisie against the anticapitalist proposals in the government's program. With the economic revival came the political revival—with one difference over the past. The antisocialist opposition was no longer divided; the Christian Democrats and the National party alliance symbolized the unity of property against further changes.

SYSTEMIC CONSTRAINTS ON THE TRANSITION TO SOCIALISM. The Allende government faces several political problems: political opposition in Congress, the judiciary, and the bureaucracy; the internal political differences in the UP; the position of the army; and the UP's relationship with the "insurrectional" Left, the MIR.

The combined opposition of Christian Democratic and National parties controls a majority in Congress, and has blocked most government legislation, at least temporarily. The limits on the power of the Congress are few. Allende can resort to a plebiscite to dissolve Congress and call for new elections but that is a risky proposition. The Congressional opposition is careful not to oppose measures that have broad popular support for fear that this may produce an unfavorable polarization of the electorate. Although the PDC is divided into left and right wings, the former has shown few signs of a willingness to collaborate with the UP on critical anticapitalist measures. There is little likelihood of further splits in the PDC, and the conservative pro-Frei faction is firmly in command. Third, although the Chilean Executive has at his disposal a great deal of potential power, especially emergency powers, it is highly unlikely Allende will use it. Executive measures can be taken on the basis of past laws, regulations, and decrees, which in fact make it possible to implement policy without Congressional approval. The government failed to use the results of the municipal elections (described as a "popular mandate") to pressure Congress into responding. Thus the power of the opposition in Congres is formidable, if not insurmountable.

The Chilean Supreme Court is dominated by the political opposition and has served to protect the interests of the national elites, the most notorious case being the Court's decision to uphold the immunity of a right-wing senator implicated in the assassination of General Schneider. Backed by a reactivated opposition, it is unlikely that the Court will take a progressive role, instead it will continue to take prorightist positions.

The bureaucracy in Chile is big and inefficient. In addition, it has always contained a substantial portion of politicized functionaries. Part of the agreement between the UP and the PDC securing congressional support for Allende's election was the decision to leave the bureaucracy intact; the PDC was thus able to insure that its political supporters retained a substantial proportion of the middle levels of the bureaucracy. The ministries of Foreign Relations, Agriculture, Economy and the Agrarian Reform Corporation have substantial numbers of Christian Democrats, who administer policies which, in many cases, they hardly favor, in key positions. Hence, while the top leadership of the government and the groups at the bottom (such as workers, peasants, and neighborhood groups) may favor a policy, the middle levels may choose to sabotage it through endless delays and maladministration. In some cases the functionaries conduct antigovernment propaganda while ostensibly administering programs, attributing difficulties to their chiefs while taking credit for achievements. The problem of how to implement a social transformation through a bureaucracy that is hostile or indifferent is one that the Allende government has been unwilling to tackle; this has caused serious political as well as socioeconomic problems. Large-scale replacements would probably provoke an immediate confrontation with the opposition, something that Allende would like to avoid. A solution more in keeping with the modus operandi of this government was the creation of new agencies, necessitating increased governmental spending.

When the "easy" phase of the social transformation ended, and the question of expropriating the properties of the Chilean industrial bourgeoisie approached, the internal differences within the UP became accentuated. In other words, as the national-democratic phase of the revolution was completed, the political forces in the coalition had to decide whether to continue the process on to socialism, or to seek a coalition with the opposition.

Up to that point, despite internal tensions and rivalry for patronage the Popular Unity government maintained its cohesion. The first defectors were members of the conservative wing of the Radical party—mostly senators and deputies, who opposed further nationalizations. Apparently this split provoked further debates and discussions in the government and led to a new political division between Allende, the Social Democrats, and the Communists on the one hand and the Socialists and the Left Christians on the other. The former argued essentially for a two-stage approach to socialism. The immediate task, argued the Communist Minister of Finance Millas, is to make concessions to the middle class, consolidate the changes that have already occurred, negotiate a modus vivendi with the Christian Democrats and at some later unspecified time recommence the process of gradual socialization. The Left opposition has argued for acceleration of change, winning the "progressive" sectors of the lower-middle class through bold new initiatives and postponing problems of production to the future. In June 1972 the debate was temporarily won by the "consolidationists"—the emphasis has shifted from change to productivity. It remains doubtful however if any serious inroads will be made to winning over the middle class or coaxing the Christian Democrats toward cooperating in bring about anything resembling a socialist society.

Besides these overtly political conflicts that the government faces, there is the question of the army. The Chilean army is not a static, homogeneous group with a fixed political position. The high army officers in Chile are predominantly from the middle class and the lower officers are closer to the lower-middle class. Under the Allende government, the social and economic position of the army and the national police force has improved; the government has paid close attention, and given ample publicity, to military services and ceremonies, thus increasing military prestige. Socioeconomic benefits have also been increased. Communication and consultation between the President and the military has increased. More important, the UP government has involved military officials in a variety of socioeconomic projects, with the result that the military is becoming directly committed to the development program of the UP. The process of mutual interchange of ideas between socialist developmentalists and military engineers could lead to a consensus regarding broad problems and solutions, or it could increase the military's decision-making capacity and encourage a coup. In any case, military participation in the development process weakens the possibility that a conservative sector of the army opposed to the UP could command the immediate and total adherence of the army. Political orientations within the armed forces varies; one sector favors Allende, another sector favors the opposition, and a third sector, not clearly defined in specific political terms, appears to uphold the Constitution and legality, and, for now, backs the Allende government. Apart from these internal constraints, the Allende government faces serious external opposition from U.S. policy makers and economic interests.

U.S. RESPONSE TO THE ALLENDE GOVERNMENT

U.S. policy toward the democratically elected Socialist president is in stark contrast to its policy to the authoritarian military dictatorship in Brazil— toward the former unmitigated hostility, to the latter lavish praise and aid. The strategy of U.S. opposition to the Allende government operates on three levels of policy making: (1) an "outsider" strategy; (2) an "insider" strategy; and (3) a regional strategy.

The "outsider" strategy includes basically three types of policy moves: (1) symbolic hostility; (2) veiled threats; and (3) overt hostility. Symbolic hostility has taken the form of not extending to the Allende government the usual courtesies on ceremonial occasions: Nixon snubbed Allende after his electoral victory; the Executive Branch canceled (over the objections of some military officers) the scheduled visit of the naval vessel *Enterprise* to Valparaiso. These symbolic gestures are meant to pressure the Chilean government and to encourage U.S. allies among the internal opposition.

The speeches of Rogers, Laird, and Connally regarding Chile's nationalization policies have been full of threats of U.S. economic reprisals. The purpose of these speeches is to make other countries aware of possible negative reactions from the United States if they follow the Chilean route.

Overt hostility has taken mainly economic form: cutting off of U.S. loans and credits—while demanding payments on back loans accumulated by previous "friendly" governments; cutting off Export-Import Bank loans, specifically blocking Chile's purchase of Boeing airplanes; and shutting Chile off from "international" bank loans, that is, Inter-American Development Bank (IDB) and World Bank loans (to pressure the Chilean government to meet United States corporate compensation demands). The United States manipulates these "international" banks since it has sufficient representation to block any proposed loan.

The "insiders" strategy is basically directed toward maintaining ties and strengthening potential replacements of the Allende government through the selective channeling of resources. Thus, while the United States has cut off all development loans, it has granted the Chilean military $5 million worth of credits to purchase military equipment. The Catholic University stronghold of the rightwing opposition received a substantial loan from the IDB—thus increasing its base for antigovernment activity.

In addition, the United States is in constant consultation with the titular leader of the opposition, Eduardo Frei, who has made several unpublicized visits to Washington. The selective channeling of money to political allies, the attempt to keep in close touch with the military, and the publicity given to the opposition is exactly the same pattern that the United States followed prior to and leading up to the overthrow of the national-popular "Jango" Goulart government in Brazil.

The regional strategy that U.S. policy makers are developing has two basic ingredients: (1) strengthening Brazil as a counterrevolutionary center and possible source of military intervention if not directly in Chile at this time— at least in bordering countries (Uruguay) if that country decides to go the Chilean route; and (2) isolating Chile on its borders—especially with regard to Peru and Bolivia. In part, this strategy has already brought about some immediate payoffs. Two days before Chile and Bolivia were to open relations the United States military (along wtih Brazil and Argentina) provided logistical support, intelligence reports, and medical supplies to aid the Bolivian army in its overthrow of the national-popular Torres government. The United States now has a loyal government in Bolivia led by Hugo Banzer, has increased border pressures on Chile, and has a passageway from Brazil through Bolivia to Chile. Regarding Peru the United States has moved in the direction of closer relations—there are agreements on most issues which have been pending, especially since the "nationalist" Peruvian military have come around to seeing the "need" of foreign investment for economic development. To the extent to which United States-Peruvian differences become narrower, the United States may be able to push the Peruvians into a more distant relationship with Chile.

The overall purpose of U.S. policy makers to which their "insider," "outsider," and "regional" strategies are directed is to create economic dislocation and provoke a social crises that could lead to either the overthrow of the Allende government by a civil-military coalition made up of the Army, the

Christian Democrats, and the extreme Rightwing National party or the discrediting of the government and its defeat in the 1973 congressional elections, thus undercutting the basis for future change.

CONCLUSION

The inability of the middle-class parties to realize the historic tasks of eliminating external domination and the latifundio, and to pave the way for national economic development, forced the working-class parties to assume these tasks. In Chile, these historic tasks, accomplished in an earlier period in Europe by the revolutionary bourgeoisie, are being realized by the political coalition headed by the Communist and Socialist parties. The question remains, "Having completed the national-democratic revolution, will the working-class-based parties go on to socialism?" The core of monopoly industrial capitalism has thus far hardly been touched. The important changes that have thus far taken place are not incompatible with "nationalist capitalist" or "state capitalist" development in the long run. The expropriation of foreign owners of natural resources, and the formation of mixed enterprises with foreign firms in the machine and manufacturing fields is compatible with the new trend of foreign capital investment; foreign investors have shifted from the extractive industries to manufacturing. In the short run, the political climate—such as the powerful working-class base of the government, the articulation of a socialist program, and the plans to expand the state sector—has been viewed by the foreign investment community as unfavorable to new commitments. Given the insecurity and uncertainty of foreign capital in Chile, new investments will probably not be forthcoming unless political guarantees against nationalizations are secure, which in effect would be to ask the government to cut off its social base of support (that is, the socialist industrial proletariat).

Nevertheless, some sectors of the national industrial bourgeoisie are presently reaping the benefits of the government's new credit and financial program. With the wage increases, new public works programs, and acceleration of agrarian reform, the demand for consumer goods has greatly expanded. At the same time, credits and loans from the state banks are more readily available, and price controls have lowered the cost of power and electricity. The more dynamic and politically "flexible" sectors of the industrial and commercial bourgeoisie, along with the workers and peasants, have benefited from the initial measures of the UP government. Whether they will want or be able to form a permanent part of a broad national coalition is dubious.

The opposition PDC and PN since early 1972 have been successful in blocking government action. It would be a mistake to underestimate their potentialities for limiting change or preventing the transition to socialism. The strategy adopted so far is to reject outright those measures that the opposition is confident the government would not submit to a plebiscite (the proposal to form neighborhood courts to try minor infractions). Regarding more popular measures, the idea is not to oppose them, but to add a series of regulations and procedures, which in practice undermine the change. Both sides prepare for the critical congressional elections of 1973. In the meantime, government experts in jurisprudence may be able to discover new laws or decrees that will facilitate changes through existing procedures.

Within the UP government, there is a tendency toward "premature consolidation." Allende's preoccupation with production is in part correct; shortages could adversely affect the living standards of the population, and generate negative political reactions. On the other hand, a slowing down of the process of expropriation has given new life to the propertied interests, who have regrouped around the industrialists and launched a new antisocialist alliance, including former sectors of the UP. The six-month period following the April municipal elections was politically the best time for expropriations; the government had a broad basis of support and political antagonisms and social conflicts had not dissipated support. A year later political support among the lower middle class slipped. Because the government maintains a private industrial sector, it has to confront labor-management conflicts that are emerging and has attempted to limit working-class demands in order to encourage private entrepreneurs to increase production. The problem of production is essentially a *postrevolutionary* problem for a *socialist* government—though, of course, efforts can be made to link the structural changes to increases in production. Demands for increases in production and personal sacrifice within an essentially capitalist society can only be successful if the government is at the same time preparing to transfer power to the working class in the tangible future.

If exhortations to produce more are not explicitly linked to socialization of industry, the class point of view will reassert itself within industries and plants: production for whom?

While some within the leadership of the UP emphasize production, most militants see production problems as part of a larger process that involves accelerating change, broadening popular participation, and fortifying the revolutionary consciousness of the protagonists of the Chilean revolution—the industrial and rural working class.

2

James Petras | Chile: Nationalization, Socio Economic Change, and Popular Participation

In a country such as Chile, where workers are found in a variety of industries, on different economic levels, in varied geographical regions, they are bound to have widely differing political experiences. Differences in outlook and attitude toward "participation" in the postnationalization period probably exist. The manner in which nationalization occurs—the degree to which there was prior politicization and mobilization—will also affect the workers' attitude toward the forms of participation. The working class is not a homogeneous entity with the same level of class consciousness; even within the same industries there are often significant variations between workers, in many cases among workers with similar backgrounds and experiences working at the same machine. Because of this complexity the attitude of workers' toward participation in industry is not easy to determine. One cannot assume either that workers are only oriented toward "participation" through higher salaries (economism) or that workers are by nature prone toward participation in the firm (workers' control).

In addition to industrial and mining workers, four additional groups linked to the productive process have potentially important roles to play in defining participatory aspects within the broad structural transformation taking place in Chile today: the agricultural and nonindustrial urban workers and the mining and industrial technicians and supervisors. The sweeping changes that are occurring in Chile have embraced almost all important sectors of the economy, although the degree of change within each sector varies considerably—and at all levels of enterprises. Socialist policy makers have to face fundamental issues: who is going to run the new nationalized enterprises? What role will the industrial workers, miners, agricultural workers, technicians, and supervisors play within the new system? Before those questions can be discussed, however, it is important to discuss the *attitudes that workers have toward their role in the process.* We conducted a series of 40 open-ended, unstructured interviews to obtain some notion of the attitudes of several different working class, peasant, technical, and supervisory groups.[1] Two copper mining enterprises (*Chuquicamata* and *El Teniente*), the textile factory (Hirmas or *ex*-Hirmas, as the workers referred to it), farms in the south of Chile (the provinces of Nuble and Cautin), and a land squatter settlement on the outskirts of Santiago (Nueva Habana) were visited.

AN OVERVIEW: THE COPPER MINERS

In discussing the nationalization of the copper mines one of the directors of the new state copper mining directorate said "consciousness is the biggest problem." At first glance this may appear to be incongruous: a plurality of the copper miners—even in Chuquicamata—voted for Allende in 1970. The proportion of left voters increased during the municipal elections of April 1971, six months after Allende took office. The majority of the industrial workers in the mines voted for the socialist ticket in the union elections (7 out of 10 of the industrial workers' *leaders* in Chuquicamata are Socialists or Communists).

Despite appearances, there are a number of political problems. Half of those employed in Chuquicamata are now classified as "empleados" (employees) as opposed to "obreros" (manual wage workers). The employees' union is led by nonleftists (such as Christian Democrats and "independents"), whose only concern is to increase salaries, to improve the financial accounts of the union treasury and, the income and expense account of the union officials.[2] The leftist unions are only nominally under party discipline.[3] For the most part, socialist trade unionists formulate trade union policy independently of the party. In fact, the union controlled party policy regarding the mining sector. In addition to the division between workers and employees, the supervisors and technicians have an Association that worked closely with United States managerial personnel and whose leadership was allied with the political Right. The introduction of modern technology reduced the number of manual workers, increased the number of employees, and thus reduced the political influence of the Left.

[1] All the enterprises visited were either nationalized or requisitioned property—no longer in the hands of their previous private owners.

[2] This "style" of unionism was also one of the by-products of the United States ownership of the copper mines.

[3] The only possible exception was the communist trade unions.

A number of factors contributed to the formation of a "sectoral economist consciousness"[4] as opposed to genuine working-class consciousness. The copper miners, especially those employed in Chuquicamata, are geographically isolated from the rest of the working class. Workers came to *Chuqui* for one reason: to make money. After a few years, many of them leave. There is little working-class community. Outside of the common pursuit of higher salaries there is little that holds the workers together; outside of work there is little of the social solidarity that one finds in other working-class areas of Chile. Geographically apart, socially isolated, uprooted from their normal class environment, in transition toward new occupational opportunities—the copper workers in Chuquicamata are *salary conscious,* not *class conscious.* The nationalization of copper was celebrated throughout Chile as a "historic national occasion"—in Chuquicamata the workers went about their routine business.

Participation in the copper mines is very low, except in some sections of the mines. The workers' representatives on the directorate of the firm reflect more than anything else the leadership of the trade unions, that does work closely with the government. Because of their support of the government, trade union leaders face continuous pressure from the rank and file to increase wages. Occasionally, trade union leaders function as if they were still combating the foreign capitalists, fail to discipline absentee workers, and have not taken adequate measures to systematically reeducate the rank and file workers and prepare them for responsible positions. In discussing the problem of the copper workers' attitudes in Chuquicamata after the nationalization of the mines, the President of the Industrial Union noted:

There was fear that they would lose their social gains. There is no change in their political level. They vote for Left trade unionists because they are more effective negotiators of new contracts. Alessandri was popular but he does not have one trade union leader. The workers may turn to conservative unions if the workers' leaders identify too strongly with the government thus not leading the struggle for improved benefits. The government can help Left trade unionists by granting a 60 percent increase. . . .

The workers' demands are the same as before and the response of the trade union leaders is no different—albeit they make attempts to square the government's overall development plans with the workers' immediate demands. The results in terms of participation are symptomatic. The same trade union leader noted:

In the struggle for [economic] demands 95 percent of the workers are active but in informative meetings there are very few. The working class

---

[4] By "sectoral economist consciousness" we mean concern with and social action directed toward issues solely related to salary and job considerations within a particular firm or sector of industry.

was accustomed to the old system, they have not entered into participation in the leadership of the administration—the workers see it as a change of owners. Presently, temporarily, the trade union leaders represent the workers in the administration.

Though salaries are high in comparison with the average wage of Chilean industrial workers, the cost of living in this isolated desert area is also high— and the location offers few extra monetary compensations. The government has begun some programs of social improvements, such as installation of private sewage systems, but this type of program has only a limited impact. Meanwhile, the business unionism fostered by companies and union officials still influences the workers occasionally encouraged by conservative middle level government functionaries and plant supervisors held over from the previous regime.

MANAGEMENT IN THE NEW CONTEXT: CONSERVATIVE ATTITUDES AND TECHNOCRATIC IDEOLOGY

Some of the top personnel of the mines are competent and have a favorable attitude toward the socialization program of the government. The new general supervisor of Chuquicamata spent five years working in the United States, has 10 years experience as a mining engineer, and sees the new responsibilities as a challenge to Chilean professionals. Regarding the new situation, he stated:

> There is much more responsibility. We have to make our own decisions —not the people in New York. Before we did most of the routine work; now we must find ways to better exploit the mines—according to our national interest. To avoid exhausting the mine we no longer want maximum exploitation for short term gains. The fundamental positions were in the hands of the U.S.—planning and operations; as a result there were not sufficient Chileans trained for executive positions. Many went to the U.S. and learned and a new mine *Exotica* was a learning experience, providing executive training. The sacking of the mine [by the U.S. companies] left waste deposits accumulating—this imposes new investments on the government. The multi-national corporation owns many mines around the world: it exploits at the least cost and takes the cream. It does not have a long range perspective because of its many holdings— this is what conflicts with the national interest of Chile.[5]

While a number of supervisors have made the transition from private to

[5] The mining supervisor at Chuquicamata provided data that suggested that despite the changeover (or perhaps because the changeover *meant so little* in terms of the organization of work and production), production had not declined but had increased over the previous year: January to June 1970—139,632 short tons, January to June 1971 —142,052 short tons.

nationalized industry, a substantial number show signs of hostility and out-right opposition, cloaking their political opposition in technocratic jargon.

One supervisor stated: "I don't have any response on nationalization. My only interest is that this enterprise produces."

Another supervisor noted: "If politics is not mixed with technical questions the technicians will stay. Politics must take second place to technical problems."

Three weeks after this interview, the supervisors walked off the job to protest government hiring of executive personnel. The top leadership maintained, "We are not in bad condition nor are we in very good conditions." Yet problems arose—serious conflicts between the government and the supervisors. The supervisors attempted to take control of the hiring of management—a prerogative they had never assumed under United States ownership. On the one hand, the supervisors claimed that they were only concerned with production and technical questions and had no objections to the government's policy; on the other hand, they attempted to convert nationalization of the mines into a vehicle for their own domination. Using technological ideology (opposing the introduction of "politics"), many supervisors attempted to control the appointment of the managers and executives to the mines—thus, in effect, controlling mining policy—a highly political issue.

WORKING CLASS BEHAVIOR AND ATTITUDES

One of the paradoxes during the first months of the nationalization was the decline in the number of strikes and the low level of absenteeism among the relatively *less* politicized and radicalized copper workers in Chuquicamata compared to the copper mining workers in *El Teniente* or *El Salvador*. The lower level of absenteeism in *Chuquicamata* was not so much a response to the revolutionary goals of the government as it was a commitment to staying on the job to make more money. In the short run, the workers with an "economist" outlook are more disciplined and more prone than the more radicalized workers to continue working as well as before. The latter may perceive the victory of the Left as a means of relaxing on the job. To the more radical workers, socialism is associated with redistribution, not production. To the more conservative workers, "a job is a job" that has to be done regardless of who is in power. In the long run, with political education these differing responses may change—and the workers may change their perceptions of their role in industry. However that will depend on the kind of efforts the government makes to mobilize, educate, and motivate the working class. Presently, the political efforts by the parties on the Left to *concientizar* (to make conscious) the mining workers has been very sporadic and unsystematic. Workers' representatives are elected by the trade union officials and the new management personnel function much the same as before. The structure of salaries, status, and the prerogatives of management are little changed. Nevertheless, trade unionists are aware of the larger political issues involved in the nationalization of the mines.

This is a long term process. Workers have to learn that the national interest comes before private interest. All profits are not to be distributed to the workers—but to be used for development of the whole country.

The militancy of the workers is most clearly seen on the issue of paying compensation to the former U.S. owners. Most workers felt that the government should pay little or nothing. One trade union leader stated:

I believe that the Company should not be paid, they should pay us for all the riches that they took out; they left us misery and sabotaged the mines. They were the thieves not the Chileans.[6]

While mining workers appear to be primarily interested in increasing their personal income, they also express considerable nationalist sentiment on the issue of compensation. This might be caused by the belief that if the Chilean government pays a high compensation, it will come out of their pockets. The combination of economic self-interest and nationalism blend and make the compensation issue a potent factor in Chilean politics and in U.S.-Chilean relations.

While more mine workers in El Teniente favored the nationalization of the mines (as opposed to workers in *Chuquicamata*), their perception of what nationalization *meant* was different from that of the leaders of the Left. For the workers, it was seen as a means of substantially improving *their* economic levels—not as a stimulus to national development—although the national development outlook was being promoted by trade union leaders. As one copper worker in *El Teniente* stated:

I am in favor of nationalization of the mines—it will bring more work for everybody—as long as we keep our social benefits (*regalias*) and they arrange our collective bargaining contracts (*pliego de peticiones*).

Another worker emphasized:

We are the ones who produce for the country therefore we should receive better salaries at the end of the year.

On the question of who should make policy within the plant the workers tend to divide between a majority favoring bipartite committees (worker-technicians or worker-professional supervisor) and a smaller group favoring strictly workers' committees. In contrast, the supervisors tended to favor a structure in which management was rooted in the upper reaches of the supervisory hierarchy and the workers' councils formed a consultative body

---

[6] The reference to "thieves" was in response to an article published by the New York *Daily News* that was reproduced in Chile and that accused the Chilean government of robbing U. S. investors.

dealing with limited areas of labor relations. In summary, the mining workers were much closer to a democratic socialist participatory position than were the supervisors. In *El Teniente* there is a closer identification between workers and government than in Chuquicamata; likewise the *El Teniente* workers' express more hostility toward their supervisors. One worker stated:

> Up to now this government has done more in six months than the previous government in six years—even though they [referring to the supervisors] don't believe it.

On the other hand, there is considerable naivete among the new socialist managers; they assume that the mere fact of nationalization—the formal change of ownership from private to public—is sufficient to motivate the workers to produce more. One manager thought that as a result of nationalization "the miners will be obligated to be more responsible." Up to now, many socialist executives have avoided the question of who will control the nationalized industries.[7]

In regard to the charge that they are "privileged workers," the miners usually react with indignation.

> We don't believe it. Here [in the mines] you have to mortify yourself a great deal. Those people in Santiago simply don't know the conditions of the mines. They don't know the kind of work involved in the mines. They think it is the same [kind of work] as they do.

These same mining workers in *El Teniente* who support Allende, who think this is the best government Chile has had, are the same workers who see the process of change in narrow economic terms *and* are among the 30 to 50 percent of the workers absent each Monday. Radical political beliefs are not linked to a disciplined commitment to socialist production.

The copper miners accustomed to struggling for welfare and redistributive programs have yet to be converted to viewing themselves as leaders of the whole of society. While trade union leaders have to some degree modified their behavior, this may lead them to misperceive the attitudes of the rank and file workers. One example is the case of a former mine leader—now a government official in Rancagua—who asserted:

> With a few exceptions most workers perceive nationalization as welfare for the country. The workers will see that there is a limit to demands. There will be increased demands for national development and less demands for individual satisfaction.

It is interesting to note that subsequent to his opening declaration the rest of his response was in the *future* tense.

---

[7] This "socialist" position is not very different from the bureaucratic collectivist position adopted by the technocratic supervisors who justify their elitist position by arguing that "workers are not prepared [to participate], the majority are campesinos who lack a [cultural] base even if they are literate."

Thus, while trade union leaders tend to perceive nationalization as a means of capitalizing the economy and developing new industries, workers tend to perceive it in terms of "better living standards" and other immediate benefits. The crucial task of the government will be to bridge the two points of view—or face a serious loss of support.

INDUSTRIAL WORKERS, PARTICIPATION, AND THE TEXTILE INDUSTRY

In May 1971 the textile workers employed in the giant, modern plants owned by the industrial magnates, Yarur and Sumar, went on strike, occupying the plants and calling on the government to nationalize them. The government "requisitioned" the plants and the firms passed over unofficially to the "social" or state sector of the economy.[8]

The major textile firms in Chile were largely in the hands of immigrant Middle Easterners—successful businessmen whose labor policies reflected a carefully organized paternalistic system: low wages and company organized social facilities, opposition to unionization, and a network of clientele groups (section chiefs, foremen, and others), which filtered information and served to check militant workers.

The industrial workers union in Hirmas textile firms were organized in 1945. Prolonged (60 day) strikes did not occur until 1961 and 1965 and were largely over wage issues. The employees union was founded in 1964 and engaged in strikes in 1969 and 1970. Until 1961, the company was largely in control of the union—manipulating it to serve the ends of the owners. Subsequently, the Left, mainly the Communist party, became active and eventually communist unionists were elected to the leadership of the union. Through pressure, organization, and struggle, the workers improved their treatment on the job, although salaries remained quite low. The union began to replace the company in the organization of the social and cultural activities of the firm. The trade union's role in the enterprise was largely confined to raising purely economic issues. On occasion, usually during elections, spokesmen for the left-wing parties were presented to workers' assemblies. In the Hirmas textile firm, union leaders estimated that 70 percent of the industrial workers and about 60 percent of the employees voted for Allende in 1970. Nevertheless, few of the workers are actually members of any political party. The Allende government had strong support from the trade union leaders and and the sympathy of the great majority of workers—yet the level of consciousness within the plant did not go very far beyond "economism"— behavior that is mostly concerned with trade union issues.

Unlike the nationalization of copper, which was almost wholly a product

---

[8] The owners are contesting the expropriation and a definitive legal decision has not yet been reached—although it is very doubtful if the ex-owners will ever return.

of executive and congressional action, the workers and employees actually took an active part in the "requisition" of the textile industry. From the time Allende was elected until the firm was requisitioned, the owners lowered production (as did almost all private industrialists). The trade unionists correctly perceived this as part of a campaign to sabotage production and to create shortages and public unrest leading to the overthrow of the government. Trade union officials met wtih the Minister of Economy, Pedro Vuskovic to discuss the problem. Subsequently the trade union called a mass meeting of textile workers in which the overwhelming majority decided to strike and proceeded to occupy the plant. After three days, the government requisitioned the plant and appointed an *interventor* to manage the firm along with the leaders of the trade unions.

While the trade union leaders were clearly acting out of socialist convictions and understood that the strike and occupation were first steps toward nationalization of the industry, many of the workers who supported the strike initially did so in response to the low salaries and intense exploitative conditions of work. Behind the general support of the trade union leaders' political demands were the workers' economic and social grievances against the *patron*. *After* the nationalization took place, the majority of workers expressed support for the idea. The idea of nationalization was not a novel one to the workers; *but* prior to its actually coming about it seemed somewhat remote in comparison to economic and job problems that workers faced on a day-to-day basis.

Once nationalization took place, sectors of the government interested in workers' control of industry immediately initiated a series of broad educational programs to prepare workers to participate in the management of the firm. Unlike the supervisors in the copper industry, the government *interventor* in charge of the Hirmas textile plant was a professional with strong democratic socialist ideas. While the textile workers shared the same "economist" orientation as the copper workers and the trade union leaders were not too different from the union leaders in the copper mines, the way in which the requisition took place, the direct and active mobilization of the workers themselves. and the active political intervention of a technically competent socialist *interventor* created a siuation where the workers *could* deepen their political understanding of the whole process.

THE SOCIALIST EXECUTIVE IN EX-HIRMAS TEXTILE INC.

The importance of the presence of a class-conscious democratic socialist in the top executive position of a newly nationalized plant cannot be underestimated, especially in light of the need to transform workers from economist to socialist consciousness. At the time of the requisition the government *interventor* acted, decisively, disposing of all vestiges of the authority of the previous owners; some workers, partly fearful of the return of the old owners, were reserved and refused to openly commit themselves. Subsequently, once the *interventor* made it absolutely clear that the owner could not "come home again," there was a general outpouring of support. Downgrading or eliminating the structure of authority, however, was only one of the tasks that faced the socialist executive. He faced two other problems— maintaining the efficient operation of the plant and creating a new structure of authority in which the workers and employees participated directly in all major policy decisions. His first step was to work closely with the trade union leaders who were in close day to day contact with the workers; second, he took measures to reassure the older professionals and employees but let them understand that they were under the orders of the *interventor* and the trade union leaders. Closely allied measures were taken: the content of the company publications was changed, publishing articles on workers' involvement; courses in workers' management were established; more important, the executive began to move toward the development of a *consejo directivo* (executive council), which would include five representatives directly elected by the workers, five representatives selected by the government, and a general administrator, appointed by the government. As a first step, in every section of the plant, workers formed production committees to advise on policy and to exercise control over the productive process.

The organizational measures taken thus far in the nationalized firm reflect in part the socialist ideology of the *interventor*. In this words:

> The goal is for workers to participate in the discussion of national politics—not only the production goals of the government. The workers should participate on all levels of the plan—both on the level of the firm as well as on the national level.

Regarding the attitudes of the workers, the interventor had an accurate perception of how much support existed as well as the problems regarding political consciousness.

> There are two tendencies among the workers: some identify with the new structure and produce more; others take advantage of the new structure and work less. To maintain work discipline we need workers' committees to pressure the workers—not administrative measures. The basic reason that workers support change is because there are better working conditions—there is more tranquility. For others there is a wait and see attitude: to see if we can run the plant efficiently and can maintain authority. Even if workers do not have the capacity to decide today, they will learn through practice.

TRADE UNION LEADERS IN HIRMAS

Most of the leaders of the industrial union were Communists who had spent many years improving working and salary conditions in the factory and urging workers to vote for candidates of the Left during the elections. They felt somewhat uncomfortable during our interview, which took place in the plush meeting room of the former board of directors. The trade unionists were men and women who were close to the level and style of life of a skilled worker. In discussing the role of the trade union in the postrequisition period one trade union leader noted:

It [the trade union] has to change without losing its autonomy.[9] We must defend the interests of the working class. With the bosses the struggle was frontal; now we have to participate directly in the firm. Now we have to know all aspects of the firm—we must consider our collective bargaining demands in relationship with the overall performance of the firm. We have to make the workers conscious and prepare them for the elections to the *consejo*. I think the trade unionist should stay in the union to make the rank and file conscious.

While the communist trade unionist favors the elimination of capitalism he favors a *gradual* transformation.

This is a government in transition: in this stage the government defines the areas to be expropriated, forms mixed enterprises and eliminates it [capitalism] little by little. Politically it may not be suitable to expropriate some enterprises in this stage—in the long run they might be expropriated as we head toward socialism.

In contrast to the socialist *interventor* who favored acceleration of the process—the communist trade union leader exclaimed:

The rate of expropriation [during the first eight months] is dizzy, the working class was not prepared for the rapid rate of change. The government is complying with its program. We are pleasantly surprised by the rate of change.

It appears that the political leadership outside of the factory took the initiatives. With the leadership of trade unions supported by rank and file workers with economic and social grievance they carried out the requisition.

TEXTILE WORKERS' ATTITUDES TOWARD PARTICIPATION

There are at least four different types of workers to consider in discussing workers attitudes: the section chiefs (foremen), the union delegates (equivalent of shop stewards), the rank and file skilled workers, and the unskilled or semiskilled workers, who were mostly women.

The foremen were deeply divided between those who favored the changes and those who were uncertain or somewhat opposed. For example, one foreman who had been with the firm for 22 years stated:

[9] All trade unionists that I interviewed throughout Chile maintained that the trade unions should be autonomous and have the right to strike. One socialist union leader stated, "The day we lose the right to strike I will stop supporting the government."

I am not sure that the social benefits gained in the past will stay because it [the change] is all new, it is not secure. I cannot say whether it will result well or not. With the *patron* it was hard to get an increase but through the trade union one could get increases. We do not know if this practice will continue.

Questioned about the issue of workers' participation this same individual responded:

The principle issue is the factor of money. With pay the workers will be successful: if there is more money there will be more work; if the present *patron* doesn't pay more we should return to the old patron.

In contrast, another foreman analyzed the situation from a totally different perspective.

This change was long awaited. We have to thank President Allende. We are content and have to produce more. The workers and employees are capable of running the enterprise. We are not *obreros* (manual workers) or empleados (white collar workers) but trabajadores (a general term, "one who works"). I participate in all the meetings and assemblies.

If lower management is divided, the skilled workers tend to be overwhelmingly favorable to the changes—although they differ somewhat in terms of their perception of specific issues. Many of the skilled workers, like the unskilled workers, felt that the lack of constant pressure—what some refer to as "persecution"—on the job was the most important change. Others felt that there was less conflict and more peaceful labor relations—social relations were more humane. Among most skilled workers interviewed there was a clear understanding that wage increases were dependent on production increases. Unlike unskilled workers, the skilled workers felt confident that the workers and employees were as capable of managing the enterprise as the previous owners. One class-conscious mechanic stated:

This is what we had always hoped for. We are going to work under a new system—socialism—for all Chileans. It is a principle to nationalize all vital industries. Of course with facilities, repair-parts, the workers can run the industry. Working twenty-two years for private owners— why can't we work for ourselves? Here [among the mechanics] all the workers think the same as me. Here and there some workers, those without culture,[10] can't understand. If there is an increase in production then there will be an increase in salary. We have to show the *interventor*. Some companeros want more money now—but we have to prove our capacity to produce first.

Most skilled workers actively participated in meetings and discussions. They felt the importance of the change and the opportunity that this change

---

[10] This may be translated loosely as "those who are not very bright."

represented from the point of view of the worker much more so than the unskilled workers. The skilled workers were more likely than their unskilled *companeros* to take a "longer view" of the process and to see the whole process.

There are articulate class-conscious workers among the semiskilled or unskilled workers, but they are a small minority. A younger worker who was a section delegate to the union, active in the nomination of the new *directorio*, summed up the meaning of the nationalization in the following terms.

> I feel integrated in the firm, before I felt alienated. The biggest change is that the very workers are organizing committees, the people are actually participating in the firm. As it is new the workers are learning and the university people with theoretical preparation will contribute. There are differences occasionally, workers who want more salary, (differences in work result in different demands), problems inherited from the past; we should equalize salaries. Workers salaries should be adjusted to take account of inflation and then the rest should be in the form of social improvements [not individual increases], something visible like child care centers for four and five years olds [in addition to the infant centers that already existed], a football field, more housing—fifty percent of us live in temporary shacks. It is important that the changes come from this government and not through strikes. I have to participate as a worker in this change. I want change for my children even if I don't see it.

However, most unskilled workers were *not very clear* about the changes and had less to say though they were generally sympathetic. One worker stated:

> It is a little better—more work. The talks are very good—they explained things I didn't understand. There is more comradeship (*companerismo*). I am in favor of increased salaries as well as increases in production.

A woman who had been a machine operator for five years commented.

> We are better off but I don't go to meetings or to talks. [long pause] Now we are more peaceful. It is better to have workers as leaders than a *patron*. Before we worked because we had to, now one knows he has to.

Another female machine helper blandly noted:

> Same conditions as before. I haven't participated in meetings. There are some people better prepared in the industry. Up to now the government has been very good. Our job is to produce good fibers (*telas*).

The main base of support for the notion of workers' participation lies with the trade union activists and the skilled workers; lower management and the unskilled workers are less involved and tend to view the process of change somewhat more in "economist" terms. The acceptability of the larger issue of workers' participation will depend on the ability of the more politically conscious workers to draw their less involved *companeros* into activity. The alternative to workers' participation is the gradual bureaucratization of the new structure—and the subsequent focus exclusively on salary demands, which in turn could cause serious strains on the governments industrial expansion program.

AGRARIAN WORKERS: FROM SUBJECT TO PROTAGONISTS

The process of land expropriation has been vastly accelerated with the election of Salvador Allende. Both organized peasant land seizures and government *initiated* expropriations have made deep inroads in the old latifundia structure, especially in areas little affected by the previous Frei government. The conservative landholding elite of the South of Chile had declared that it would never surrender; many landowners armed themselves and some were implicated in the aborted plot to overthrow the government, which began with the attempted kidnapping and actual assassination of the commander in chief of the army. Despite this intransigent opposition, the large farms are being expropriated—the political power of the agrarian elite is being undermined. Massive unionization has taken place. Equally important left-wing organizers —socialists, MIR, and MAPU[11]—have been organizing peasant assemblies, which elect peasant representatives who help formulate postagrarian reform policy—putting an end to bureaucratically administered agrarian decisions and nonpeasant-directed agrarian policies.

Due to intense party competition in the countryside and the organizational and political breakthrough during the past six years, we can distinguish essentially four types of peasant organization: (1) The Socialist, Communist, MAPU-led peasant unions, closely linked to the official left-wing parties. These peasant unions contain a variety of social forces from moderate "legalist" Communist peasant unionists to militant Socialists who work closely with MCR; (2) The Christian Democratic peasant unions, which contain a variety of moderate as well as left-christian (*izquierda cristian*) peansant unions; (3) The MCR, largely MIR-led peasant movement, which took the lead in the organization of peasant land occupations outside of official legal channels. (4) The traditional peasantry—loyal to the large landowners' association; this type of peasant is a vanishing phenomenon.

Obviously the degree of politicization in the countryside has risen considerably in the past few years, as has the complexity of political affiliation.

With the victory of Salvador Allende, the agrarian reform was accelerated both by peasant as well as by government action. Parallel to the overall politicization was the growth of rural radicalism; within this radical peasant

---

[11] MIR stands for Movement of the Revolutionary Left; MAPU is a former left-Catholic group now closer to Marxism-Leninism.

movement, a revolutionary socialist peasant movement emerged, largely composed of left-socialist and MIR-led peasant unions.

It is apparent that in the South of Chile—an area of extreme poverty and tyrannical landlord rule—the organization of the peasantry was delayed. Peasants were violently prevented from unionizing; the repression was much more intense than in the rest of the country. With the election of Allende, the "late" developing peasant consciousness of the South responded to the most "advanced" revolutionary ideas, methods of struggle, and organization. Rural collectivism and nonlegal land occupations under the leadership of the most resolute and determined revolutionary organization characterized the Southern peasant movement. The sudden and radical change expressed the latent political demands that previous governments had inhibited. The election of Allende was the green light for a rapid and thorough transformation. Consciously or not, depending on the level of awareness of each peasant, throughout the South of Chile scores of farms were occupied as peasants learned that the Armed Forces would not be used to repress them. Whether with tongue in cheek or not, many peasants interviewed claimed that they were "only helping President Allende to carry out the agrarian reform and to increase production for the country." There may be two elements involved in this response (or a mixture of both). The peasants may have genuinely thought that they were helping Allende or they may have felt that this was a historic opportunity to bring about changes tht Allende might later be unable or unwilling to carry out. There is some rational basis for peasant doubts about government action and "do it yourself" agrarian reform: in the past Chilean leftists have promised far more than they have ever actually carried out.

A local peasant leader of a recently seized farm describes the process of political action in the following terms.

Trade union activity began in 1965 but there was no unity among the workers, most workers were afraid that the owner would cause trouble, they would lose their job. With the Allende victory the owner disappeared[12] and the son managed the farm. After September 4, 1970 they started to sell the [farm] machinery and the animals: of 400 cows only 140 remain.[13] In October we formed a union—108 of the 120 workers participated in the assembly. On November 13 the farm was taken by 78 peasants, the employees [management] did not participate—they were allies of the owner. On November 25 CORA[14] arrived with an *interventor*—we lost only one half day of work. During the intervention the Socialist Party gave us legal aid. There is little "politics"—work and

[12] It appears that the owner fled to Argentina, implicated in the Schneider assassination plot.

[13] After Allende's victory September 4, 1970, the large landholders began selling and slaughtering animals and dismantling farm machinery.

[14] The government's Agrarian Reform Corporation.

technical assistance is basic. There are no Christian Democrats . . . before there were some Alessandristas. The majority are with the Socialist Party though few attend meetings. Allende is very good: on all sides he is wih us. The Program is being fulfilled. Before I was with the Right: always eat with the Right but vote with the Left.

On the issues directly affecting the peasantry, local peasant leaders have moved closer to the Left—shedding their inhibitions and openly collaborating with the government. Concerning other areas of the government's program there is some radical spillover, but the local unionists were not as sure of their opinions.

I understand very little about copper. It is a big step. The riches will not go abroad but will stay in Chile. To have the State own the banks is not a bad idea. The funds of the rich will be controlled.

In discussing their relationship with peasants outside and inside of the farm, the unionists had a realistic appraisal of their possibilities.

Production on this farm will increase—we are expanding the amount of land to be seeded from 50 to 100 hectareas. Milk will drop since the cows were sold. . . . The peasants on the adjoining farm are with the boss he is very paternalistic. We are surrounded by small proprietors—there are no direct discussions. We participate in the municipal peasant council—which seems to unite the peasants. We agree that, in principle, we should work the farm collectively ("en comunidad"). Work discipline varies: we levy fines but we cannot throw out offenders. Concerning drinking: he who doesn't drink is an evangelist—with this cold we all take a drink.

The more radical peasants—many of them Mapuche Indians from the South of Chile—are attracted to the MCR. Living in abysmal poverty—even by Chilean peasant standards—many of their children walk barefoot on the frozen mud. In the Camilo Torres *campamento* (municipality of Lautaro in the Province of Cautin), a local MCR peasant leader of an illegal land occupation clearly articulated their revolutionary socialist outlook.[15]

We favor collectivizing the land. This land seizure was self-organized. We support the government by land seizures. I am with Allende. This was an abandoned farm that we are making productive—which is what the President has asked us to do. We support the nationalization of copper.

When asked to identify Camilo Torres, the MCR militant confused him with Che Guevara. Nevertheless, this peasant militant represents one of the most advanced social forces in Chile today; in the breadth and scope of his

[15] As we approved, the MCR militant came toward us menacingly, carrying a thick club—apparently mistaking us for the former landowners.

ideas he is thoroughly imbued with the socialist ethos—considerably more advanced than many urban industrial workers.

In general, most peasants describe this government's performance favorably in comparison to previous governments—although a good many still think the agrarian reform is too slow. Most ascribe a possible decline in production to the sabotage of the former landlords, the slowness of the expropriation procedure, and the inefficiency of government agencies in the delivery of supplies. Peasants in areas of intense conflict where farms have been seized or expropriated during the Allende government favor collective ownership.

It is in the areas of the organization of agriculture after expropriation that the left-wing parties are in disagreement. The relationhip between the Socialists and Communists in rural areas is tense; the more militant Socialist organized unions are growing rapidly and threaten the existing Communist leadership in the unions. In the upcoming peasant council elections, the Socialists may displace the Communists as the leading force in the country-side. On the other hand, the relationships between the socialist militants and the MCR—in rural Southern Chile—are very good. One socialist peasant stated: "The MCR are intelligent, they are not like they are painted—they are a great help to the government. They helped organize the trade unions not undermine them." In summing up his position regarding the government, one rank and file peasant from Coihueco (Province of Nuble) put it very succinctly.

> Our hope is with the government that we have, it is completely with the *campesino*. It is more or less good—better than before. We are begin-ning, much has been done, more to be done. The opposition is strong. We need to organize trade unions to put the opposition to rest.

For the peasantry, the electoral victory in September 1970 presented an opportunity to act without reprisal, stimulated land seizures, and accelerated legal expropriations—the snowball effect provided the massive popular sup-port for the Left in the April 1971 municipal elections.

The President of the "Socialist Lands" Federation of Nuble claimed that 80 percent of the peasants favored collectivizing the land. The other 20 per-cent who favored individual holdings were described as still under Christian Democratic influence. According to this militant leader, son of a rural proletariat,

> We should work the land collectively, and not divide the land because then conflicts will continue: conflicts between small proprietors and workers.

The process of radicalization in the countryside continues: first the Christian Democrats displaced the traditional Right; now the Communists, Socialists, and Chrisian Left (ex-MAPU and ex-Christian Democrats) are displacing the Christian Democrats; at the same time the MIR has begun to put pressure on the official left and has put itself in a position to become a major force if the government failed to carry through its promise to accelerate the agrarian reform. The peasant commitment to the government, although strong, is *conditional*: performance is stressed; comparisons are made with the past; and support is hedged with the proviso, "Up to now it is completing its program . . .," which suggests that the government's support will depend on its ability to keep up with radical peasant demands.

LAND SQUATTERS: THE NEW URBAN REVOLUTIONARIES

Comparing the best years of the two previous presidents to the performance of the Allende government in the area of public housing, we get an idea of the specific improvements that have led to increased support of the Left among the lower class.

Time Period	Number of Houses Built
Allende (November 4, 1970 to March 26, 1971) [16]	31,018
Frei (1965) [17]	26,196
Alessandri (1961) [17]	28,297

In many areas, unemployment committees in the land squatter settlements (*campamentos*) provide the labor force to build the houses. The *campamentos* themselves vary a great deal in terms of their internal structure, degree of organization, politicization, and capacity to make basic decisions concerning community development. The *campamentos* around Santiago under MIR leadership are generally recognized as the best organized; there is a greater degree of participation, law and order, and sense of purpose among the *pobladores* (residents).

The most recent major land squatter movement began in January 1970: groups of houseless ("sin casa") families (endlessly given the runaround by Frei's housing officials) began a massive occupation of unused land sites. Not infrequently these squatters were attacked by special units of the riot police (*grupo-movil*) established by the Frei government to deal with mass movements. As a result the *pobladores* set up self-defense units—*milicia popular*—to defend the settlers from external government sponsored violence as well as to maintain internal order.

After the election of Allende, government policy began to change, as did

[16] By July 1, 1971 nearly 50,000 houses had been built; by the end of 1971 the government hopes to build 100,000 houses.

[17] We are comparing the best years of the Frei and Alessandri governments to the first five months of Allende. Raw data taken from CORVI *Sub-Oficina de Campamentos*.

the attitudes, policies, and organization of the *campamentos*.[18] Mike, chief of "Campamento Nueva Habana" ("New Havana")—population 7000—discussed these changes."

After September 4 there was a fundamental change. Before, the Housing Ministry (Ministerio de Vivienda) was enemy No. 1. After September 4, the doors of the Housing Ministry were wide open. The *grupo movil* was dissolved, and our popular militias in part also were dissolved because some [milicianos] became delinquents for lack of sufficient political education. We are re-organizing the militia. After September 4, mobilization and confrontation ended—in part because the *pobladores* began to criticize leaders of the Campamento; they said 'Allende is now President and you have to change your politics.' The land here was given over to the *pobladores*. All the *campamentos* began to divide. Some went to the Socialists, many stayed with the MIR. The pobladores demanded that the leaders solve their problems. When the national health workers (Servicio Nacional de Salud) came to our campamento they had to join the Campamento's Health Front (*Frente de Salud*). Thus the nurses and doctors had to discuss the organization of the poli-clinic with the *pobladores*—thus avoiding paternalism. A doctor is just one more *companero* who happens to know more. . . .

The high degree of active participation in the *Campamento* reflects the stress given to it in the ideology of the MIR and the MIR's capacity to create organizational structures and tangible goals that allow individuals to channel their energies. In discussing *New Havana's* housing policy, Mike[19] reveals the degree of political and organizational sophistication that the pobladores have achieved.

CORVI [the Housing Corporation] came with their little shanty houses. The *pobladores* demanded that they participate and discuss the planning of the houses. Along with the *pobladores* were a group of left-wing architects who advised them in their discussion with CORVI. The *pobladores* make the architects conscious of the need to work together. The *pobladores* rejected private construction firms and provided voluntary labor to build. CORVI set up a construction firm to work with the *pobladores*. With the money saved, the size of the houses was expanded from 36 square meters to 46 square meters and up to 65 square meters. We know how we want to live even if we are not architects. We discuss and approved the plans. *Pobladores* who are paying for their house want a

---

[18] Campamento Nueva Habana has several "fronts" or organizations that deal with different areas, such as health, education, and cultural activity. In other words, community "development" is expressed through functional differentiation and organizational specialization.

[19] Mike, the leader of the New Haven campamento, was formerly an electrician in construction. He left his trade to become a full-time poblador organizer for the MIR. He lives in the campamento and receives less than $1.50 (official rate) per day.

say in how it is going to be built. The bureaucracy of CORVI resisted but we mobilized and threatened to seize their building. In private enterprise workers don't care about materials because they have no say in the organization of work. The *pobladores* organize Tri-partite committees: (a) poblador leaders and workers (b) university technical advisors (c) CORVI officials. Once New Havana is finished the workers will have the experience to form a construction firm; they will elect their foremen and supervisors and there will be no inequality between workers and management.

Regarding the internal structure, the *campamento's* fundamental unit is the block, each block and each *frente* elect delegates to the *directorio* or leadership which meets on weekly basis. In July 1971, the community was completing the construction of a community cafeteria, laundry, and supermarket. Mike pointed out that these social services are built to "allow women to participate in the tasks of the community."

New Havana is not a "typical" campamento—it is exceptional. The degree of order, organization, and achievement is a function of the *political* level of the *pobladores,* which in turn reflects the policies of the political leaders.

In comparing the MIR to the official left (Communist and Socialist parties) Mike made some interesting distinctions that may be relevant to our understanding of the political and social basis of popular participation in basic community decisions.

The traditional left organizations organize the *pobladores* until the next elections when they introduce lighting, water, etc. The MIR rejects elections in principle—we work continuously with *pobladores.* The leaders of the campamentos of the U. P. [*Unidad Popular*—the coalition of left parties in the government] don't live in the campamento, they come in a car twice a week—to attend meetings. The absentee leaders are not present to execute the program. MIR leaders are totally integrated in the campamento—involved in all relations within the campamento. We work because we believe in the revolution. There is a strong sense of *companerismo.*

Among the land squatters of New Havana we see the first Socialist experiment and the building of the new Socialist man, that Che *Guevara* spoke of; the self-organized community, in which state property is an instrument of the democratically organized community. Socialist political organization and behavior appears to be higher among the pobladores of New Havana than any other working-class strata in Chile.

3

M. C. Tavares & J. Serra | Beyond Stagnation: A Discussion on the Nature of Recent Development in Brazil[1]

This essay opens a discussion on the fundamental characteristics of recent economic development in Brazil. The subject is not alien to other Latin American economies, considering the varying degrees of similarity between them and the Brazilian economy. For this reason, whenever possible, we make reference either to Latin America as a whole or to a particular country.

In the first part of the essay, we will try to demonstrate the weaknesses of the argument for economic stagnation—as it is currently understood—as a tendency that affects the Latin American economies. We have given great importance to this topic, since, in our opinion, the stagnation thesis has

Source. Reprinted by permission of the author.

[1] Several aspects of this essay make use of and develop the ideas of Anibal Pinto and Pedro Vuskovic as presented in the following articles: A. Pinto, "*Concentración del progreso técnico y de sus frutos en el desarrollo Latinoamericano,*" *Trimestre Económico*, No. 125, 1965, also included in Andres Bianchi (ed.) : *America Latina*: *Ensayos de interpretación económica*, Santiago, Editorial Universitaria, 1969; A. Pinto, "*Diagnósticos, estructuras y esquemas de desarrollo en América Latina,*" Boletín ELAS, No. 2, Year 3, June, 1970, and P. Vuskovic, "*Distribución del ingreso y opciones de desarrollo,*" *Cuadernos de la realidad Nacional*, CEREN, Catholic University of Chile, No. 5, September 1970.

The authors thank Anibal Pinto for his immense contributions to the form and content of this essay. We nevertheless assume complete responsibility for the ideas expressed here. We also thank Luis Souza, Claudio Salm, Fernando H. Cardoso, Luis Barros, and Francisco Weffort for their valuable comments. Finally, we wish to state that the ideas expressed in this essay are strictly personal and do not necessarily represent the ideas of the institutions that the authors are connected to.

significantly hindered the progress of interpretations of the ways certain economies operate, as in the case of Brazil.

After making a general presentation of the problem, we will analyze in detail the thesis of stagnation as it has been presented by its principal exponent: Celso Furtado, in his article: "Desarrollo y estancamiento en América Latina: un enfoque estructuralista."[2] We chose this article because it explains in detail the thesis of stagnation.

Part One ends with a brief interpretation of the process of crisis and recuperation in the Brazilian economy during the middle of the last decade.

Part Two presents some characteristics that define the nature of recent economic development in Brazil. Our perspective will allow us to distinguish the various ways in which the basic elements of a capitalist economy manifest themselves within the Brazilian structure, in relation to the processes of expansion, distribution, and incorporation of technological progress and economic concentration.

Lack of space and time prohibit a more detailed analysis of some important aspects of the system (that is, the financial system), that are fundamental to an understanding of the processes of expansion and concentration of capital.

Since our analysis is exploratory, we will dedicate ample space to the discussion of some concepts and ideas that have traditionally been understood in an inaccurate way or that are simply erroneous.

Part Two concludes with some ideas on the decisive contradictions and crises of Brazilian capitalist development in order to outline some ideas for a subsequent analysis.

It is important to emphasize that the ideas we develop here must be seen as basic hypotheses for a more profound and extensive interpretation of the various topics. This fact is reflected in the examples given and in the lack of statistical evidence.

PART ONE: STAGNATION OR CRISIS?

Prevalent in certain political and intellectual circles is the belief that the majority of the Latin American economies face a situation of long- or medium-range structural stagnation. This theory is prevalent because of the exhaustion of the forces of industrial development that had been created by the import substitute industries. This conviction has given rise to and has been strengthened by numerous analyses, which range from simple empirical studies to theoretical, explanatory, and predictive models.

We believe that the crisis that follows the weakening of the substitution process in essence represents—at least in some countries—a transitory condi-

---

[2] See A. Bianchi (ed.), *América Latina: ensayos de interpretación económica*, Santiago, Editorial Universitaria, 1969, pp. 120–149.

tion toward a new strategy of capitalist development. It can present very dynamic characteristics, at the same time reinforcing some aspects of the "model" of substitutive growth in its more advanced stages: social margination and geographic concentration, as well as the falling behind of certain economic subsectors in the areas of production.

Because of this last factor, perhaps, many academicians conclude that the Latin American capitalist economy lives in a state of economic prostration. Observing that a great part of the population in Latin America is, and will tend to remain marginated from the benefits of economic growth and at very low levels of productivity through underdevelopment, they maintain that such a situation demonstrates capitalism's dynamic unfeasability in Latin America. The evidence is obviously correct, but its use in these studies avoids the differences between the interests of the dominant sectors of Latin America and the national interest. Margination, structural unemployment, underconsumption, and so forth, do not necessarily constitute in themselves fundamental problems of the economic dynamics of capitalism (as opposed to, for example, the case of the problems related to the absorption of savings and investment opportunities). In the developed capitalist countries, the modernization of agriculture, the maximization of the use of the labor force and of the consumer market have, in the past, constituted important factors for the expansion of the system at given points in time.[3] This does not occur in the Latin American economies, but this is not a basis for stating that capitalism lacks vigour in the region as a whole. The capitalist process of Brazil, in particular, although it is more and more developing in an unequal fashion, incorporating and excluding sectors of the population and the different economic strata in order to deepen a series of differences related to consumption and productivity, has also created a model that allows for a self-generation of internal impulses and of expansion, which gives it forcefulness. Thus, one could say that while Brazilian capitalism is developing satisfactorily, the majority of the population continues to live under conditions of great economic deprivation because of the dynamics of the system, or, because of the *type* of dynamics under which it operates.[4]

Other analyses attempted to explain the material stagnation through the manipulation of some method extracted from Marxist economics, or from neoclassic economics. It is even postulated that as the Latin American economies keep growing, the market will decrease, because more people will become marginated from it. It would seem, then, that the size of the market would depend more on the number of people that integrate it than on the amount of the economic surplus available for exchange. More refined analyses, obviously possessed of a static perception of the economic process, try to

[3] See Antonio Castro's introduction to his book *Sete Ensaios sobre a economia brasilera*, Río de Janeiro, Ed. Forense, 1970.

[4] Fernando Mendes' article, *La situación económica social del pueblo brasileño: la otra violencia*, Santiago, 1971, has ample statistical documentation on this matter.

identify the problem of the declining rate of profit, which is essentially related to the increase through time of the organic composition of capital. Without neglecting this idea completely, others emphasize the problem of a lack of investment opportunities, compounded by the heterogeneous nature of the economy. Undoubtedly they deal with problems more pertinent to the object of this study, as they are concerned with the manifestations of a basic contradiction in the capitalist system: production versus surplus value. Even though Latin American capitalism suffers more from this contradiction than the metropolis does, we cannot assume that because of this contradiction the tendency toward stagnation in our economies will be more pronounced than in the centers of capitalism. Even though the contradiction between production and the realization of surplus value is at the roots of the capitalist system, it is difficult to sustain that such a contradiction is also responsible for any lasting stagnation in economies possessing a significant amount of production goods.

An important consequence of the belief in the stagnation thesis is that it hinders an understanding of the current dynamics of capitalism in the more advanced regions. The conviction that capitalism does not work, or will not work in the future, breeds a disinterest in making an analysis of how it works and expands,[5] which would be an essential starting point for those who propose changing the system.

CELSO FURTADO'S "MODEL." In the last part of Furtado's previously mentioned essay, he analyzes two cases of economic stagnation in Latin America. One case corresponds to countries that were industrialized while at the same time retaining an important precapitalist sector; the other case corresponds to countries that industrialized without holding on to the remnants of a traditional sector, or else absorbing them. According to Furtado, in the first case—contrary to what is observed in the second—an unlimited source of labor, and of wage levels regulated by the prevailing life patterns of the precapitalist sector, will be maintained throughout the industrialization process. As this is the case in most Latin American countries, particularly in Brazil, we will focus on it in our analysis.

Furtado links economic stagnation to the loss of energy of the import-substitute industrialization process. In this sense, he focuses his analysis on the evolution and behavior of the structure of demand, which depends, in turn, on the distribution of income. He considers that industrialization was

[5] We by no means believe that the apologetic analyses of domestic capitalism—so common in Brazil—reveal more than the critical analyses of authors who insist on the idea of a prostrated capitalism. In the latter, perceptions and partial explanations of importance appear, and there has been evident progress. In the former, the real explanations are obviously hidden, through either open apology or through so-called "scientific" analyses, which restrict their focus so much that in the end they say only that which is not important.

definitely not capable of substantially altering the patterns of distribution of income, which were highly concentrated and inherited from the primary export economy, and failed to create a socially integrated market, becoming increasingly oriented toward satisfying the diversified demand of the upper-income groups. The range of possible and profitable substitutions became progressively more restricted to the higher-priced durable consumer goods, and to capital goods that generally necessitate a higher capital per worker coefficient than do the "traditional" activities. The size of the demand, in each new heading to be substituted, was shown to be relatively small, which created significant problems of scale.

In the first place, we should view the economy as a whole. There has been a reduction in the product-capital relationship in terms of an alternative allocation of resources within the different industrial subsectors of industry (due to the concentration of investments in activities with a larger capital-worker coefficient), which results in a slower rate of growth for the whole economy. Similarly, the lower demand for labor per investment unit creates a relative reduction in the rate of assimilation of labor, which, in a situation of wage stability, reduces the total wages in proportion to the industrial product. Since the increase in productivity is barely reflected in the lowering of prices, and would only be concentrated in nonmassive consumer goods even if it were done in large proportions, the rise in the capital-labor coefficient leads to a greater concentration of income, which reinforces the strategy of orienting the production resources toward the sectors with a lower product-capital relationship. On the other hand, it implies a relatively weak growth in the demand for goods produced in sectors whose capital-product relationship is higher (for example, agriculture). Thus, the factors slowing down the growth of the economy increase.

Nevertheless, the situation could appear more optimistic at the level of "dynamic" activities. This is not the case. The capital goods industries can only develop if the relative prices of the sector are extremely high, since they confront greater obstacles resulting from a limited market and the lack of adequate finance resources. In this situation, the capital-product relationship tends to decrease, which, under conditions of wage stability, implies a reduction in the rate of profit. The situation is compounded by the prevalent margin of idle capacity in the durable goods industry. The reduction of profits in modern industry excludes the possibility that the rate of savings can increase to compensate for the decline in the capital-product relation. So, from the point of view of the total economy, as well as from that of the dynamic sector of industry, economic growth tends to diminish under the influx of a capital-product relationship, which rapidly decreases in a situation of wage stability.

Furtado's "model" can be examined from three interrelated angles. The first angle is related to the categories he selects for his analysis, the second is related to the basic assumptions and the internal consistency of his model, and the third is related to the greater or lesser relationship with and account-ability to what has actually taken place in some countries.

We shall now try to develop some observations that are concerned with the first two points; the following section makes implicit or explicit reference to the third point. Finally, we would like to point out that these three points of view are present throughout all our comments.

It seems evident that we consider the development of the product-capital relationship an essential aspect of the economic process of stagnation, although this category is actually a *result* of the economic process and, contrary to what can happen in the categories related to behavior (such as the expected rate of profit), does not constitute an explanation of the dynamics of a capitalist economy. When an entrepreneur makes a decision to invest, he is concerned with the rate of profit that he can obtain. That is, the funda-mental consideration will be the rate of profit expected from the investment he will make. The product-capital relationship does not form part of the entrepreneur's calculations, so it constitutes a technological parameter in physical terms, and a consequence in terms of value for each sector or activity in operation.[6]

The distinction given is not only theoretically important; it is also relevant to an interpretation of stagnation as it has been observed in certain areas. In Brazil, as we shall see later on, the crisis that accompanied the draining of

[6] In terms of conventional economic procedures, it is easy to mistake the expected profits or "marginal efficiency" of an investment with the product-capital relationship. The former is related to the behavior of the entrepreneur and depends on his expectations according to certain given circumstances or variables of the market. The latter is deter-mined by given technological conditions in the process of long-range accumulation.

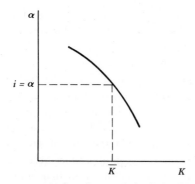
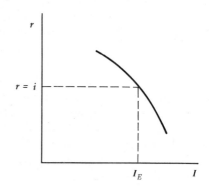

α marginal product-capital relationship
i "normal" rate of interests
K capital
I investment
I_E investment balance
r marginal efficiency of the investment

The determining factor in the dynamics of a capitalist economy is the entrepreneurial behavior that takes into account the changes in the given technological parameters.

the substitutive process is related more to the reduction in the rate of investment and the factors responsible for it than to an eventual decline of the product-capital relation.

Let us look at Furtado's model in order to examine in more detail the author's conclusions regarding the evolution of the product-capital relation and its consequences on the economy.

In examining the alleged decline of this relationship in the industrial sector, Furtado admits a rise in the allotment of capital per worker derived from the concentration of investments in the subsector of metal mechanics.[7] The author then reasons that if "the rate of profit tends to level off among the different industries (otherwise one could not explain how investments are attracted to industries with notoriously inferior profits on capital), taking into account that the wage rates are the same, then we must assume that the product-capital relationship tends to be lower as the capital-per-worker coefficient increases."

In stating this, Furtado uses, in our opinion, an unrealistic premise regarding the equalization of the rate of profit, given the condition of a notably "imperfect" market, where some branches are dominated by large production units that are highly monopolized technologically. There is no reason to state that the rates of profit among the different industries can be equalized. On the contrary, they are always larger in the modern sectors of industry,[8] even though they might have a smaller product-capital relationship.[9] The causality that Furtado establishes in the sense that equal rates of profit imply that the product-capital relation varies inversely to the capital-per-worker coefficient is

[7] In refering to the subsectors of greater concentration of capital and therefore, as he says, of a lower product-capital relationship, Furtado does not refer to the branches of intermediary goods, which are precisely the ones that in advanced stages of the substitute industrialization process are bound to demand a higher allotment of capital per worker, more complex technology, and, in many cases, greater dimensions of scale. For this reason, they constitute important headings in the "difficult" areas of export substitution.

[8] These larger rates of profit are due to the fact that in the more modern industries the rate of labor exploitation tends to be higher as a function of higher productivity, which is not transferred to salaries or to prices by either increasing the first or decreasing the second.

[9] The rate of profit can be expressed by

$$r = a \; \frac{m}{m-1}$$

r rate of profit
a product-capital relationship in terms of value
m rate of surplus value or rate of exploitation

$$m = \frac{p-w}{w}$$

p product per worker
w wage

In spite of its simplicity, there seems to be a great deal of confusion regarding the relationship between the rate of surplus value (surplus value on wages), the product-capital relationship, and the rate of profit. In reality, the product-capital relationship can be considerably smaller in one branch (I) than in another (II) and the rate of profit can nevertheless be much higher, due to the incidence of the rate of surplus value.

also erroneous because it is based on purely formal relationship. If we continue with his analysis, we see that given the product-capital relationship, the relationship between the rates of profit (expost) are a result of the rates of surplus value, or, in other words, of the surplus-wage relationship.

On the other hand, the idea that the product-capital relationship necessarily declines when the capital-worker coefficient is increased (an idea derived from an analytical model of a neoclassic nature), does not take into account the effects of technical progress linked to the accumulation of capital. In effect, the increase in the capital-labor coefficient in a given sector or activity occurs simultaneously with the generalization of technical progress, even though this last one might be limited. The "new" equipment incorporated into the economy is always more "efficient" within the dynamics of the sys-

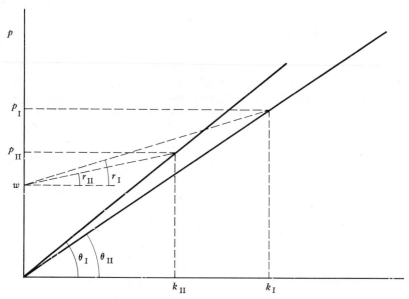

w	rate of wages (given as a constant in the different branches)
k	capital per worker
$t_g\theta$	product-capital relationship$=a$
r	rate of profit
m	rate of surplus value$=\dfrac{p-w}{-w}$
p	product per worker

$r\mathrm{I}>r\mathrm{II}$ in spite of the fact $a\mathrm{I}<a\mathrm{II}$. Why? Because $m\mathrm{I}<m\mathrm{II}$ ("a punto") to compensate $a\mathrm{I}$ lower than $a\mathrm{II}$, that is:

$$\frac{\dfrac{m\mathrm{I}}{m+1}}{\dfrac{m\mathrm{II}}{m\mathrm{II}+1}} = \frac{a\mathrm{II}}{a\mathrm{II}}$$

tem than the existing one.[10] Thus, if technical progress saves capital, the needs for capital input per production unit will decrease, which tends to counteract the possible negative effects of accumulation on the product-capital relationship. Nevertheless, the most common case (that Furtado takes into account) is that in which technical progress cuts back on labor force. But even under these circumstances, the product-capital relationship will only decline if the relative increase in labor productivity turns out to be lower than the relative increment in the allotment of capital per worker.[11] Furthermore, if, in this case, the product-capital relationship declines, it is possible that the rate of surplus value will increase enough to provoke an increase in the surplus available for investment.[12] To sum up, either the product-capital relationship does not decline, in spite of the increase in the capital-labor coefficient, or if it does, its negative effects on the surplus available for investment can be counteracted by an adequate increase in the surplus taken from the labor force. The possibility of compensating for the effects of the decline in the product-capital relationship on the growth rate will depend on whether or not the surplus is transformed into new investments.

There is no doubt that at least in some activities, the actual product-capital relationship in the more advanced stages of the substitutive process tends to remain far below its highest possible degree, even though an increase need

[10] Even if theoretically that is not the case in a perfect competition model of general equilibrium.

[11] This is because the product-capital relationship equals productivity of labor divided by the capital-labor relationship.

[12] The following demonstrates the logic of the statement.

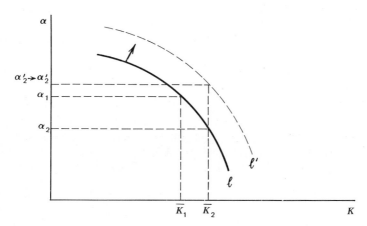

The accumulation of capital $(K_2 - K_1)$ would lead α_1 to α_2 if there were no technical progress. As there is technical progress, α_1 goes to α'_2. The final result, of course, depends on the form of ϑ, allowing $\alpha'_2 \lessgtr \alpha_1$; but in any event, the product per unit of capital input plus labor increases. In other words, there is an increase in the surplus available for investment.

not be the result of the capital-labor coefficient. In some cases this is due—as Furtado himself says—to the process of import substitution; domestic manufacturing of equipment is carried out only after relative prices reach certain substantially high levels, as a result of the problems created by a limited market and the scarcity of adequate means for financing sales. Consequently, the physical product-capital relationship is reduced for the equipment industries (in their role as producer), and in value for the industries using these equipments.

In other cases, the same situation of overextension in the durable goods industries could also apply, because of either special circumstances favoring the acquisition of equipment or problems related to its indivisibility.

Nevertheless, there is no reason to state that at the level of macroeconomics the product-capital relationship is necessarily reduced at the stage in which the returns on the infrastructural investments that allowed for the installation of the metal mechanic and basic industries are beginning to materialize. One can also assume that with the passing of time, adequate complementary conditions and demand will develop, which will result in a better utilization of the installed capacities. Both situations tend to increase the product-capital relationship.[13]

If there were a crisis—for reasons unrelated to the evolution of the product-capital relationship—the problem would obviously be different, given that the reduction in average demand creates an increase in the margins of idle capacity and a subsequent reduction in the product-capital relationship. But that would then be a consequence, not a cause of the crisis.

Paradoxically, a more detailed examination of Furtado's model suggests that if the categories with which he works are the most pertinent ones, one can scarcely conclude that stagnation is inevitable in the type of economy he examines. At most there would be a slight and short-lived deacceleration, until those forces that counteract the tendency of the product-capital relationship to decrease were strengthened. In no case would the stagnation be permanent. As it turns out, by using a "Category Result" mode of thought, he assumes that the rates of profit of the various industries tend to level out among themselves as wages do; this mode of thought separates the intensified use of capital from the generalization of technical progress and does not take into account the effects of this on investment productivity nor the effect of the various modalities of foreign economies. Furtado seems to have bound himself in the "straitjacket" of a neoclassical model of general equilibrium,

---

[13] Furtado forgets the possible significance of the amount of available investment resources. This is not only due to the fact that he does not take into account the effects of technical progress; even though Furtado mentions that the increase of capital per worker (in wage-stable conditions) leads to a regressive redistribution of income (given the increase in the rate of surplus value), he does not conclude, as would be logical, that the surplus available for investment would consequently increase. Were this to happen, it would occur in an opposite direction to the decline of the product-capital relationship, as far as the effects on the rate of growth are concerned.

which is as elegant as it is inefficient in explaining the dynamics of a modern capitalist economy.

CRISIS AND RECUPERATION IN THE BRAZILIAN ECONOMY. There is no doubt that the economic crisis that Brazil went through during the 1960s was closely related, at the structural level, to the draining of its industrial dynamism, which had been built on the substitution of imports. After having carried out a "package" of complementary investments—fundamentally of durable consumer goods and production—which exhausted the reserves of the existing market and which led to an expansion of income and the diversification of consumption, the economy lacked a group of projects for new investments that could be introduced in an adequate temporal sequence, that is, after the investments of the "Plano de Metas" (Goal Plans) (corresponding to J. Kubitschek's government, 1956 to 1960) had ripened. The new "package" of investments should have played a role similar to that of Schumpeter's wave of innovations, which tend to provoke pronounced fluctuations in the development of capitalism if they are not carried out regularly over a period of time.

The lack of massive new investments capable of securing and maintaining a high rate of economic expansion was not strictly related to a limited productive capacity (which was already adequate in some branches of the production sector, such as metal mechanics, electrical equipment, tools, and construction material), but to problems related to the structure of demand and to finance.

Regarding demand, the problem consisted of a highly concentrated distribution of income, which hindered the diversification and adequate expansion of consumption in the middle sectors, precisely the type of consumption that would allow for the better utilization and expansion of the already available industrial capacity and that would give great impetus to the development of the economy as a whole. On the other hand, the means needed to finance new private investment projects were limited by the evolution of the wage-surplus relationship, as were the public investment projects limited by the expenditures-fiscal load relationship, in addition to existing problems that related to the nature of the projects themselves.

Thus, it would seem that the system's growth possibilities were restricted by the lack of means for financing new investments and by the demand for high profits, in spite of the fact that a considerable productive potential was available, although never fully utilized. Under these circumstances, the system's answer was to alter the composition of demand: upward redistribution of personal income and of its future increases in favor of the middle and upper strata, and an increase in the wage-surplus relationship through cutbacks, on occasion even absolute ones, in wages for the less skilled working masses.

Nevertheless, financing in terms of mobilizing available resources was not the only problem; there was also the matter of *how* this was to be done.

The prevailing mechanisms during the process of import substitution were inserted into an inflationary model that played an important role as an "accelerator" of the crisis. Inflation had allowed for a relative relaxation of wage-profit tensions through the maintenance of a deceptive rate of profit for countless new investments, especially in those areas of production goods linked to the strong process of material accumulation during the period 1957 to 1961. The expected profits on additional capital were artificially maintained through increasing the value of the real assets in the face of a parallel monetary devaluation, as well as by socializing the costs of certain basic inputs and capital goods (the exchange policies) and the financial costs (thanks to the financing created by the public sector and other external sources unrelated to the enterprises). Consequently, a physical overinvestment took place which tended to lower the corporations' marginal product-capital relationship.

With its dissemination mechanisms out of control, inflation became rampant and disfunctional; not even the high growth rates could curb it. The greater solidity of relative prices did not permit an intersectoral transference of costs; it demystified the illusory profits and financially strangled the corporations. The high rate of price increases caused an intensification of labor pressures, and wages followed fast on prices. This limited the possibilities of forced redistribution.

The decline in the expected profits on investments, the crash of paper profits, and a reduction in the total means available for investment led to a strong reduction in the rate of total investments—public as well as private.

The product-capital relationship in industry seems to have grown during the period 1955 to 1960. There is no information available on the growth rates from 1960 to 1963, the period when their decline began. In any event, it seems that the reduction in the rate of investment was the decisive element in the economic crisis. What is absolutely certain is that once the economic crisis became acute, either because of a reduction in the prevailing level of activities, or a reduction in the investment rate, a significant margin of idle capacity was created with negative consequences on the product-capital relationship.

THE FIRST STAGE OF THE CRISIS. A conjunctural crisis during the economic slowdown was superimposed on the search for a solution to the slowdown itself. In the first stage, different circumstances coincided in shaping this situation. Primary among them was the government's attempt to redistribute income in favor of wage earners through the implementation of a wage-price policy, while simultaneously trying to halt inflation through a slowdown in public expenses or private credit, and the reduction of the liquidity of the system through the programming of rigid monetary policies (1963). These measures were depressive, granted that it was not possible to link them to an effective reorientation of investments and of the production mechanisms and to support them with a reduction in the income rate of the upper classes on a short-term basis (nor was the government serious about doing so).

The reduction in public investment, and a frontal attack on foreign capital (legal restrictions on and control over repatriation of profits) put a stop to investment plans in the newer and more dynamic sectors that the multinational corporations had set their sights on (mining, steel, petrochemicals, and heavy equipment), eliminating self-sufficient elements that could have offset the effects of the existing crisis in the area of demand in the economy.

THE SECOND STAGE OF THE CRISIS (1964 TO 1966) AND THE RECOVERY. The transition from the first to the second stage was conditioned by the change in regimes in early 1964. The immediate perspectives for Brazilian capitalism did not improve. The depression worsened. But this time its causes were not accidental; instead, it was deliberately set off by placing the finance mechanisms that had prevailed since the 1950s (those relating to exchange, credit, wage, and public deficit policies) under almost complete control. The fiscal load increased greatly, there were more cuts in public expenditures, and new restrictions on credit. A harsh policy of contraction of wages was put into effect along with these measures. The effects on the economy were twofold: they relieved corporation expenditures, but reduced the existing demand on the other.[14]

In spite of all this, these measures can be seen as "functional"; they confronted the crisis and made the transition toward a new phase of capitalist development possible. Many marginal enterprises were dissolved (the financially weaker ones and those with lower credit ratings), opening the way for an industrial and commercial concentration of activity. This had the obvious positive effect on production efficiency of eliminating much of the "excess" production capacity, at least in terms of dynamics.[15] The wage control program substantially altered the functional distribution of income in favor of profits for those corporations strong enough to survive. Along with some emergency measures designed to attend to financial problems, this program permitted the recuperation and expansion of later stages.

Two institutional reforms in the areas of taxation and the capital market paved the way for a new private and public financial strategy. By 1966 the government was already increasing its rate of investment; it succeeded in

---

[14] As a consequence of the rapid decline in demand for imported capital goods—the result of a reduction in investments—the notorious "external stranglehold," which was the pretext for some theories of stagnation, disappeared as if by magic during 1964 to 1965. For the first time since World War II, a strong surplus in the balance of payments was generated, which allowed for a considerable outward flow of capital in spite of radical changes that openly favored foreign capital.

[15] This process was accompanied by an accelerated take-over by foreign capitalism, not only because foreign corporations were more competent, but also because they were offered huge incentives to bring in financial sources (Decree 289).

attracting foreign capital on a short-term basis (Decree 289) to finance the recovery of the dominant industries; it backed the development of a series of private financial enterprises; and it prepared the new cooperative agreement between long-term foreign capitalism and the state (in the areas of minerals, capital equipment, petrochemicals, naval construction, transportation, and electric power).

One must keep in mind that in Brazil, as opposed to many Latin American countries, the stage of industrial development during which the important substitution process begins to lose impulse allowed for the physical substitution of some of the imported articles. In other Latin American countries, the substitution process was exhausted before their respective economies had a chance to form a material base that would allow them to produce the production goods necessary to undertake relatively heavy capital-intensive and technologically complex investments.

The conditions of Brazilian capitalism allowed it to develop an expansive strategy built on its own incentives. This did not mean that its dependence on foreign capital decreased; on the contrary. With the material conditions at the economic level, this new strategy necessitated readjustments in the structure of demand, a greater accumulation of investment sources, and profitable projects complementary to the existing production capacity. It also implied some "corrections" in the production structure, such as elimination of some activities installed under the protection of inflation that were not important to the new expansive strategy. Such a corrective program was only viable if the public economic policies (financing, distribution of income, orientation of expenditures, allocation of resources, and a restructuring of the monetary-financial system on different terms), were reordered.

All these prerequisites shaped the transformation and accompanied the economic recovery. As we indicated before, they were carried out in the early years of the military regime. We have also pointed out one of the more important problems; the problem of the resources needed to finance the new investments and the expansion in demand for durable goods (which obviously reflected on the industrial product-capital relation) was resolved basically by an absolute control of wages. This takes us back to Furtado's "model," which posits that real wages in industry are kept stable and regulated by the subsistence sector throughout the industrialization process.

We can see this clearly if we keep in mind the development of the 1950s. Although industrial employment grew at a rate of 2.6 percent annually during this period, it is very probable that urban employment increased at a greater rate as a consequence of the transference to other activities of the surplus created in the industrial sector, through various services and expenditures of the state. Because of this, there was a 6 percent annual increase in the demand for nondurable goods, which allowed for the substitution of imports to develop dynamically through to the more advanced stage, thanks to an increased demand in the "traditional" subsectors. The fact that wages were increased allowed for their subsequent restriction after the crisis in the mid-1960s. This fact, in turn, permitted the creation of a source of financing which was doubtlessly crucial to the economic recovery.

PART TWO: SOME CHARACTERISTICS OF THE RECENT DEVELOPMENT OF BRAZILIAN CAPITALISM

Between 1966 and the end of 1970, some significant characteristics emerged that clearly express the new style of Brazilian capitalist development. The lack of background research, the very incompleteness of the process itself, and a certain difficulty in overcoming certain outmoded analytical patterns would make a coherent analysis of the new system particularly difficult.

Given these factors, we shall limit our survey to an examination of the traits characteristic of the expansion process: the incorporation and spread of technical progress and the concentration of the economy. We find that a better explanation of the nature and dynamics of contemporary Brazilian capitalism can be made in this manner, instead of by using the more traditional methods, which begin with an analysis of the particulars of the system and then proceed to a general overview, focusing in turn on the inefficiency, deviations, or "evils" of the system. We must also remain aware of the fact that this focus, by concerning itself so exclusively with what "should be," is often incapable of explaining "why it is so."

Knowing the limitations of this essay, we will leave aside a specific examination of those aspects related to the structural changes in Brazilian society, especially those that refer to the forms of economic and social organization: the sectoral and spatial links and interconnections and the concrete forms of integration of the national economy into the international system. In any event, the literature on these problems is relatively abundant.

EXPANSION

EXPANSION AND GROWTH. Sometimes it is said that an economy is stagnant or tends toward stagnation because its growth slows down at a given point. Nevertheless, while the total per capita product is growing at a reduced rate, important advances and setbacks may be taking place in the different economic sectors or strata inside the economy at the same time that new leading activities are appearing on the scene.[16] In this sense the use of the term "expansion" might be more adequate than that of growth, as it applies to a category that embraces the cyclical fluctuations of economic activities in the heart of a capitalist economy, as well as to the uneven and mixed character of the development of that system. Economic growth, as such, is a

[16] The activities that at each stage free the expansion of the forces of production, as a consequence of the process of accumulation and of innovation or technical progress.

measurement that is an *outcome* of the economic process and that does not take into account its fundamental characteristics.

The normal definition of the concepts of growth and expansion probably derives from the fact that in developed capitalist economies, the assimilation of both is easier, because its greater structural homogeneity expresses and allows for a high level of integration between the leading dynamic sectors and the rest. However, this does not mean that capitalist development does not retain its uneven and mixed character. Nevertheless, an interpretation using the concept previously referred to is extremely harmful to an analysis of economies having highly heterogeneous production structures, as it distorts the viewpoints and interpretation of the occurring economic transformation.

An interesting example of this theory is the Cuban case, even though we are not dealing with a socialist society. The fact that its total growth rate has been very small does not in any way mean that the economy is stagnating in the literal and conventional sense. On the contrary, the Cuban economy is passing through a process of marked expansion in new undertakings, strong accumulation of capital, and diversification of production. It has been precisely the combination of a drastic change in the economy's direction, a search for new forms of economic and social organization, and a slowdown or fluctuation in the traditional basic activities (that is, sugar cane and urban services), of the pre-1960 economy which has been principally responsible for the low total rate of growth. As we have already pointed out, this is not a form of "stagnation," instead, it represents a necessary dynamic transition toward a new type of economy.

In the Brazilian case, we have stated previously that the economic crisis of the mid-1960s also represents a period of transition, not into a new economy, but toward a new type of capitalist development. Given the existence of an adequate production base, the transition presupposes a new strategy of concentration of power and of income, as well as new incentive mechanisms geared to the next stage of integration with foreign capitalism. We believe that the upheavals experienced by the Brazilian economy do not correspond to the usual definition of stagnation despite the reduction in the total growth rate observed between 1962 and 1967.

THE DETERMINANTS OF THE NEW EXPANSION. In reality, Brazil, along with Mexico, constitutes one of the more representative cases of integration of the national economic expansion—with or without a crisis—into that of international capitalism, resulting in a soaring growth rate. This process has been taking place for some time now in Mexico and more recently in Brazil (1968 to 1972).

If we examine the situation in other Latin American countries we will see that one of the key factors determining its possibilities for expansion has been precisely the greater or lesser degree of isolation of their economies from international capitalism. In addition, the impetus provided by the emerging dynamic sectors has determined whether or not the expansion has resulted in a high growth rate at each individual stage. What determines its dissemination potential is the relative weight of the "leading" sectors within the total structure, as well as their degree of internal and external interrelatedness. Furthermore, the prevailing relationships between the pivotal agents of the process (the state and foreign capitalists), primarily in the area of allocation of resources, is crucial.

It is important to emphasize that the results, in terms of investment patterns and growth, vary depending on the prevailing objective relationship in the strategic sectors between the nation and foreign capitalism, and on national behavioral patterns in the decision-making process.[17]

In some Latin American economies it is clear that the expansive process has been hindered by a contradiction between their structural patterns—subordinate to the old patterns of foreign dependence—and the need for assimilating themselves into the new regional and worldwide evolution of capitalist development. This has been the case in countries such as Bolivia, Uruguay, Ecuador, and, until recently, Peru.

On the other hand, "adequate" adjustments to the new forms of dependence (technological and financial) will apparently permit an expansion process of a new type in some countries. Even so, either because of the relatively small dimensions of the new emerging sectors (in Chile, until recently), or because the "old" urban and rural capitalism plays a contradictory role in adapting to the necessary functional patterns of the modern sectors (Argentina), the total growth rates have been unsatisfactory.

In the case of countries like Mexico and Brazil, a flexible adaptation to the "new dependence" took place after overcoming their internal contradictions (among the different classes and sectors or subsectors) and they were able to expand and grow at a reasonable rate. In Mexico, no crisis took place; thus, its growth was sustained, supported by its domestic market, which is superior to the others in absolute terms.

Returning to the case of Brazil, it will be helpful if we specify some characteristics that distinguish it from the rest of Latin America, based on the observations we have made up to this point.

First, it is necessary to emphasize the greater weight and complementarity of its leading sectors in relation to those of the other Latin American countries. A greater organic affiliation between the state and foreign capitalism can be seen; both are the principal participants in the key dynamic investment and production sectors, and there is no important contradiction between them as far as the decision-making process is concerned. In addition, the

---

[17] These patterns can be characterized as either submissive and antagonistic, or as tending toward tolerant and negotiable attitudes. They are obviously not unrelated to the aforementioned objective relationships which, in their turn, can be based on either organic homogeneity or, at the other extreme, on a certain lack of complementarity or disfunctionality, with a gamut shaped by the clear division among these areas in between.

leading sectors, controlled by the state and foreign capital, have been increasing their participation in the economy and constituting themselves as an integrated nucleus of the recent expansion.

The following table enables us to see its potential in terms of intersectoral relationships and organic "complementarity."

Integrated
Expansion Core

Foreign Capital	State
Domestic Market	
Transportation equipment	Land and sea transportation program
Mechanical equipment	Steel industry
Electrical equipment	Federal construction
	Electric energy program
	Communication systems
Chemicals	Petroleum and its derivatives
Financial services	Public utilities services
Foreign Market (Exports)	
Cattle	Coffee (policies relating to)
Vegetal and mineral extraction	Iron minerals
Industrial surplus	

In the current stage of its capitalist development, the Brazilian government, contrary to what has occurred at other times, has not established any major links with the so-called "national" bourgeoisie or put forward any populist-style programs. Because of this, it is free to carry out these institutional reforms corresponding to an accelerated modernization process, and even to promote a more specific division of labor with foreign capital in its state role as manager. This has made possible an increasing interrelation between both in the areas of investment and production in the so-called strategic sectors: petrochemicals, mining, steel industry, electricity, transportation, and communications.

In this division of labor, the state is generally responsible for the heavier part of the load, providing the domestic market with cheap inputs of general consumption and also with foreign goods, which is, of course, to the advantage of the multinational corporations. It enables them to expand their market (and eventually to export) by exploiting commercial conditions that are frequently under their direct control.[18]

[18] Private national "initiative" plays a relatively minor role in the industrial sector where it is only important—and ever decreasingly so—in the area of production of nondurable consumer goods. On the other hand, it is dominant in the sectors of commercial and financial activities, in spite of the fact that here, too, they have also been losing relative importance in favor of foreign capital.

ACCUMULATION IN THE PROCESS OF EXPANSION. The distinctive characteristics already mentioned in the Brazilian case have emphasized the mutual support and the role of the two main agents of expansion: the state and foreign capital. For this reason it seems appropriate to analyze some aspects of the accumulation process. It is essential to place in evidence the mechanisms of generation, appropriation, and utilization of surplus, as well as the different possible and prevailing forms of accumulation in economies such as ours.

Within the capitalist system, and given the availability and quality of resources, the role of surplus is fundamentally determined by the relationship between the value of the product created and of the producers' consumption of goods. In the case of Latin American capitalism—to a greater degree than in the developed capitalist states—the leading corporations and the more modern industries are better able to generate and appropriate a portion of the economic surplus. This is not only due to their higher physical productivity—a result of their more advanced and efficient technology—but also to their ability to hold wages far below the real production level, owing to, among other things, the direct or indirect pull of the considerably lower level of wages in the economy as a whole. On the other hand, there are no competitive forces pressuring the corporations to continually and proportionately transfer their production advantages to their prices. Finally, the presence of the traditional enterprises within the same market allows them to obtain a differential rent or quasirent from their surplus.

As concerns the allocation of surplus, one of the most important forms, and one that implies its transferal, is that which is carried out directly to feed the expansion of the service sector and those made directly or indirectly by the public sector through their policies relating to income, employment, expenditures, and prices. It is particularly important to take into account the marked expansion in the use of personal services, which can be seen as a form of surplus transferal by the bourgeoisie and the upper-middle income groups to the sectors that have not been able to incorporate themselves into the system as a regular labor force—a highly necessary step in their development. This transferal is intrinsically functional, as it allows the incorporation of the urban masses into the consumer economy. Their demand, in great measure, supports the expansion of the traditional sectors.

If we think of the possible forms of accumulation in our economy, we would have to give priority to those that are potentially adaptable to the "primitive" forms of accumulation, which are particularly meaningful when we are dealing with the marginal population and with agriculture. This strategy is only of interest to the system in the measure that it allows for the expansion of residue activities which retain labor that otherwise would not be needed in the productive system. In addition, this type of investment increases in importance when it becomes tied to the general process of accumulation. One example of this is the expansion of the agricultural frontier through the construction of roads or of large public works that serve as basic social capital in the implementation of new activities, at the same time that they maintain or increase production in the investment goods industries.

In our type of economy, the "traditional" form of capitalist accumulation has been based on the internal accumulation of profits within the corporations, sustained by the strong inequality between the growth rates of wages and productivity, and by a series of explicit or implicit subsidies granted to capital by the public sector.

More recently, new forms of accumulation, which we would term financial, have been gaining in importance.[19] A series of agencies, especially foreign ones, have begun operations, organizing an embryonic "capital market" that has as its fundamental objective the accumulation of profits without direct relation to the process of generation of a real surplus. Its basic function is to contribute dynamically to the creation of this surplus. On the other hand, this possibility allows all the economic agents: consumers, corporations, and the state to increase their margins of indebtedness. It also allows the modern sectors that have a surplus with no profitable prospects for investment to transfer it to the newer sectors, or to those with higher growth rates and credit ratings. Furthermore, it allows for a more organic control over capitalist expansion and gives direction to the integration of national capital with foreign capital.

This scheme has not evolved evenly in the different Latin American countries, but it can be observed in its most advanced stages in Mexico, Argentina, and Brazil. In Brazil, financial accumulation linked to an enormous expansion of the nonbanking financial sector and to speculation in the securities market, has become almost a caricature of the old financial capitalism of the 1920s in the United States. It would seem anachronistic were it not for its close ties with the multinational corporations that represent the most modern stage of contemporary capitalism.[20]

Brazil also presents specific characteristics regarding other means of accumulation in relation to the other Latin American countries. Its opportunities of maintaining and increasing the primitive accumulation of capital together with the accumulation of capital by the strategic national and foreign sectors are great. In this context, the exploration of new geographic areas for natural resources, agricultural development, and other primary or secondary

---

[19] Financial accumulation was always present, but under traditional forms: variations in the evaluation of assets and the speculative and normal operations of the financial system.

[20] Paraphrasing Baran, it could be said that Brazilian capitalism combines the worst of two worlds: it is socially exclusive and presents the typical problems of advanced capitalism. Advanced capitalism is compelled to search continually for new investment opportunities through finance capitalism and technological obsolescence, because of its tendency to generate excess surplus. In Brazilian capitalism, there is at the same time an excess and a shortage of surplus due to the polarized character of its accumulation process, which determines the coexistence of internal problems of lack of investment opportunities—"excess savings"—and profitable investment opportunities.

activities destined for foreign trade or domestic distribution among the dynamic sectors of the economy are particularly relevant. The most notable recent example of this type of initiative is the opening of the Trans-Amazonian Highway, undertaken for a multitude of reasons related to the occupation of new land and the exploitation of natural resources. This represents another instance of close cooperation between national and foreign capitalism, be it in the construction of the highway itself, or in the related stages of exploitation (of timber, mineral resources, and cattle).

The corporations' internal accumulation was noticeably increased in the last years by the increase in surplus extracted from the labor force in the urban areas in a proportion not equalled by any other Latin American country during the last decade. Workers' real wages have declined so radically that the legal salary reverted to its post-World War II subsistence level. Consequently, the leading corporations have been able to achieve very high rates of profit, and the minor or traditional commercial and trade enterprises maintained a reasonable rate of profit on the capital invested.

THE INCORPORATION AND DISSEMINATION OF TECHNICAL PROGRESS. It is well known that in Latin America, and more particularly in Brazil —because of the nature of the historical process of capitalist expansion—the incorporation and dissemination of technical progress has been restricted in each historical stage to those leading dynamic sectors that have been most tightly integrated into the international capitalist system.[21] Thus, the dissemination of modern technology has been fundamentally centered in the leading industries and its assimilation has been limited to some complementary sectors whose productive efficiency was an important prerequisite for any opportunity of expansion for the new industries. In the so-called primary-export stage, modernization[22] was limited in general to the export sector and to its infrastructure.[23] In the first stage of industrialization, based on the substitution of imports, it was limited to certain consumer goods industries and to some urban services. In the second stage it was concentrated in the metal-mechanics complex (durable consumer items, input of capital and

[21] See Anibal Pinto's essay, "La concentracion del progreso tecnico y de sus frutos en el desarrollo Latinoamericano."

[22] By modernization, we understand precisely the process of incorporation and dissemination of modern technology. In this sense, when we talk about the forms of modernization, we are referring to the way technology is incorporated and disseminated. There is no similarity at all with the use given to the term by certain sociological trends, related to the idea of an unilinear and continuous development process. The use of the term in this essay—in spite of the misunderstanding it might occasion—is only to facilitate discussion.

[23] Ramifying to a greater or lesser degree into the economy according to a series of determining factors—among them the type of products exported, the form of exploitation, the ownership of property (national or foreign) in the export sectors, and so on.

capital goods) and chemical industries.[24] Finally, in the current stage, characterized by a deepening and diversification of consumption, as well as by the development of forms of financial accumulation, modernization has been present not so much at the level of improving and broadening the productive structure as in the diversification and commercialization of products (change of brands and models, advertising, and financing services).

Going further into the matter, we can see that the nature of the process of incorporation and dissemination of technical progress depends on a series of dominant expansion forms in which any form can be preceded by one that has rapidly fallen behind because of a loss in its relative capacity to create and retain surplus, which is limited by a tendency toward technological "paralysis." Thus, activities, sectors, or areas that were dynamic and modern in the past are relegated to the middle strata or, in the long range, are even assimilated into the so-called primitive stage, at least as far as the contrasts in levels of production within the economic system are concerned.[25] This implies that the process tends to accentuate the structural heterogeneity of the system and also to modify the concrete conditions on which it is built. This is reflected in the fact that it is not always the same areas or strata of the production sector that are left behind in terms of productivity over a period of time, but the relative position of the principal sectors that are changed.

[24] In Brazil, the rate of expansion was so great that it gave a powerful impetus to some branches of "traditional" industry that were then emphatically modernized, for example, textiles and food products.

[25] The concepts of modern, intermediate, and primitive production strata are most thoroughly explained in A. Pinto's article, *"Notas sobre la heterogeneidad estructural en America Latina,"* Trimestre Economico, No. 145. It is helpful to transcribe here a fragment of the essay by Pedro Vuskovic cited in footnote 1. ". . . thus a pronounced heterogeneity has been created in the economic structure, with their strata clearly differentiated, quantitatively as well as qualitatively, in terms of their productivity. A group of these strata constitutes what could be called a 'modern' sector, made up of those economic units that are relatively efficient in terms of organization, production increase, and their relative high levels of technology and of capital allotment per employed person. The opposite extreme could be classified as the 'primitive' sector, formed by economic units working at very low levels of productivity. These units barely have mechanized, have an insignificant capital density, and are extremely backward technologically. Between these extremes there is an 'intermediate' stratum distinguished from the 'primitive' one by its levels of productivity and its integration into the national market. The middle stratum tends to progressively remove itself from the patterns characteristic of the modern sector. These differences between markedly different strata of the economy in their methods of production apply not only to the total economy, but also within each one of the principal sectors of economic activity. In other words, not only are some sectors' average productivity conspicuously inferior to the rest, the problem is that within each of the sectors themselves there is a marked and prolonged difference in the level of productivity among their individual strata." (Vuskovic, p. 42, cited in footnote 1).

It is estimated that in Latin America, one-eighth of the active population is part of the modern stratum and generates approximately half of the national product. One third of the employed population corresponds to the primitive stratum, which generates 10 percent of the total national product.

HOMOGENEIZATION OR HETEROGENEIZATION? In examining the process of incorporation and dissemination of technical progress in Latin America, the question arises: When the modern activities reach a certain absolute dimension within the total sphere, will there eventually be a strong push toward generalization of technical progress that will contain, almost by definition, a tendency toward a standardization of the production system?

In this regard we believe that even though the potential productivity of the Brazilian economy might be sufficient to allow for its standardization, other factors characteristic of dependent and underdeveloped capitalism intervene. These factors inhibit the generalization of a process of assimilation and dissemination of technical progress.[26] We shall try to establish some of the reasons for this belief.

In the first place, it should be firmly established that the existence of that generalized modernization trend imagined by some analysts requires that an ever-increasing proportion of the total surplus of the economy be transferred —in the shape of investment—to the backward sectors, in such a way as to eventually eliminate the differences in the levels of productivity. We know that this is not the case in the reality of most Latin American countries, and the cause is to be found in the conditions governing the allocation of investments in the capitalist economies, which are obviously related to their relative profit capacity; that is, with the rate of profit that can be obtained from different activities. In the Latin American economies, the nature of the leading activities, together with the dominant character of the social groups that control it, allow for a larger rate of relative profit for the developing modern sectors precisely in the same measure that a polarization of the circulation of surplus is maintained; that is, that the dissemination of technical progress is restricted. Let us examine these ideas more closely.

If we observe the economic process from the point of view of the modern sector, we can see a whole series of strictly interrelated circumstances that make up a strongly centripetal force in relation to the circulation of surplus. It is well known that the development of the patterns of distribution of income that has accompanied the recent development of the Brazilian economy (see the coming section entitled "The Tendencies of Concentration") has guaranteed growing margins of demand for the industries of conspicuous consumption by the upper and middle income groups in the urban and especially in the metropolitan sectors. They are directly or indirectly linked to the leading sectors, allowing a profitable expansion of those sectors. This situation has been doubly reinforced by the actions of the state: (1) In the direction given to public investment with the purpose of providing diverse economic modalities unrelated to the activities of the modern sector or of

[26] We disagree in this respect with Antonio Castro's thesis that refers to the generalized modernization of agriculture; see *"Agricultura, Emprego e Desequilibrios Regionais— Perspectivas,"* in *Sete Ensaios sobre a Economia Brasileira,* cited in footnote 3.

directly benefiting the consumption of groups within that sector; and (2) in the economic program itself; this would apply to the wage, exchange, and even financing policies, tending to benefit the industries of modern consumption directly or indirectly.[27] This concentration of private and public investments and of consumption, together with the given institutional opportunities, tends to allow the accumulation of the surplus created by the modern sector to maintain a relative state of profitability.

Although it can be seen that there are great possibilities for maintaining the level of profit through a scheme of polarized accumulation, it is important to note that implicit in this very scheme is a permanent contradiction between the creation of a rapidly growing surplus and its possibilities for realization within its restricted sphere of circulation. As we shall see further on, this system seeks to escape the contradiction through a permanent process of deconcentration and reconcentration of income which allows it to enlarge its market successively according to the characteristics of each stage of expansion. If we look at this process from the angle of enlarging the production capacity and incorporating technical progress, we can observe that those contradictions give way to cycles of modernization.

In effect, as the effects of complementarity wear out within the modern sector at each stage of expansion, the surplus it has created tends to infiltrate into some of the traditional industries or into those corresponding to intermediate production levels, but it does so in a restricted fashion, only in those activities that can be rapidly modernized. What is this restricted character due to?

To begin with, we have to consider that the vast majority of modernized industries are those that maintain a functional relationship with the modern sector, that is, industries producing primary input for industry or food for the markets of the privileged urban sectors. In both cases, there are forces pressing for a more or less inevitable modernization, but at the same time, important factors inhibit the ability of that process to move forward without decreasing the profit rate which is related to the modernization process itself.

Let us see what those limiting factors are: first, the limited income elasticity in the demand for food among the middle and upper income groups who constitute the privileged markets; second, the fact that the direction of technical progress in recent times indicates a trend of increasing "savings" of rudimentary inputs or to their substitution by industrialized products—that is, synthetics that correspond to the appearance on the market of the new modern activities. For this reason, the relative importance of the activities that maintain an industrial relationship with the modern sector is decreasing

---

[27] It could be thought that the state could "redeem" its past through its development policies and social expenditures. Nonetheless, this is not so; not only because the doubtful relative significance of its social expenditures but also because the regional development that it promotes tends to repeat the concentration and exclusion patterns of its total development. The Brazilian Northeast is a notable example of this.

in relation to the whole. Last, we could look at what happens to the intermediate and primitive activities producing for the same market as the modern industries. In this case, modernization implies the destruction of the existing traditional activities. This destruction, nevertheless, is not carried to its ultimate consequences. Were this the case, the overall homogeneization of production could be achieved, given that the operation within the same market of activities with significant differences in their productivity permits the more efficient ones to receive a differential income at each new stage of expansion and protects their rate of profit in the crisis stages.[28] Consequently, the generalization of modernizing investments in the nonmodern activities that are competing with modern ones implies a decline in the rate of profit which tends to inhibit a permanent modernization in this direction.

One might think that the situation would be altered when the demand for certain "traditional" articles of general use became more dynamic at certain points, for example, food articles, whose consumption is more widespread. Nevertheless, it seems more likely that the "modernizing" investments tend to satisfy any increase in demand without losing their restricted character, either because they are made by corporations that are already more productive, or because their level of technical progress allows them to generate a considerable increase in production through the creation of new corporations or the modernization of the few remaining backward ones.

If the hypotheses that we have formulated are correct, we may conclude that technological modernization and intensification of capital tend to project themselves at each stage of expansion in a restricted manner in some areas and subsectors. This means that at the same time that the modern strata are enlarged, a necessary consolidation of the structural heterogeneity takes place. In the three basic sectors of the economy, primary, secondary, and tertiary, all the possible technological patterns coexist; the intrasectoral differentiation by productive strata becomes as important or more so than the classic intersectoral differences.

NEODUALISM? It is relevant to ask at this point if the consolidation of structural heterogeneity that accompanies dependent, underdeveloped capitalist development represents some sort of disintegration between the modern and primitive productive strata. In our judgment, no valid argument supports this conclusion.

The idea of social or economic disintegration appears as a vestige of certain "dualist" models a la Broeke, which admit the evolution of two

---

[28] The income differential for some activities occurs because they operate at a lower physical cost and sell at prices regulated by those activities of greater physical cost. We are referring to income differential in the Ricardian sense; in no case should this be misunderstood as monopoly excess profits which exist in any oligopolic structure in which small and large enterprises coexist; both are modern but the smaller ones are subject to the larger ones in their price policies, the smaller enterprises serving as a cushion.

practically independent subsystems within the same society as a possibility. Even some authors of the Latin American "structuralist" school who use the integration of our economy into the new international capitalist system as the starting point for their analysis of structural change have been influenced by the trend. However, they tend to emphasize the internal disintegration caused by this form of relationship.[29] In contrast some authors, taking into account the complexity of the internal structural relationships that are established with the evolution and transformation of the patterns of dependence recognize that the structural heterogeneization process is not a phenomenon of disintegration, but rather a superimposition of transversal and horizontal cuts that produce an economic and social stratification with different and asynchronous levels of integration.[30]

Although we do not agree with Antonio Castro's analysis with respect to his idea that the trend is toward generalized modernization of the system, we do recognize and agree with him that the process of incorporation and dissemination of technical progress current in Brazil is taking place at every level. We also recognize that the total integration of the system manifests itself through the mass media and transportation, which facilitates, among other things, the creation of a national market generally unified in the field of commercial production, and a greater geographic mobility for the labor force.

Similarly, in terms of dynamics, we may affirm that the idea that modern and primitive strata get disassociated from each other, tending to grow progressively more separate and autonomous, is responsible in its simplified form for the neodualist theories. In effect, although the heterogeneity is deepened, a continuous change takes place in the relative positions of the different activities that accompany the process of cyclical expansion and modernization within the total system in movement. Thus, the "composition" of the different strata is not an absolute constant; primitive activities become modern and modern activities become intermediate, in the same way that intermediary activities become modernized, retain their position, or regress. We are far from the idea, then, of a compartmentalized takeoff having a limited mutual relationship. We are dealing with a single system whose heterogeneity can be deepened without provoking a single split among its different parts.[31]

[29] See Osvaldo Sunkel's essay, *"Desarrollo, subdesarrollo, dependencia, marginalización y desigualdades espaciales, hacia un enfoque totalizante,"* Santiago, 1970 (mimeographed).

[30] See Anibal Pinto's article, *"Diagnósticos, estructura y esquemas de desarrollo en América Latina,"* and Luciano Martin, *Industrializaçao, Burguesia Nacional e Desenvolvimento,* Rio de Janeiro, Ed. Saga, 1968.

[31] These considerations bring our attention to the danger inherent in the use of the terms "sector" or "modern strata." In effect, when we talk of a secondary sector, for example, we think of a unit of transformation activities producing goods with specific characteristics. When the term "modern sector" is used, one does not think of a given spectrum of goods produced within it, but of relatively high productivity or "leading" activities.

EXCLUSION AND MARGINALITY. In the process of incorporating and disseminating technical progress throughout an economy, two contradictory effects arise with respect to the absorption of labor: those of exclusion or expulsion, and those of incorporation into the new emerging activities. It is a well-known fact that the net result in terms of total productive employment in Latin America, and particularly in Brazil, has been highly unsatisfactory. This negative evolution is commonly attributed to an "excessive" modernization. Such an argument is usually based on the idea that the sectoral composition of the product in our economies advances in a "normal" pattern of development while that of employment is absolutely deflected from its course. The situation would be explained by an exaggerated use of imported technology that with its more modern system and greater degree of capital intensity would be "maladjusted" to our particular configuration of factors. In our judgment, this thesis deviates from a true explanation of what actually takes place. We consider that the cause of the unfavorable evolution of productive employment is not related to an excess of modernization but to the form that the modernization assumes. Reasoning from the perspective of dynamics, the problem does not lie in the fact that technology is imported or is capital-intensive but in the way that the greater surplus it creates is used.[32]

In effect, the way in which surplus and its subsequent increase is used clearly indicates the character of the modernization process. In talking about the concentrated nature of the incorporation of technical progress, and of the appropriation of its benefits, or of the circulation of dominant surplus inside the modern sector—a sector that expands spasmodically, giving way to a process of concentrated accumulation of capital and income—we are referring precisely to the way in which the surplus created by the labor force is being used, and to its consequences on the model of economic development.[33]

We will now examine in more detail the relationships of modernization and exclusion and marginality.

We should first point out that when the modern sector expands vertically, that is, without absorbing or liquidating traditional activities, the exploitation of the incorporated labor force is more intensive, and at the same time, that the workers not incorporated into the modern sectors are kept "excluded" in great measure from this form of exploitation. Thus, there is an even greater reduction in the relative levels of productivity in these strata, and heterogeneity is affected in the area of technological cutbacks.

Conversely, when modernization extends into certain areas of the traditional productive activities—that is, when it becomes more extensive—the base for the creation of the absolute and relative surplus is widened (as

---

[32] As long as it increases—in Ricardian terms—the product per input of capital-labor.

[33] It is clearly important to develop these ideas both theoretically and at the level of practical examples. Nevertheless, we will leave this task for anothr essay. The statement we made is due only to the need of bringing attention to an important idea that is, as we see it, erroneous and that is usually accepted with excessive complacency.

productivity rises and wages are kept stable), but the expulsion of labor employed in the activities that were modernized increases. In other words, at the same time that the base of production of the increased surplus is enlarged, the social margination process, which implies a concentration of the labor force in the economically residual area of activities, gains force. Thus, the enlargement of the modern sector paradoxically magnifies economic heterogeneity in the area of margination. In this sense, incorporation and expulsion become two simultaneous and contradictory trends of the expansion and modernization process which presents, at its peak, an unequal and combined character.

ASPECTS OF BRAZILIAN MODERNIZATION. In Brazil, during the first stage of import-substitute industrialization, from the end of World War II to the mid-1950s, there were great expectations for total homogenization, especially because of the possible great impact of urbanization, in terms of absorption of labor from the rural areas and the extensive modernization in the urban industrial complex. Nevertheless, toward the end of the 1950s, this image began to fade under the influence of the situation in the northeast, made worse by a terrible drought. This was reflected in the evidence obtained in an analysis of the regional imbalances. Several theses were put forward regarding the exploitation of backward areas by modern areas of polarized capital accumulation. In our opinion, the relative importance of the surplus that will eventually be extracted from the backward areas to feed the accumulation of capital in the southern centers has been exaggerated.[34] This area had a physically self-sufficient expansion capacity and was not dependent on the interregional relations.

During the most intensive period of industrialization, even though an expansion of the economic frontier might have been observed, together with an expansion of modernization into several agricultural areas as well as an incorporation of new contingents of the population into the service sectors of the various urban areas, heterogeneity was aggravated along wtih a concentration of capital and the reduction of the rate of productive absorption of the labor force in the urban centers. Faced with the crisis and subsequent recuperation of the rate of growth, the relationship between the nonmodern and modern sectors was weakened, not only because the enlarged modern complex was in a period of "digestion" of its own capacity, but also because the weight of the crisis fell on the traditional activities (agriculture and raw

---

[34] This is not to denigrate the long-range effects of the exchange policies and of an effective extraction of surplus from the northeast on the economy of the area. Nor does it leave aside its short-range importance for the southern centers between 1953 and 1958–1959. The problem is that it is not legitimate to extrapolate these events to explain the later trends. See Antonio Castro's article on the northeast in the second volume of his book, cited in footnote 3.

materials for the traditional industries nondurable consumer goods industries, and some civil construction).

Nevertheless, the links with the more backward region—the northeast— were tightened, since the southern sector was able to invest large amounts of surplus in the industrialization of the region, taking advantage of the tax incentives offered by the government as of 1963 and revitalized in 1965 to 1966, creating in this fashion a kind of regional division of labor for the industrial sector. This partial invasion of the intermediate and primitive strata by modernization once more provoked a deepening of the structural heterogeneity—this time in the northeastern area. It precipitated a violent and combined process of restricted incorporation, ejection, and margination of the population of that region.

In spite of the opportunities for investment to be found in the northeast, the problems of realizing a surplus became more difficult for the central-southern complex. Within the complex, a considerable deterioration of the economic intrastrata relationship in the modern and nonmodern sections (at the level of product input) took place; the demand for labor and for new inputs from the modern activities to the backward ones diminished noticeably. Brazilian capitalism was faced with the problem of drowning in surplus and not being able to convert it into assets. As we have seen, an attempt to find a way out was made by increasing the rate of surplus value extracted from the labor force and increasing the concentration of income and of economic activity. All of this was carried out with the explicit or implicit objective of enlarging the middle-class market, intensifying the capitalization process, and promoting a new expansion.

Thus, Brazil achieved a level of heterogeneity unequaled by the rest of Latin America (except possibly Mexico), which, did not, however, interfere with its dynamics. This was possibly due to the impetus provided by its modernization process, amplified by its spatial dimensions. High rates of incorporation, margination, and expulsion coexist in this process, and they have not yet proved themselves to be in contradiction with the process of expansion. Up to now this process tended to obscure the violent social and political contradictions within the process of capitalist expansion, which are a result of the "exclusive" nature of Brazilian capitalist development. Even though the economic foundation for a class struggle is present and has increased, the masses' capacity to press for their demands has not grown proportionately, either because of their low organizational level, or because of the oppression they suffer. Brazil is also an exception in relation to other countries with a comparable degree of economic development in this respect.

THE TENDENCIES OF CONCENTRATION
GENERAL CHARACTERISTICS OF CONCENTRATION. The development of capitalism is deeply marked by the process of concentration; it influences not only the shape it will assume but also the economic and social results to

be achieved at each stage. For this reason it is a decisive element in explaining the operations and expansion of the system.

Before we go on to examine certain aspects of the Brazilian economy, it is necessary to clarify some ideas on the concentration process itself with the purpose of making a more accurate analysis.

The idea that the process of concentration is linear is extremely common in our economies. In other words, the prevalent notion is that there is a permanent trend toward the concentration of property and production in the hands of a few corporations, and that consequently, income is flowing increasingly into the hands of only an insignificant portion of the population. These factors would imply a progressive and inexorable relative narrowing of the market. The statement needs to be qualified, as it involves excessive doses of simplification and abstraction that are harmful to an interpretation of development in our economies. We will try to present some qualifying factors that we deem important.

Any process of concentration is always closely followed by one of deconcentration and reconcentration and the result may or may not represent an increase in the total coefficient of concentration. Nevertheless, during this process, the relationships and the internal composition of the different productive strata, property, the size of corporations, and the size of income undergo significant change. Consequently, the market and the operations of the system are reorganized but all of this is done without necessarily bringing about a higher degree of concentration.

Similarly, in considering the relationships between the various types of concentration, one can observe that the concentration of capital in the hands of a few corporations, in the urban centers, does not necessarily imply their ownership. Financial and technological control are sufficient to dominate the decision-making process and to eventually withdraw the surplus necessary to realize the superprofits required by the big corporations.

On the other hand, the tendency of the small and medium enterprises to disappear as a consequence of corporate concentration determined, in turn, by the dimensions of the minimum scale in the face of a narrowed market, does not necessarily materialize. First, this minimum dimension does not exist for all branches of enterprises. Second, at the same time that the small and medium traditional enterprises disappear and are replaced by large ones, the small and medium modern enterprises—client or supplier of the great leading corporations—appear on the scene. Simultaneously, the luxury crafts industries, which are a concomitant of increasing urban consumer sophistication, develop at great speed. We are not even mentioning the small and medium commercial services and small businesses.

In reality, there is no such thing as a large isolated enterprise. There are instead macromolecules, each with their dominant enterprises and a constantly renewed constellation of small- and medium-size complementary enterprises. Let us not forget that it is only possible to imagine a process of urbanization free from forward and back interlockings in countries with an extremely low level of industrialization or with "enclave" economies. This protective "cushion" of small enterprises can shrink or expand in accordance with the system's periodic fluctuations, but generally, it does not tend to monopolization.

The concentration-deconcentration-reconcentration process is permanent, and at certain stages it can result in a greater participation by the large enterprises in production and employment, although this does not necessarily happen. What does increase unavoidably is the control of the exchange surplus through mechanisms that can involve independently, either commercialization (purchase or sale oligopsonies), financing (greater predominance of finance capital), or technology (compulsory "patternization" imposed by the mother company or by its affiliate). In the cases where control involves all these elements simultaneously, we are before the most current and sophisticated of the concentration forms, expressed by a type of "conglomerated" organization. The "conglomerate"[35] is not a centralized and monopolic type of organization similar to the early production corporations in North America, such as Ford, General Motors, and Standard Oil. Nor does it necessarily require a horizontal and vertical integration of production in each dynamic sector (as monopolization does)—a form of integration that corresponded to capitalist expansion up to the 1950s—as in the well-known cases of DuPont-Carbide in chemicals and General Electric-Siemens in the electronics industry. The essence of the conglomerate lies in its control of surplus and the market, and it only leads to the integration of production, or technological adaptation when this is the only way to reach the goal that gives it meaning. In other words, the purpose of the conglomerate is to concentrate production, regulate the assimilation of technology, and increase productive efficiency by taking advantage of the economies of scale and interlinkage or complementarity; its objective is to capture the surplus of several sectors or enterprises and search for new and diversified uses for it. It is a question then, of expanding the market and of realizing an increasing amount of surplus in a much more flexible way than by the superaccumulation of the giant production molecules.

Although the structure of a large capitalist oligopolistic enterprise is maintained for certain functions of production, technology, and accumulation,[36] the formation of a conglomerate becomes more and more necessary to a strategy of control and reallocation of surplus on a national or international scale. It is the most efficient way of forming real capital, compatible with

[35] There is ample literature on the origins and characteristics of the conglomerates. See, among many, the work of Celso Furtado (Revista de estudios internacionales de la Universidad de Chile), Stefen Hymer, and selected issues of the *Monthly Review* and of *Developing Economies*.

[36] Which in some less dependent countries is still "national."

financial accumulation without aggravating the crisis inherent in the capitalist system.[37]

As it acquires significance in the underdeveloped capitalist countries, this new form of finance capitalism permits the preservation of a majority of production organization forms using varying degrees of technological development and with different-size corporations. It is also able to control the surplus of those activities whose production forms are not connected to each other and even to unify enterprises and groups that would ordinarily be antagonistic in conditions of normal oligopolic competition. (See, for example, the case of DELTEC in Brazil).

With respect to the process of concentration of personal income, the distribution of income cannot be directed inexorably toward its exclusive concentration in the hands of a few (the top 1 percent of the population, for example) while excluding the rest of the population from participating in the increases in income. If this were to happen, the system would be condemned to live in a permanent crisis. What *can* be observed is a trend toward a continuous redistribution or reconcentration of income, in which the widened consumption of certain social strata and the generation of the necessary surplus are united.

The total coefficient of concentration or the level of absolute inequality can increase or diminish throughout this process. It can be stated that in our countries it increases as an extensive process of industrialization is followed by another intensive process, and after that by a deepening and diversification of consumption among the middle and upper urban classes.[38] However, there is a change in the relative positions of the income strata that represent the different social groups incorporated into the expansion market as a function of the demand required by the system. It is even possible that the partial concentration of the subgroup of middle and upper layers of the distribution scale will be reduced, even if the total concentration increases.

It is evident that in the larger Latin American countries, in the current stage of development through diversification of consumption, a sustained incorporation of the middle classes is necessary.[39] When the system is not able

[37] In Japan, much earlier than in the United States, the formation of conglomerates overcame the old dichotomy between production corporations and finance corporations that is even now dominant in the North American economy. This is a source of strong contradictions between its expansion as a nation and its condition as the head of contemporary imperialism.

[38] See again on this subject Anibal Pinto's *"Diagnósticos, estructura y esquemas de desarrollo en América Latina,"* and Pedro Vuskovic's *"Distribución del ingreso y opciones del desarrollo,"* both cited in footnote 17.

[39] In the same way that the wage-earning classes had to be incorporated during the stage of extensive industrialization. It was not by chance that this period corresponds to the golden age of populism for several Latin American countries. Populism was compatible with the system. Wherever the populist forms arrived late on the scene or were delayed until the following stage of industrialization, there was a rupture in the scheme of vertical alliances. See Francisco Weffort's work, for example, *"Estados y masas en Brazil,"* Revista Civilizaçao Brasileira, No. 7, May 1966, and Luciano Martins, cited in footnote 30.

to carry this process out satisfactorily, either in the area of employment or of expenditures (financing the increasing debt of the middle groups), or finally, with respect to income, through an ever-increasing differentiation of salaries in favor of the bureaucracy and the technocracy, crises tend to occur. Whether the system is able to overcome them or not depends as much on the structural realities, with a certain degree of historical permanence, as on the conjunctural picture created in a period of transition. During the middle of the past decade, both factors were favorable for Brazil.

THE TWO BASIC MECHANISMS OF BRAZILIAN RECONCENTRATION. The process of concentration in force in Brazil since 1964 has been fundamentally supported by the state's new power mechanisms and the growing financial and technological control by international capitalism.

The reconcentration of property, production, income, and markets is a consequence of this new unified form in which the moving forces of expansion operate through more and more centralized mechanisms. They are, then, the simultaneous result of the policy which has been put in practice and of inexorable laws of internal operation of underdeveloped capitalism that leads to a closed process of accumulation of capital and of the fruits of technical progress.

In the case of Brazil, we are more concerned with the dynamic sector's mechanisms of control, and the problem of the restricted participation of the masses incorporated into the expansion process, than with the concentration of property and production. Regarding the first aspect, it is fundamental to mention what appears to be the most efficient form of controlling the dominant dynamic sectors, which is related to the "new" and increasingly important role of finance capitalism. Regarding the second, an examination of the process of reconcentration of income can throw some light on the matter. In this essay we shall deal only with the second aspect of the problem.

THE RECONCENTRATION OF INCOME IN BRAZIL. It is convenient to present the following schematization comprising five different income groups in order to visualize the distribution of income and its changes, which are a result of the capitalist transformation.

Group A. Upper class, bourgeoisie: (property owners, managers).

Group B₁. Upper middle class (some liberal professions, executives, administrators).

Group B₂. Urban middle class (public and private bureaucrats, small merchants).

Group C. Base wage earners.

Group D. Rural workers, independent marginal urban workers.

It would seem to us that the fundamental dynamic of distribution is practically limited to Groups B and C. The upper class maintains or increases its

		Annual Income	
Groups	Total Population	Percentage of the Total	Absolute per Capita Level (in dollars)
A	700,000 (1%)	28	8400
B₁	2,800,000 (4%)	16	1200
B₂	10,500,000 (15%)	21	420
C	21,000,000 (30%)	20	200
C	35,000,000 (50%)	15	90

Source. Estudio de la distribución del ingreso en Brazil, CEPAL, Rio de Janeiro, 1967.

participation, while Group D does not participate in any significant way in the production gains of the system. The following table is an estimated break-down of the distribution of income in 1960.

Even though in 1960 Brazil had a market for sophisticated durable goods —approximately the same size as those of Argentina and Mexico—the patterns of income and consumption of the middle groups were remarkably inferior because of the high concentration and the absolute size of the dominant sector. Consequently, the economy had almost no possibility of sustaining a unified participation of the middle groups and the progressive increase of concentration in the dominant sector, without restructuring the distribution scheme.

As of 1961, the acceleration of inflation began to undermine real urban wages, and, consequently, the relative position of Groups B₂ and C. As a result, the base of the market for popular consumption began to contract, without a substantial parallel expansion of the diversified consumption market taking place because of the low participation of the middle classes. It was because of this that the consolidated luxury patterns of the upper classes provided the only element of dynamic impulse in the area of consumption.

Perhaps to counteract these developments, in 1963 the government tried to implement a redistribution strategy in favor of the working classes. The strategy was condemned to failure, considering the previous trends of the expansion process and the continuance of the basic parameters of the system's mode of operation.

The policies of the new military government made it possible to reorganize the distribution strategy in a way that would be "convenient" to the system. It began by redistributing income in favor of the urban middle class, and against the working class. This redistribution began first at the level of expenditure, through the new expanded strategies for financing durable goods, and later on, through income. It maintained the deterioration of the real minimum wage, but kept the average wage constant and permitted a fanning-out of the salary scale of the new emerging middle classes. Everything would lead us to think that the concentration in the dominant sectors continued and increased in vigor in 1967 with the substantial increase in surplus. This increase was made possible by a reduction of almost 50 percent in the real minimum wage, and of 30 percent in the average industrial wage, (in respect to 1961), under conditions of recuperation and accelerated expansion of the urban economic activities. Similarly, the incorporation of labor resulting from the expansion made it possible for the number of working members per urban family to increase significantly in 1969 in respect to the previous decade. This is what made it possible for the average family income in 1970 to descend to the levels registered at the beginning of the decade.

THE DISTRIBUTION OF INCOME IN 1970. If we accept the very optimistic hypothesis that during the last decade, the average income per agricultural worker has increased proportionately to the average productivity of the sector, and if we accept, with even more optimism, that the rhythm of margination has not intensified, we may estimate that the strata corresponding to the lowest 50 percent of the population increased its average income by around 1 percent annually.

In spite of this definitely rosy supposition about the lower classes, the scheme of distribution of income in 1970 would actually show a larger total rate of inequality and a greater concentration in the dominant sector with relation to 1960. By way of compensation, the upper middle groups' relative participation in the total income and the average level of the middle-class groups as a whole would increase significantly. If we admit, for the sake of simplicity, that the average yearly income in Brazil was about US$400 in 1970,[40] and supposing that the class structure remained the same—a very optimistic hypothesis—and taking into account the changes in distribution that we have already mentioned, the breakdown for 1970 would probably be as follows.

[40] It was actually not more than US $380.

		Annual Income	
Groups	Total Population	Total Participation (Percentage)	Absolute per Capita Level (in Dollars)
A	900,000	30	12,000
B₁	3,600,000	20	2,000
B₂	13,500,000	22.5	600
C	27,000,000	15.0	200
D	45,000,000	12.5	100

Source. The authors' estimate.

Accordingly, Groups A and B_1 represent 5 percent of the total population. They absorb the bulk of the profits on the total productivity of the period and receive 50 percent of the total income. Group B_2 also improves its relative position in respect to 1960. And, in addition, if we take into account the absolute increment of income, its absolute weight within the consumer goods market grows considerably.

The importance these five income groups have for the market can be roughly outlined as follows.

Group A. Appropriates the surplus that sustains the process of accumulation and diversifies consumption.

Group B_1. Fundamental core of the modern market.

Group B_2. Base for the modern market.
$$\left\{ \begin{array}{l} \text{Largest} \\ \text{absolute and} \\ \text{relative} \\ \text{position} \\ \text{during this} \\ \text{period} \end{array} \right.$$

Group C. Base for the extraction of surplus and principal support for the traditional market. Its buying power fluctuates with the minimum wage.

Group D. Excluded from the modern consumer market. Part of Group D represents the base for extraction of surplus of the traditional sectors and has little relative participation in capitalis consumption; the remainder, whose dimensions are not known, constitutes the marginated population.

The total absolute income of the three groups that are truly important for the modern market was US$14,650 million in 1960, and it will be closer to US$26,600 million in 1970. This sum is greater than Brazil's gross national product in 1960. Thus, during the decade, the modern market grew by 80 percent, as against the per capita income's 33 percent. That is, of the US$15,000 million increase in the national income during the period, US$12,000 million were distributed among 20 percent of the population, contributing to feed the expansion of the dynamic market. Only US$3,000 million were distributed among the remaining 80 percent of the population, which helped to expand the traditional market.

Obviously, these are not rigorous estimates, and have an extremely weak empirical base. Their only purpose is to give an approximate idea of the dynamics of the reconcentration of income during the last decade and to demonstrate the error of the relative narrowing of the market as an argument for the stagnation thesis.

CONTRADICTIONS AND CRISIS. After having outlined some important aspects of the dynamics of Brazilian capitalism—which are probably very similar to those of other dependent, underdeveloped, capitalist systems—it would be appropriate to enter into a more detailed examination of the fundamental contradictions and the character of the system's potential crises. Nevertheless, for various reasons, this will remain a subject for future essays. In the first place, a more profound analysis of the development of the system's financial organization—a nucleus that is fundamental to an understanding of the Brazilian capitalist "movements"—would be necessary. In the second place, we would have to reexamine the industrial development of the last two decades through a lens that would permit us to see the process of expansion, modernization, and concentration of income in retrospect. It is obviously necessary to make this analysis in the context of the transformation of world capitalism.

We will formulate only some partial indications that could be useful "clues" for more thorough studies.

If we consider the dynamics of incorporation and dissemination of technological progress in the Brazilian economy, we can observe a significant difference in relation to the developed capitalist countries, a difference that tends to shape a contradiction peculiar to the system. In effect, its expansion gives impulse to the spread of modernization as a result of the search for new "investment opportunities" for realizing a surplus. Nevertheless, there is a tendency for this modernization to be restricted (because of the defense of superprofits), which is a result of the presence of backward activities within the same market and of the demand for traditional articles that develop very feebly.

Thus, the full attainment of the modernization potential is continually frustrated. This means that it has to sustain the dissemination of technological progress and of its products inside an orbit that only expands very slowly and spasmodically. Nevertheless, if on the one hand, modernization is restricted precisely in order to preserve the rates of profit in the modernized activities, the surplus, on the other hand, tends to be kept increasingly within the circuit of the modern sector. This inhibits the attainment of its goal. Besides trying to deepen and diversify the "modern" consumption of goods and services, the system seeks ways out through the already mentioned modes of combined accumulation that can be favorable in the measure that they are unified, in terms of their productive results, with the dynamics of international capitalism.

Before considering the problems of realizing a surplus in Brazilian capitalism, it would be worthwhile to insist on one point. The specificity of the crises of realization of a surplus in the Brazilian economy is not related to any periodic fluctuations in economic activity. These fluctuations are associated with the presence of a domestic sector of capital goods which tends to expand any variations in the level of effective demand, or to generate crises of demand because of the existing disproportion between the growth of the two "departments," those of consumer goods and those of capital goods. In this sense there are no important differences in relation to the cyclical character of any other capitalist economy.[41]

Our hypothesis is that the tendency toward a crisis of realization of surplus —inherent in any capitalist system—acquires more dynamic and specific characteristics in the heart of dependent and underdeveloped systems like Brazil's. These characteristics are related to the need for permanent and discontinuous changes in the form of allocation of resources (generation, appropriation, and utilization of surplus) explained, in turn, by the unification of the economy to the renovated scheme of an international division of labor. Historically, the Latin American, and especially the Brazilian economies have "burned" with increasing speed the stages of expansion brought on by the behavior of their leading sectors, dependently integrated into the scheme of an international division of labor. Given conditions of a lesser or greater generation of domestic bases for a self-propelling process of expansion, the result is that our economies, which are not able to generate or control their forms of incorporation into the technical process endogenously, have almost no possibilities of integrating themselves into the international market. Together with the infeasability of a domestic generalization of modernization this abbreviates the periods during which the exchange surplus must be even more intensely reoriented.[42] The sometimes drastic reorientation of economic activity would only be possible through intense periodic changes in the schemes of income and product concentration, in such a way as to adjust to the new schemes of allocation of resources. This situation implies that a reordering of the mechanisms of power is required at the beginning of every new stage of capitalist development, from the state's control apparatus and the new forms of unification with foreign capitalism to the problems of a new class alliance.

This can lead us to the conclusion that along with a tendency toward a periodic crisis of realization of surplus, social and political crises occur more frequently, especially when it is not a question of a simple fluctuations in the economic activity, but of important changes in the patterns of capitalist development.

A few countries have been able to go from one mode to another without any major crises, thanks to more adequate connections in their forms of expansion or a greater political control of the system—as is the case of Mexico. In other countries, the capitalist system has suffered profound ruptures in its prevalent institutional and political strategies and, even under

[41] We can also add that it would not be pertinent to state that the crisis—in the case of certain underdeveloped economies with a greater degree of industrialized diversification—has only a reflective character in respect to the crisis of the central economies.

[42] In the case of an eventual integration into the international market, it would be possible to ease the process of transformation, since the external market would increase the operational scope of the domestic economic process.

extremely coercive conditions favoring the dominant groups, it has not been able to carry out a stable reorganization of its strategy or create more than a mediocre caricature of a modern "consumer" capitalist society.

After a critical rupture in its political structure, Brazil seems to be the country that has best turned the key variables of accumulation and modernization to its advantage. It has even acquired a modest, relatively privileged standing within the new strategy of division of the regional and international market that is being carried out by the international corporations. Nevertheless, it still has serious problems of realization of surplus that caused it to accelerate the development of the financial system since 1968. This system sustains inflation at a rate of around 25 percent, a rhythm that is tolerable and even functional within the expansion system, but that inhibits the preservation of the buying power of the basic salary and aggravates the already soaring rate of extraction of surplus from the labor force.

Although we reject the stagnation thesis and do not see any limitations to the potential for Brazil's capitalist expansion in the current stage of its development, we do believe that it presents constant and recurring problems related to the realization of surplus. As we mentioned before, a more thorough analysis of this topic will be the object of another essay.

4

J. Serra | The Brazilian "Economic Miracle"*

During the middle of the last decade, the Brazilian economy went through a profound crisis which resulted in a strong contraction of the growth of industrial production and of the gross national product, together with a marked increase in urban unemployment. The depression lasted almost six years, starting in 1962 and reaching its lowest depths from 1963 to 1965. It was closely related to the overthrow of President Joao Goulart in April 1964, and the emergence of the military regime that has remained in power to the present. The depression was also responsible, to a large degree, for the military government's increasing "rigidity" during its first years in power.

There are abundant, though not always satisfactory, analyses of the origins and evolution of the crisis. This is not the case in regard to the period of economic recovery that began in 1967.

Much of the economic literature dealing with interpretations of the recovery phase has been restricted to a superficial analysis with a strong propagandist tendency in favor of the military regime.

The more "vulgarized" versions of the implicit or explicit content of this literature, disseminated in the national and international press, have tried to characterize the Brazilian recovery as an "economic miracle" similar to those that took place in Germany, Italy, and Japan after World War II.

* This essay was edited at the end of October 1971. Subsequently, an extended and corrected version was prepared, updating the 1971 data. Unfortunately, because of time, it was not possible to include it in this volume. As such, we are presenting the first version.

The propagation of the image of an "economic miracle" has apparently been encouraged with a double objective in mind. On the one hand, on the domestic front, it tries to foster a climate of "optimism" for the bourgeoisie—indispensable if favorable expectations for investment are to be created, and consequently, to guarantee a rate of accumulation compatible with the acceleration of growth. Economic theory teaches that in order for the economy to "go well," it is indispensable that the capitalists believe that it will do so. The Brazilian technocracy seems to have learned its lesson well. On the other hand, at the international level, the promulgation of Brazil's alleged success not only favors the expectations of investors and financiers, it also helps to improve the military government's public image throughout the world.

The image of the regime's economic efficiency would seem to compensate for its violence; it would even appear as a kind of "advantageous" counterpart to the authoritarian state. Authoritarianism would be presented as a concomitant necessity to impose the "social peace" that ensures economic efficiency and the improvement of the masses' standard of living.

The promulgation of this thesis has achieved certain acceptance in different countries interested in the Brazilian experience. It has also contributed to the censorship of the domestic information and communications media and to the control of the political, trade union, and intellectual sectors that dissent from the official policies. In addition, the use made of Brazil's alleged economic success by the conservative sectors of several nations—especially in Latin America—to further their own political interests, has played an important role in this scheme.

The theses put forth by the conservative sectors are precisely the ones we listed earlier: the authoritarian Brazilian state manages an efficient economic policy, guaranteeing the social stability that allows dispassionate technocrats to lead the economy—within the freest of free enterprises—toward an accelerated expansion and democratization, resulting in a growing expansion of economic opportunities.

The importance given to the "Brazilian Miracle" and the desire to shed some light on some aspects of the process of economic recovery that has taken place since 1967, has prompted us to write this essay. Our evaluation of the recent socioeconomic experience of Brazilian capitalism is manifestly critical.

The essay is divided into four main parts. In the first part some commonly used indicators of the "Brazilian Miracle" relating to the growth of the gross national product, the halting of inflation, and the increase in foreign reserves are analyzed. The second part analyzes in more detail the fundamental points of the governmental policy in reference to the distribution of income, as well as the practical consequences of implementing this policy.

In the third, briefer, part we make a short examination of the conditions and trends of international participation in domestic productive activities. Finally, the fourth part attempts a brief outline—through the introduction of new elements and the integration of others already mentioned—of some aspects that define the nature and contradictions of Brazilian capitalism in its current stage.

INDICATORS OF THE ALLEGED MIRACLE

In its editorial of October 13, 1971, *El Mercurio** published a brief summary of facts that purport to account for the economic explosion.

• A 9 percent average annual increase in production during 1968 to 1970.

• A reduction of the 86.6 percent inflation rate of 1964 (the year President Goulart was overthrown) to a 19 percent rate in 1970, after the application of a gradualist approach.

• An accumulation of US$1.5 billion in monetary reserves by mid-1971.

Let us analyze these facts more closely, trying to uncover their true significance.

DATA ON THE TOTAL GROWTH. First, it should be recalled that what we could call the myth of growth rates has been completely discredited. In fact, the prevalent notion today is that mere quantitative data give a very partial, and at times distorted, vision of the economic and social reality of a nation. In sum, and in order to avoid digressions on a subject already familiar to intellectual and political circles, it is a question of the relevant differences between growth, development, and social progress.

Thus, the display or compiling of growth rates in themselves is not definitive, although it may always be important. Instead, what is fundamentally interesting is the *content* of this process, or if one will, the knowledge of who benefits, and to what degree, from the distribution of the fruits of economic expansion.

Turning now to the specific topic of the growth rates of Brazilian economy, it would be in order to take a broader period as references for the analysis, especially if our objective is to formulate an opinion on the political economy of the military regime.

It is evident from Table 1 that there was a 6 percent average annual rate of growth for the last seven years. While this is not a "bad" growth rate, it is far from being an astounding rate for that time period. One could argue that what is most important are the more recent results, which would express the outcome of the policies inaugurated in 1964. But, without straying too far from the mark, it could be asserted that the low growth rate for 1962 to 1967 was precisely one of the factors that made the subsequent acceleration possible. It permitted a takeoff to occur from a very low absolute level, and based the recovery process on a high coefficient of idle capacity. This is of particular importance in an economy that has the highest and most self-sufficient production potential of Latin America.

* The leading Chilean daily newspaper, published in Santiago, Chile.

TABLE 1

Variations in the Brazilian Gross National Product (Percentage Relative to the Preceding Year)

Year	Variation
1960	9.7
1961	10.3
1962	5.3
1963	1.5
1964	2.9
1965	2.7
1966	5.1
1967	4.8
1968	8.4[a]
1969	9.0[a]
1970	9.5[a]

Source. Getulio Vargas Foundation.

[a] Preliminary estimates.

The better use of that idle capacity permitted an acceleration of the rate of growth without having to resort to a parallel investment drive. Nevertheless, it must be said that this reserve has already disappeared in a great number of activities. It remains to be seen if from now on the government can promote a true expansion process based on the generation of complementary productive capacities that are realizable from the viewpoint of demand.

Returning to the question of total growth rates, it is interesting to note a fact that *El Mercurio,* always so concerned with statistics, surely cannot underestimate. We refer to the interview with Delfin Netto. In it, the data for the last three years are considered "provisional," as are those in Table 1. Is this due to an econometric inefficiency of the Brazilian technocracy, always so proud of its talents in this area? Or is it, rather, a practical application of the economic theory that states that expectations must be inflated and optimism created, even at the cost of public honesty?

Let us take 1969 as an example. A significant recession in the last quarter of that year reduced the expansion rate of the entire urban economy. Agriculture, for its part, had a bad year; the harvests were inferior to those of the preceding year.[1] An optimistic estimate would place the total growth rate at about 6 percent. Nevertheless, the government continues to publish flagrantly unrealistic estimates which place the growth rate in the range of 9 percent.

[1] In the *Anuario Banas,* a publication associated with the Brazilian industrial bourgeoise, a similar point of view is presented (1970 edition).

THE BRAZILIAN "ECONOMIC MIRACLE"   103

Moreover, the government's desire to inflate expectations and promote itself is so blatant that it has no modesty in predicting exorbitant expansion rates. In December 1970 Delfin Netto affirmed, for example, that there would be a 10 percent increase in production during the present year. These same predictions have been repeated throughout 1971. If the 10 percent rate is not achieved, it should not prove very difficult to present "inflated" data. After all, four or five years from now, when they are reviewed, who will remember?

TRENDS AND NEW CHARACTERISTICS OF THE INFLATION. It is worthwhile to point out some elements that place in their proper perspective the government's vaunted antiinflationary triumphs, which seem so important when it is stated that the price index has been cut down from 80 plus percent in 1964 to less than 20 percent in 1970. In effect, the "triumph" is what becomes considerably deflated when one considers that although the factors to which inflationary pressures were attributed have virtually disappeared, the price index continues to float at around 20 percent annually, a rate that cannot be considered negligible.

In the opinion of the "dispassionate" technocrats, the public deficit, the pressures on wages, and the disorderly monetary policies were the three elements responsible for inflation. Let us see what happened with each one of them.

The treasury cash deficit went from 4.1 percent of the gross national product in 1962 to 1963 to 0.4 percent in 1970.[2] The federal government's growing debt in the form of public securities allowed it to finance this small deficit and even to achieve a *deinflationary* surplus in its account after 1969.

On the other hand, with the government in control of the labor unions, with job stability virtually eliminated, and with the harsh repression, there has been almost no pressure by labor on wages. Thus, between 1964 and 1970, the readjustments on minimum wages have been at a rate systematically lower to the rise in the cost of living, reducing the average buying power in Sao Paulo by 20 percent in real terms. The average real salary of federal civil servants decreased even more, as shown in Figure 1.

Finally, the government monetary policy has never been so thoroughly implemented and "correct" from the orthodox point of view, as during the period of the dictatorship, at least in comparison with the years prior to 1964.

Despite these achievements, the inflation rate has stabilized, after the drastic breakdown of 1965 and 1967, at around 20 percent, a level that is by no means low. By 1970, only Chile had surpassed this rate among all the Latin American countries (see Table 2).

[2] The elimination of the deficit was not due to cuts in the public investment sector, which rose from 45 to 60 percent of the total fixed capital investments of the economy from 1959 to 1964 and 1965 to 1969. The explanation lies in the increment of 50 percent in the tax load and in a relative reduction in current expenses due, in large measure, to the heavy contraction of the real wages for federal civil servants.

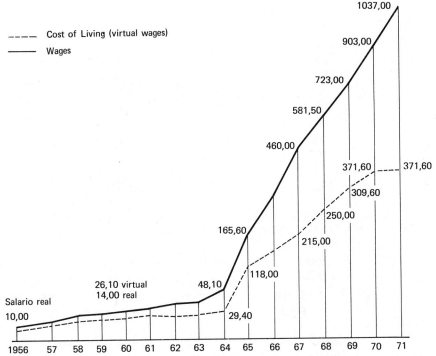

Source. Union Nacional de los Servicios Publicos (UNSP) (National Union of Public Employees), with data from the Getulio Vargas Foundation.

So we see that the much publicized gradualism of the antiinflationary policy has been just a euphemism to justify the failure to reduce inflation to the minimal or "normal" level in an expansively balanced capitalist economy.

Actually, the factor that allowed Brazilian capitalism to withstand the break in the growth rhythm of prices in 1965 and 1967 was the violent reduction during that period of the wages of urban workers, including civil servants. The credit reductions were principally withstood by industry and the public sector, thanks to the reduction in the cost of labor, which thus bore the brunt of the antiinflationary policy.

Beginning in 1968, the reduction of wages, although it has continued, has lost strength, mainly because of the extremely low remuneration level that it had reached. Since then, the acceleration of growth and the utilization of idle industrial capacity allowed enterprises to produce considerable surpluses, which, in turn, permitted them to expand without affecting the rhythm of prices level increases.

It is easy to conclude that any disturbance to the growth reached up to this

TABLE 2

Cost of Living Increase in Guanabara State (Percentage Relative to the Preceding Year)

Year	Variation
1960	23.8
1961	43.6
1962	55.2
1963	80.6
1964	86.6
1965	45.4
1966	41.1
1967	24.5
1968	24.0
1969	24.0
1970	20.9

Source. Getulio Vargas Foundation.

point will tend to reaccelerate the inflationary process which, because it is already at such a high level, could rapidly go out of control. But a descent from that level has proved very difficult for the government, because the present inflation is structurally connected to Brazil's mode of capitalist development.

In retrospect, the increase in the rate of exploitation of workers and of the return on investments, the more orderly fiscal and monetary planning, and the development of the capital market did not—in *ex-post* terms—lead to an increase in the national monetary reserves. Rather, these tended to reinforce a production scheme oriented toward expansion and above all toward the diversification of consumer goods for a minority, namely the bourgeoisie and the upper-middle class. The durable goods industries—the leading sector of the expansion—have been living with the constant problem of demand needed to maintain profitable growth, given the concentration of the national income and its relatively low per capita level in the face of the consumer patterns implicit in its privileged production. The principal solution was to increase the income of some restricted sectors and, since 1966, to accelerate the development of consumer financing schemes for wide sectors of the middle income groups, and even of the better paid working class. The debt level of these sectors reached suffocating heights; in 1970, for example, it rose by almost 50 percent. The drafts that largely financed consumption totaled more than US$1.6 billion[3] that year, 4 percent of the gross national product.

[3] *Correio de Manha*, September 27, 1971.

That credit load represents a cost uncompensated for by any real returns since it is not associated with productive investments. This cost, which nourishes a giant sector of financial services, is paid for by the price increase, which serves as a defense for the profit rate and absorbs the real income of persons depending on a fixed income, mainly the wage earners.

The very price of credit becomes greatly relevant in this scheme. It is believed that the rate of interest continues in the range of 40 to 45 percent annually, that is, 17 to 20 percent in real terms, allowing for the rate of inflation.

The need and advantage of satisfying the wide demand for credit for current expenses by the public and private sectors has created great competition among the financing sources. The government tried to develop these sources through highly generous inducements which sought to promote investments in financial securities by the high income groups. This has led to a keen speculative process, whose effects have been to preserve or raise the returns on those investments, which, in terms of alternative uses of capital, makes the interest rates on loans more inflexible. Adding this to the guarantee monetary correction for all types of financing, the financing costs of the enterprises excessively burden their expenses, and are then partially transferred into prices, as a way of preserving the rates of profit.

The problem of inflation is unquestionably complex; considering that it is a product of the economic structure, breaking its spinal column would be similar to curing the illness while killing the patient. On the one hand, Brazilian inflation represents precisely the price that must be paid so that such a concentrated economy might be supplied with the demand necessary for expansion. On the other, in terms of its effects, it cuts down on the preference for liquidity, causing immobilizations, whether real or financial, that end by nourishing effective demand, which is highly beneficial to economic activity.

A sharp change in the situation would seriously endanger the level of production. Governmental technocrats know that that could imply a profound crisis. Minister Delfin Netto, in the debate with Roberto Campos—within the plan of internal opposition to the regime—sustains that holding down inflation would mean a four-year crisis and a loss of US$15 billion in terms of reduced production. The powerful Sao Paulo Industrial Federation almost sent roses to Delfin Netto in gratitude, stating that it would "reiterate its unconditional support for the manner in which that young man from Sao Paulo has been handling national finance" (October 16, 1971).

THE FICTITIOUS EXTERNAL SOLIDITY. The third fact mentioned by *El Mercurio* as proof of the Brazilian government's economic success refers to the high level of foreign reserves reached by the nation. As is well known, these reserves act as an important safeguard according to the specialists in international economy, enabling the country to negotiate freely abroad and thus reducing the costs of imports and financing. Brazilian reserves—among the largest in Latin America—seemingly would carry out this function. They would also indicate a condition of exceptional solidity for the Brazilian economy, capable of growing rapidly and in surplus conditions with respect to the rest of the world.

Nevertheless, in the Brazilian case these reserves are not the result of any particular solidity. Quite the contrary, the country has increased its international reserves in the last three years at the cost of a significant expansion of its foreign debt.

Brazil's small trade surpluses in the last few years have been widely canceled out by the costs of transportation, tourism abroad, payments on interests, profits, and technical assistance, as can be seen in Table 3.

TABLE 3
Brazil's Balance of Payment (in Million of Dollars)

Breakdown	1964 to 1968	1969	1970
Balance of trade	335	318	213
Services	−476	−602	−845
Transportation, tourism and others	−239	−270	−417
Profits, dividends, and interests	−198	−261	−351
Technical assistance, patents, and trade mark	−39	−71	−77
Balance of current accounts	−80	−253	−622
Income of capital	599	1291	1748
Amortizations	−372	−533	−632
Miscellaneous	−164	−92	−137
Balance	−32[a]	−549	−545

Source. Banco Central de Brazil.
* For 1968.

In spite of the magnitude of such payments and those corresponding to commercial services, travel and "miscellaneous," whose meaning the Banco Central does not clearly explain, the nation's reserves have grown from US$257 million to US$1,187 million between 1968 and 1970, and by April 1971 had almost reached US$1,380 million. (See Table 4.)

This increase was due to a considerable growth in the flow of foreign capital, especially in the form of loans and financing, which has caused a rapid increase in the national debt.

It can be seen that from the end of 1967 to April of the present year, the reserves grew by almost US$1,200 million and the debt by more than

TABLE 4
Brazil's Reserves and Foreign Debt (in Millions of Dollars)

Period	Debt	Reserves
1963 to 1964	3161	—
1967	3372	199
1968	3917	257
1969	4403	657
1970	5295	1187
1971[a]	6000	1378

Source. Banco Central de Brazil and *Visao* Magazine, September 1971.
[a] For 1968.

US$2,600 million. *Thus, for every dollar increase in the reserve, the foreign debt grew by US$1.8.*[4]

The picture is even more discouraging if one considers the composition of the debt. Cash loans, which have grown rapidly since 1968, represented around 43 percent of the total external debt by the end of last year. The total was close to US$2,300 million which greatly surpassed the level of reserves. Generally, these are short-term loans, over half of which are made on credit lines renewable on a yearly basis. They serve to increase reserves and to partially cover the deficits resulting from the disequilibrium in the balance of payments, thus allowing a high and growing level of superfluous imports.

Translated into cruzeiros, those dollars are largely used to finance circulating capital for corporations or simply to finance the national enterprises' purchases abroad. The first case applies primarily to foreign enterprises, which have the most foreign credit. In that sense, these dollars imply a redistribution of enterprise property in favor of foreign interests, or subsidies to foreign companies. With the rhythm of exchange devaluation inferior by 50 percent to that of internal inflation, the cost of short-term external financing is 4 to 5 percent lower than internal credit.

As can be concluded from this, Brazil's much publicized international reserves represent only a kind of "poker chip"[5] that a losing player borrows from a winning player in order to continue playing—and losing.

---

[4] The government technocrats argue that reserves yield interests that benefit the country. Nevertheless, the debt also implies the payment of interest to creditors, and since it grows faster on an absolute scale than the reserves, the nation is the loser. Furthermore, interest on loans tends to be higher on the average than interest that the reserves can accumulate.

[5] "Cacife" in Portuguese, to use the expression that Delfin Netto coined to impress the public.

THE DETERIORATION OF WAGES AND THE
DISTRIBUTION OF INCOME

Over half the interview that Delfin Netto gave to *El Mercurio* in Santiago, Chile was on the subject of wages and labor's participation in Brazil's economic process. Despite the wide coverage given and the algebraic formulas displayed, created with the purpose of fostering an "objective and technical" image of the dictatorship's economic program, no data was given on the evolution of the purchasing power of wages.

We shall present some information on the subject and examine in more detail the government's wage policy.

THE REGIME'S WAGE POLICY. The readjustment formula adopted since 1965 for private and public employees and workers assumed that wages would be readjusted to equal the average prevailing wage of the last 24 months. A compensatory amount that took into account the expected rate of inflation during the readjustment period would be added. As an additional benefit, a rate representative of the rise in national productivity would be taken into account, equivalent to a real wage improvement. The attempt was to maintain the participation of the working sector in the distribution of income.

The following formulas are used to determine the rates of wage readjustment. They are not essential to the subsequent analysis, but it is interesting to show them and relate them to this study, since they were presented in the interview reprinted by *El Mercurio* with the apparent aim of portraying detachment and technical rigor. That this was the principal objective is clearly demonstrated by the notable number of elementary mistakes that appeared in the newspaper's formula, which thus ended by transforming its presentation into a mere display for the reader unused to algebra and mathematical calculations. We will not point out the errors, since that would take up too much space, but the interested reader can identify them by comparing *El Mercurio*'s version and the one we present:

$$(1+R_t) = \frac{W_3}{W_2} = \frac{W_r \ (1+R/2) + aW_2 P}{W_2}$$

$$W = \frac{W_1 \displaystyle\sum_{i=1}^{12} I_i + aW_2 \displaystyle\sum_{i=13}^{24}}{24}$$

$$a = \frac{1 + \dfrac{T_{-1}}{2}}{1 + \dfrac{R_{-1}}{2}}$$

R_t rate of wage readjustment

W_1 index of the recorded nominal wage during the first 12 months of the year

W_2 index of the recorded nominal wage from the 13th month to the end of the 24th-month period

W_3 the new wage, corrected and adjusted, to be paid in the next period

W_r average wage during the last 24 months

R expected rate of inflation for the effective period of the new readjustment

P rate of production increase given for the new readjustment

a percentage relating to the correction of the residual error made in the preceding period

I_i correction indexes based on the monthly cost-of-living index

T_{-1} rise in the cost of living from the 13th to 24th month

R_{-1} rate of inflation—calculation based on the rise in the cost of living— foreseen previously for the period from the 13th to the 24th month and used for the computation of W_2

The key to the manner in which these calculation were made lies in the expected inflation. If this turns out to be inferior to the actual resulting inflation, the worker is the one who loses out, even if the error is subsequently corrected, although, obviously, in the latter case, he loses less. Let us examine this matter more closely.

Compensation for the differences between the expected rate and the real rate of inflation did not exist until 1967. That is, the formula for readjustment did not include the corrective factor. Table 5 shows that there were substantial differences between the two rates between 1965 and 1967. These differences were to be the determining factor in the violent drop in wages during that period.

TABLE 5

Rate of Expected Inflation[a] and Effective Rates in the Guanabara State (Percentage)

To July of	Expected	Effective
1966	25	45.0
1967	10	30.1
1968	15	21.5
1969	15	21.1
1970	15	21.3
1971	12	20.0[b]

Source. Getulio Vargas Foundation.

[a] For computing wage readjustments.
[b] Estimates.

Beginning in 1967, a change in the regime's wage policies took place through the introduction of the correction factor. Nonetheless, there was no compensation for the differences in previous years and the correction was actually carried out a posteriori. In other words, if the wages fixed at the beginning of the work year turn out to be lower than what they should have been as a consequence of an underestimated price growth rate, wages corresponding to the year $+1$ will be calculated based on what the worker received, plus what he lost through the difference between the expected rate and the real rate. However, that difference is not returned to him; it is only used as a calculation to prevent the error from being repeated in the year $n+1$.

In terms of the formulas presented, n is equal to the year 2, when the worker received W_2 per month. Nevertheless, W_2 is not used as the basis for the calculation of W_3; aw_2 that is, the corrected wage, is used instead. But, $aw_2 - w_a = W_2\,(a\text{-}1)$, which is what the workers lost in each month of year 2, *is not returned.*

Thus, the difference between the rate of inflation used for the calculations and the actual cost-of-living increase was the principal factor for the wage reduction. The reduction on wages in the year n would be equal in percentage term to:

$$\frac{\overline{W}_r\left(\dfrac{T_n - R_n}{2}\right)}{w_n}$$

$\overline{W}_r$ average salary in the period n-2 and n-1
T_2 the actual increase in the cost of living during n
R_n the expected inflation coefficient used to calculate
W_n which would be the salary during n.

If $w_n = 100$, $w_r = 90.3$, $R_n = 16$ percent, and $T_n = 24$ percent, the worker's wages during period n will be 3.6 percent less than it should have been according to the official policy. It could be argued that this is an inevitable reduction between periods of wage readjustment in any inflationary economy. Nevertheless, the government's wage policy, precisely because it takes this factor into account, carries a built-in salary reduction, since it only readjusts the rise in the cost of living by half the actual amount. Thus, the contraction due to the fact that T is bigger than R is added to the one previously imposed.

Table 5 shows that the government has systematically underestimated the rise in the cost of living—even under Netto's management—using estimates in its calculations inferior by as much as 25 percent to the real rate of inflation. Contrary to the government's boasts, this situation has been repeated up to the present year. The consequence of this has been a steady reduction in workers' wages as of 1964, as Tables 6 and 7 demonstrate.

Another object of the government's propaganda has been the alleged incorporation of the rate of growth of the total economic production into the readjustment calculations. According to the secretary of the treasury, "It is possible to preserve the buying power of wages and even to progressively improve the average real wage." (Delfin Netto in the interview with *El Mercurio*). Netto's blatant deceitfulness is made clearly evident when one examines Tables 6 and 7, which use data from official and semiofficial sources.

In practice, the wage increases attributable to the growth of the average

TABLE 6

Variations in the Cost of Living Index and in the Minimum Nominal Wage in the City of Sao Paulo (February 1964 = 100[a])

	Indexes	
Date[b]	Cost of Living	Minimum Nominal Wage
March 1965	189	157
March 1966	272	200
March 1967	365	240
March 1968	451	309
May 1969	571	371
May 1970	691	445
May 1971	843	537

Source. Statistical Annual of the IBGE, 1970 and 1971 and of the Getulio Vargas Foundation.

[a] February 1964 can be taken as tax index year because it does not distort the actual results, in the sense that it does not overestimate the relative variations between the cost of living and nominal wages through the years. This has been confirmed by the mentioned sources.

[b] The data indicated correspond to the readjustment period.

TABLE 7

Evolution of the Real Minimum Wage in Guanabara State[a] (1964 = 100)

		Annual Variation
1965	96.9	−5.1
1966	90.0	−7.2
1967	87.0	−3.3
1968	85.9	−1.3
1969	83.6	−2.7
1970	81.9	−1.2

Source. Information from the Statistical Annual of the IBGE and from the Getulio Vargas Foundation, *Conjuntura Economica.*

[a] Mean monthly salaries, deflated on a monthly basis.

per capita product has been far from sufficient to compensate for the drop caused by the underestimation of the price growth rate. Up to 1967, of course, this was not even included, despite the fact that the dictatorship had legally committed itself to doing so. In 1967 to 1968, the rate of product increase was fixed at 2 percent, and at 3 percent and 3.5 percent in 1970 and 1971. This was determined without taking into account the official statistics which show that the per capita product rose by 6.5 percent in 1967 to 1968, by 6.4 percent in 1969, and by 6.9 percent in 1970. The difference between the two sets of figures might be attributed to the fact that the growth rate of the gross national product is consistently overestimated for propaganda purposes: but even so, the actual rates of increase in the per capita product have probably been greater than the ones used for the wage calculations.

In addition, the increase in productivity used for that estimate in year n, for example, is given as a proportion of the nominal wage in the preceding period, $n\text{-}1$ and not the effective average wage in that period, which, at the prices given at the beginning of n, would be greater than the nominal wage current during the $n\text{-}1$ period. In algebraic terms, as we have shown in formula (I), the increase rate of productivity becomes a factor in the wage readjustment for year 3, multiplied by aw_2, and not by

$$aw_2 \sum_{i-13}^{24} I_i$$

To sum up:

1. Up to 1967, the increase in the rate of production was not included in wages.
2. The rates included since 1967 to 1968 are inferior by 60 percent to those given by the regime as indicators of the overall results of the economy.
3. The included rates were multiplied by a quantity inferior to what would be—according to the government—the average worker's wage during the period in which a rise in productivity was confirmed.

Theoretically, one can see that if inflation were to materialize at the expected rate, the workers might benefit. But the Brazilian government, in all its optimism, would hardly predict an inflation rate greater than the real one. This would be tantamount to creating inflationary expectations, and that would challenge the basic tenets of a stabilization policy.

It should also be remembered that during the readjustment period, the worker has no guarantee of automatically recuperating his wage buying power. Everything depends on a predicted rate of inflation, the estimate of which will be determined by the government, and which will depend much more on their hopes or intentions with respect to the evolution of prices than on a realistic and well-founded prognosis.

Finally, from the point of view of the antiinflationary struggle, the wage policies are remarkably convenient in that they allow for a kind of inverse correction of wages by reducing them beforehand. In this way the level of inflation necessary to appropriate the wage earners' income is restricted, as the current economic model requires.

These assertions can be confirmed by a study of Table 8, which shows the evolution of prices of essential food products in Sao Paulo in terms of the minimum wage between 1965 and 1969, and which irrefutably demonstrates the extreme damage inflicted on the buying power of workers in only four years.[6]

TABLE 8
Working Time Needed for the Acquisition of Certain Essential Goods in Sao Paulo

Kilos of Food	Minutes of Work	
	1965	1969
Bread	78	147
Rice	75	107
Beans	95	199
Pasta	169	184
Potatoes	76	94
Meat	264	354
Salt	74	37
Sugar	76	62
Milk (liters)	34	46

Source. Departamento intersindical de estudios estadisticos socioeconomicos, DIEESE (Intersyndicate Department of Socioeconomic Studies), published in *Vega* magazine, No. 87.

[6] In its propaganda about the "economic miracle," especially when it is directed at the national public, the Brazilian technocracy has insisted that it is promoting an economic model similiar to Japan's. The task of destroying this historical and theoretical absurdity is a relatively simple one, but would require a separate essay. For now, it is sufficient to mention only one aspect of the Japanese model, related to the evolution of salaries, which, were it to be promoted in Brazil, would be considered a subversive incitement for the Brazilian workers. The following table will avoid further digressing.

*Average Annual Rhythm of Growth of the GNP and of
the Real Wages of Workers in the Manufacturing Industry*
(1960 to 1968)

	PIB	Wages	PIB-Wages[a]
Japan	10.8	6.0	4.8
Brazil	5.6	−4.84	10.5

Sources. Japan: The Developing Economies, December 1970, No. 4, p. 466.
Brazil: Getulio Vargas Foundation, *Conjuntura Economica*; minimum wages given.
[a] Differences between the rate of growth of the GNP and wages.

REALITY AVOIDED. The unfavorable progress of wages is an aspect that seriously damages the positive image of its model that the Brazilian regime has sought to foster. This is why the dictatorship has been so eager to distort reality, resorting to various methods in order to accomplish this.

One of the principal techniques used has been to give scarce and vague information concerning the evolution of income. It is symptomatic that in the five apologetic articles published by *El Mercurio,* no specific information was presented on the matter. An accumulation of terms very much in vogue among the international financial organizations and the "dispassionate and objective" technocracy which the newspaper refers to have been substituted for specific information. There are constant references to such things as a "realistic," or "austere" wage policy. They represent an attempt to foster the notion that this restrictive conduct is a necessary sacrifice for the economy's and the workers' good, even though, as we have already pointed out, the average purchasing power of the minimum wage has radically declined.

Another device consists of denying the validity of minimum wages as indicators of workers' incomes in favor of the average wage, which has increased in recent years.

Notwithstanding its greater sophistication, this argument remains invalid. According to the 1970 census, the monthly salary of 42 percent of all the urban workers was inferior or equal to the minimum wage. This figure makes the minimum wage a valid indicator. Furthermore, it is well known that the relative variations in the minimum wage are generally a good indicator of the variations in workers' wages.

It is also fundamental to take into account the fact that the calculation of the average salary—industrial or urban—includes the income figures for people such as directors, managers, and technocrats, whose real earnings have tended to increase enormously in recent years, thus widening the wage spectrum. Even in 1966, the distribution of income among wage earners in manufacturing industries, for example, was noticeably unequal and concentrated, and benefited an extremely small percentage of the population. One percent of the workers received almost 20 percent of the total wage income, and 5 percent of the wage earners received 30.4 percent, a higher proportion than that received by 60 percent of the wage earners.[7] There have undoubtedly been changes in this distribution as of 1966, but they have all served only to augment the initial inequality.

Another example of the general contraction of income for the majority of the wage earners is the evolution of wages of federal public employees, a very important sector of the so-called middle class. The income of the members of this group, generally larger than the average wage, has been reduced by approximately 40 percent between 1964 and 1971.

Finally, an investigation of the level of income of working-class families in

---

[7] See the *Estudio economico de America Latina,* published by CEPAL, for 1969.

Sao Paulo, recently made public, allows us to dispel any doubts that may still remain as to the progress of the real minimum wage as representative of the wage conditions of workers. This study is a comparison[8] of the data, corresponding to 1958 and 1969, relating to the income situation of a "typical" working-class family. It was observed that although the number of wage earners per family doubled (one for every two family members), the monthly average family income was reduced by 9.3 percent. The real earnings of the head of the family decreased by 39.2 percent in the same period. The index year 1958 is significant in defining the differences noted, since they correspond to the period in which the real minimum wage reached its lowest point ever during the second half of the 1950s, at a level similar to that of 1963. It can therefore be considered that the given differences have been formed especially since 1964.

THE IMPACT OF CONSUMPTION. Such a regressive evolution in the income of the working class has had negative consequences in the field of production of popular consumer goods. At the same time, given that this evolution has had as its counterpart a disproportionate increase in the income of the higher strata of society, the area of production of essential goods has become remarkably active, especially if we consider that the average per capita income in Brazil is around US$400 per year.

Table 9 gives a better view of what occurred during 1964 to 1970.

TABLE 9

Average Yearly Variations in Production During 1964 to 1970 (Percentages)

| Goods | Production | | |
	Total	Per Capita	Urban Per Capita
Food	1.8	−0.8	−3.8
Textiles	0.1	−2.5	−5.4
Clothing	1.8	−0.6	−4.9
Automobiles	14.3	11.7	8.8

Sources. Taken from IPEA (Department of Planning) data and the ANFAVEA (Association of Automotive Vehicles Manufacturers).

It can be seen that due to the annual wage readjustments—always smaller than the rise in the cost of living—*the per capita consumption of basic consumer goods has been drastically reduced during the military regime's seven*

[8] Departamento intersindical de estadisticas y estudios socioeconomicos (DIEESE), (Interunion Department of Socioeconomic Statistical Studies) : *Pesquisa do padrao de vida da classe trabalhadora de cidade de Sao Paulo,* 1970.

years in power, with highly damaging effects on the social condition of the vast majority of the population.[9]

Conversely, the production of automobiles increased by 350 percent during this same period. In an economy whose gross national income is close to US$35 billion while in per capita terms it barely reaches the US$400 mark, the production of 250,000 automobiles whose sale value is about US$800 million clearly demonstrates and gives impulse to a strong process of concentration of income. This concentration is so important that the automobile industry—Volkswagen, for example—has had to diversify its production toward the more expensive and luxurious models as a dynamic way of increasing its sales in response to the demands of the higher income strata.

A brief analysis of the data recently published in the 1970 census gives a more accurate idea of the true dimension of the reduction in wages for the working class. While the total active population increased by 3.3 percent a year, that of industry increased by 5.9 percent (in the decade of the 1950s it increased at an average rate of 2.3 percent), which might seem a significant decline in the level of unemployment and underemployment, since the industrial occupations are more "productive" than agriculture or the service sectors. The data from the previously mentioned Sao Paulo study, which show an important increase in the number of employed persons per family, also suggest a possible relative reduction of idle labor in the total urban population.

The important element to keep in mind, however, is that in spite of the probable increase in productive employment in the cities, the contraction of wages per worker was so intense that it has produced a drastic reduction, in absolute terms, of popular consumption, as Table 9 suggests.

CHANGES IN THE DISTRIBUTION OF INCOME. The *"Plano de Accion Economica del Gobierno"* (the Government's Plan of Economic Action) of late 1964, and all the subsequent plans and programs—including the Decennial Plan of 1967, the Triennial Plan of 1968, and the *Plan Nacional de Desarrollo* (National Development Plan) of 1971—made a firm commitment to preserve the participation of the working class in the gross national product and to improve the distribution of income. In the interview with *El Mercurio*, Delfin Netto even went so far as to say, "All the policies of the government are based on two key objectives: the growth of the national product and its better distribution among all Brazilians."

In spite of such declarations, repeated over and over again by the ministers

---

[9] In a more recent period (1968 to 1970) the production of durable consumer goods increased at an average annual rhythm of 27.4 percent; at the same time, the production of nondurable items increased by only 2.2 percent. This indicates that per capita consumption of nondurable goods continued to decrease because the population has an average growth rate of 2.6 percent.

and even by the President of the Republic, the inequality of the social distribution of income in Brazil worsened considerably in the 1960s.

This deterioration has been closely related to the government's policies on wages, taxation, social services, and agriculture. In this area, the margination and exploitation of the working masses has been systematically increased.

It can be observed in Table 10 that 80 percent of the population (I and II) reduced its participation in the total national income from 45.5 percent in 1960 to 36.8 percent in 1970. Consequently, its average income increased in absolute terms by only 5 percent, while the average per capita income increased by over 30 percent. On the other hand, in 1960 the wealthiest 5 percent (IV) received an income equal to 20 times the average income of the poorest 40 percent; this proportion increased to 32 times in 1970.

TABLE 10

Distribution of Income in Brazil by Population Strata

Population Strata	Percentage	Percentage of Income		Per Capita Income[a]	
		1960	1970	1960	1970
I	40	11.2	9.0	84	90
II	40	34.3	27.8	257	278
III	15	27.0	27.0	540	720
IV	5	27.4	36.3	1,645	2,940
Average				300	400

Sources. Computations based on the primary data from the 1960 and 1970 censuses. The methods adopted for the estimation of open intervals underestimates the concentration of the apex and the total inequality. Its advantage lies in the fact that, being the same for both years, it allows us to make a more accurate comparison of the relative variations of the nuclei of income of the different strata. A similar underestimation was in having supposed that the number of dependents per active person remains identical for all sectors of the population. It is well known that the poorer sectors have a greater number of dependents.

[a] Dollars.

Fifteen percent of the population maintained its participation in the national income, which allowed it to increase its average individual income by 30 percent. Even though arithmetically this is not a privileged sector, in the overall view it is privileged in respect to the lowest 80 percent. In 1960 it received 6.3 times the average income of the poorest 40 percent (I), and slightly more than twice the average income of the next 40 percent (II). In 1970, those proportions changed to 8 and 2.6 times, respectively.

An analysis of the trend in individual distribution of income confirms the nature of the Brazilian capitalist economic model and its so-called "miracle," which rests on the concentration of the fruits of the labor of a majority in the hands of a few. The "miracle" has consisted in the reinforcement of that scheme, deteriorating the relative situation of 80 percent of the population (72 million people), preserving the relative situation of 15 percent (13.5 million people), and remarkably improving the conditions of 5 percent of all Brazilians (4.5 million people).

THE MYTHS OF INDIRECT REDISTRIBUTION OF INCOME

THE SOCIAL INTEGRATION PROGRAM. In September 1970, the government announced an aggressive policy of redistribution of the national income in favor of the poorer classes. This redistribution was to be carried out by the PIS (Programa de Integracion Social—Social Integration Program). Let us briefly analyze its contents and meaning, not so much because of the importance of the PIS itself but because of Delfin Netto's enthusiastic references to it in the interview with *El Mercurio*.

The program stated that the government would form an investment fund by contributing 2 percent of its corporation tax to which would be added a percentage of the total corporation sales (more or less 0.15 percent). Both coefficients would grow yearly until they reached a set limit of 5 and 0.5 percent, respectively.

This fund would be put in trust in the name of the working class, which would be able to use it by drawing from the quota for such special situations as disability, marriage, or death. The only money the worker would withdraw at his own discretion would be the interests—with a monetary correction—on the amount deposited: a truly insignificant sum, as we shall see later.

The regime's technocrats, always so willing to display their alleged econometric talents, declared themselves incapable of handling the quite elementary matter of estimating the workers' future income from the PIS. In effect, the fund's probable total for one year must be calculated by computing the total revenue taxes of the corporations and of their sales. A 3 percent interest is figured on this and the total is then divided by the number of workers. In 1971, for example, the fund totaled US$100 million; the interest would then be US$3 million. As the project does not include rural workers, public employees, or workers in the public sector, the sum is divided by 3 million workers.[10] This would mean an average income of about US$1 a year for each worker, an amount that could reach US$6 in four more years.

Consequently the PIS is almost totally useless to the workers. On the other hand, it is extremely convenient for the industrial bourgeoisie. Before this program was put into effect, the government reduced taxes on industrial products and circulation of merchandise; in addition, the money deposited by the enterprises is tax deductible. In this way, the government found a way

---

[10] A similar fund was created for public employees. No such plan was completed for the workers in the rural sector, who represent 45 percent of the population.

to compensate for the deposits made by the enterprises so that the PIS would not represent any effective outlay of funds.

Similarly, and this is fundamental, the program's funds are destined for use as loans to private enterprises at a low rate of interest, in accordance with the government program of economic stimulus. The plans under consideration range from projects of industrial reequipment to the financing of circulation capital for private enterprises.

As can be seen, the PIS, which is supported by fiscal subsidies, represents a way of subsidizing the reallocation of the government's resources to private enterprises, following its scheme of extending the current expansion cycle of Brazilian capitalism. The income, instead of going to the workers to compensate in even the smallest way for their lost income, is going to subsidize the programs of the already oversubsidized industrial sector. There is nothing especially noteworthy about the tactic, except for the government's incredible audacity in presenting the PIS as an instrument of redistribution of income in favor of the workers.

THE FISCAL POLICIES. "Brazil clearly manages its fiscal policy in the interest of a better distribution of income," affirmed Delfin Netto in the interview published by *El Mercurio*. However, as is often the case with the minister's declarations of intent regarding the social consequences of the policies he introduces, the actual results are exactly the opposite.

In the first place, indirect taxation, which is the most important source of tax revenue (such as taxes on merchandise and industrial products) and the burden of which is directly passed on to the consumer, has a relatively greater impact on the lower-income classes' consumption.

In addition, income tax does not lighten the burden of indirect taxation, but rather reinforces it. This is true in spite of Delfin Netto's statement that personal income tax "obeys to a progressive table which in reality discriminates in favor of the lower-income classes." Besides the fact that direct taxes are mild, there are numerous exemptions and loopholes that favor those having higher saving rates, that is, the upper-income sector, which permit them to satisfy their costly consumer patterns and save the rest. The law makes interests on personal debts, fiscal incentives for investments, and so on, up to a total of 50 percent of the gross income, tax deductible. Furthermore, after the tax has been computed, the law authorizes a deduction of up to 12 percent for the purchase of stocks in public or private enterprises, as well as a deduction of 50 to 25 percent of the purchase value of bonds from the Banco Nacional de Vivienda and the Banco del Amazonas, respectively. Similarly, undistributed corporation profits are not taxed.

The lower- and middle-income working classes who spend all or most of their income on consumer goods obviously do not benefit from the generous incentives that have been briefly described, thus becoming in practice the *sector most affected by income tax.*

MORE EDUCATION, BUT FOR THE FEW. Another policy of indirect redistribution of income, supposedly linked to a democratization of social opportunities, has to do with education.

In the interview, Delfin Netto mentions a statistic concerning the reduction of illiteracy in Brazil during the 1960s, implying another triumph for the regime. Furthermore, in *El Mercurio's* editorial (October 15, 1970), there was an article of one Tomas P. MacHale praising the educational programs of the dictorship and specifically of the Minister of Education, Colonel Jarbas Passarinho.

Delfin Netto made a comparison between 1960 and 1970. By adding the information corresponding to 1940 and 1950, we can compose Table 11.

TABLE 11

Literacy Among Persons Over 10 Years of Age (Percentages)

Year	Rate
1940	43.0
1950	48.4
1960	60.6
1970	68.0

Source. 1970 census.

It can be seen from the data of Table 11 that the advances made in the decade of the 1960s were due to a historical tendency, and were actually even lower—in relative terms—than those obtained in the 1950s. The last 10 years' gains, then, are not a specific and remarkable result of the dictatorship's educational policies. Without fear of exaggeration, we can say that during that period the educational situation of the majority of the population deteriorated because of the relative and absolute deterioration of living standards.

The 1970 census considered all persons capable of reading and writing a simple sentence as literate. Educators know that this simple requirement is not nearly enough to make for a well-prepared citizen. There are other indicators that compare the educational situation of the active population between 1960 and 1970. (See Table 12.)

TABLE 12

Formal Schooling of the Active Population (Percentages)

	1960	1970
Incomplete elementary education	41.7	64.2
Complete elementary education	50.6	21.2
Secondary schooling	6.3	12.2
Higher education	1.2	2.3

Source. 1970 census.

One can observe a considerable deterioration in the conditions of the great majority of the active population enrolled in formal schooling. The proportion of the active population that has not completed its elementary schooling increased by 50 percent, while those who have completed their elementary education decreased by more than half.

The educational situation improved for only a small part of the active population; those who completed their secondary and higher education increased in percentage from 7.5 percent to 14.5 percent between 1960 and the last year given. Therefore, if there has been any democratization in education, it has been for the benefit of a minority of 15 percent. For the rest of the population, the total situation deteriorated. A comparison between the distribution of income and the benefits of the economic growth among the Brazilians is unavoidable: a relative and even absolute decline in the situation of 85 percent of the population and an improvement for the remaining 15 percent of the privileged population.

PASSARINHO'S UNIVERSITY. McHale's article on education in Brazil is mainly centered on the question of the universities. Aside from making an infantile apology for Colonel Passarinho's personality, he makes the remarkable affirmation that the reforms introduced by the dictatorship in the field of higher education are very similar to the ones carried out in Chile. He leads one to believe that there is ample student participation in the university organizations, and that the students carry on a fruitful dialogue with the Colonel. The Minister is so attentive and democratic, according to MacHale, that he challenged Bishop Dom Helder Camara to a public debate, which the clergyman refused.

Apart from the fact that the anecdote is not a plausible one, because Monsignor Camara is black-listed in the Brazilian press and continually labeled a communist, a Fidelista and a subversive, no formal invitation to a public debate is known of; had there been one, Dom Helder would certainly have accepted it. Any comparison between the reforms carried out in Chile and those adopted in Brazil is purely fictitious. The Chilean reform is based on university autonomy and presupposes an effective process of self-government through elections, truly democratic plebiscites, and universal representation of the students and the administration in all the decision-making processes of the university.

In the Brazilian case, there is no procedure even approaching a democracy in the election of university authorities. There is no academic freedom, nor freedom of speech. Agents from the federal or state police attend classes to check on what the professors say. According to Executive Decree 477, if a professor or a university functionary is considered to be practicing so-called "subversive acts," the accused is expelled and forbidden to practice his profession for five years. Students can be expelled from their school on the same grounds and not allowed to enroll in any other educational establishment for three years.

The gamut of acts classifiable as crimes leaves the students at the totally arbitrary mercy of the dictatorship. Here is a sampling of some of the "crimes."

1. Promoting activities whose purpose is to paralyze student activities, or participating in such activities.

2. Taking part in organizing acts of a subversive nature, demonstrations, or nonauthorized meetings, or participation in them.

3. Conducting, writing, preparing, printing, possessing, or distributing subversive material of any kind.

The government's de facto intervention in the nation's legal apparatus thwarts any possibility of repealing these measures.

Colonel Passarinho has faithfully upheld as law these judicial deviations for the university. Under Executive Decree 477, student representation is purely symbolic. The "open dialogue" that the Minister carries on with the students has been reduced to the demands by students that the Decree be repealed and Passarinho's refusal to do so. The Colonel has not hesitated in applying the sanctions legalized by the Decree to anyone who has dared to break this peculiar form of "dialogue."

SETBACKS IN PUBLIC HEALTH. In the area of public health—another possible tool for improving the masses' standard of living—the situation has not been any more promising than in education for the broad masses.

To begin with, as Table 13 shows, one can observe a drastic reduction in the absolute and relative amount of resources allocated to Public Health. Together with the evolution of distribution of income, it reinforces the negative trend in the public sectors' physical well being.

In relation to infant mortality, Minister Delfin Netto said that the rate declined from 120 deaths to 90 deaths for every thousand live births between

TABLE 13
Federal Expenditures on Public Health

Year	Index of Real Value	Percentage of Total Federal Expenditures
1967	100.0	3.03
1968	94.7	2.53
1969	79.5	1.60
1970	70.0	1.11

Source. Inspectoria General de Finanza, Ministerio de Hacienda (General Inspector of Finance, Ministry of the Treasury).

1960 and 1970. The source of this data is not known. What is known is that the Special Service of Public Health stated in 1969 that the rate was 105 deaths per thousand, and nothing leads us to believe that it has declined so rapidly from that figure in only one year. One may reasonably think that if infant mortality has increased in Sao Paulo, the most developed city in the country, it has also done so in many other less developed areas. (See Table 14.)

TABLE 14
Infant Mortality in Sao Paulo (Number of Infants Dead in Their First Year for Every Thousand Born Alive)

Year	Mortality
1960	62.9
1961	60.2
1962	64.4
1963	69.9
1964	67.7
1965	69.4
1966	73.8
1967	74.4
1968	76.6
1969	83.8

Source. Anuario estadistico del IBGE (Statistical Annual of INGE).

"PRAGMATIC" NATIONALISM OR GROWING DEPENDENCY

The Brazilian Government has tried to present an image of "pragmatic" nationalism, which defends the national interests but does not discriminate against foreign investments; on the contrary, it allows the economy to profit thoroughly from them. On different occasions, including the interview with *El Mercurio*, Delfin Netto has maintained that:

1. Foreign reserves play a crucial role in the internal development of the country.

2. Participation of foreign capital in domestic economic activities is actually quite small.

3. Control of the key areas of production of the Brazilian economy is in national hands.

The first affirmation has only an accounting value. Since 1964 the country has preserved an almost uninterruptedly favorable balance of trade, which means, in real terms, that *external participation is nil, or even negative.*[11]

[11] The surplus disappears if one takes into account FOB exports, COF imports, and tourism. But the resulting deficit is low, and does not alter the logic of the statement.

However, with the evolution of payments to the growing foreign debt and of foreign investments (aside from other services), the country will be forced to become increasingly indebted, as we said before, in order to pay for the necessary imports. Foreign contributions do exist in this sense, but they are of a strictly financial order. The need for them has grown considerably due to the government's borrowing policies.

This financial reality aside, perhaps Delfin Netto is right in affirming that the participation of foreign capital in the national economy is minimal, if this refers to the merely quantitative aspects. Between late 1957 and late 1969, slightly under US$600 million destined for industrial investments entered the country. All in all, the capital stock of foreign investment, by the end of the 1960s, accounted for no more than 5 percent of the active total of the economy, using the book value figures, which probably underestimate the real rate.

Nevertheless, what is really striking is that in spite of this restricted quantitative participation, foreign capital effectively controls a vast proportion of the key sectors of the economy. In industry it operates in the most active, dynamic, and modern areas of production that have the highest growth rates, and controls the largest enterprises in each sector.[12] They are monopolistic or oligopolistic units that rely on their own supply of technology and solid external and internal finance resources. They have a decisive influence on the type of articles to be produced and consumed as well as on their quality and prices. They are, in short, the manager corporations of a larger part of the economy.

As far as consumption is concerned, one can see the role and orientation of foreign investment in Table 15.

Table 15 shows that around 1965 the 12 principal advertisers in the country were foreign corporations, producing for the domestic market.

According to Delfin Netto, "The decision-making centers for the essential economic activity of the country are not outside the country but inside it." From Table 16 we can see that this statement is false.[13]

It is evident that the state controls mainly those infrastructural sectors that are outside the range of private enterprise (electric power) or of low profit capacity (railroads, sea transportation). The exception is in the oil industry, a state monopoly, and steel, in which the state participates together with foreign and national capital. In both cases they are leftovers from the

[12] Control in many enterprises is acquired through ownership of shares. Therefore to estimate the importance of foreign capital by its participation in the ownership of the total capital stock is to use a method that underestimates the real degree of control involved.

[13] The data presented by F. Fajnsyler (*Sistema industrial y exportacion de manufacturas*, IPEA-CEPAL), in relation to the top 500 corporations existing in 1968 confirms the tendency observed in Table 16. Notwithstanding the fact that the samples used are small, it is useful in that it classifies the different activities according to the function of the articles they produce.

national-populist period, which the armed forces have held on to for "security." Nonetheless, the distribution of petroleum derivates is in the hands of foreign capital. Furthermore, not only is the participation in steel production already substantial but it promises to become more so under the new massive investment program, which plans to double the production of steel within the next few years.

TABLE 15
Principal Advertisers in Brazil (According to the Advertising Agencies' Account)

1. Willys Overland
2. Sydney Ross
3. Volkswagen
4. Gessy Lever
5. Gillette
6. Nestle
7. Ford
8. Rhodia
9. Fleishman & Royal
10. Coca-Cola
11. Shell
12. Colgate-Palmolive

Source. *Visao* magazine, September 1967, Sao Paulo.

On the other hand, foreign capital has control over the production of capital goods and of durable consumer goods, and it has majority participation in the larger enterprises producing nondurable goods. *In other words, it is dominant in all those sectors that decide the basic direction of the production processes.*

In addition, with the exception of the commercial sector, and of various services, where it is homogeneous, and in finance (not included in Table 16), where it shares the investments with the state, private national ownership is relatively limited in the larger enterprises of each sector. But even in the financial sector, the participation of foreign capital has been increasing. The opportunities for direct foreign financing, legalized by the government, have grown greatly since 1968. (See the section entitled "The Fictitious External Solidity.") They have not only benefited the international corporations in Brazil but have given rise to a number of finance companies that administer funds, thus acquiring control over significant portions of the domestic credit institutions. A great many of the investment banks are owned by foreign credit institutions. Eight of these already control 38 percent of the resources of that branch in the financial system.

TABLE 16

Participation in the Ten Major Enterprises of Each Sector[a] in 1968
(Percentages)

Sectors	Foreign Capital	National Capital	
		State	Private
Infrastructure	17.2	73.1	9.7
Intermediary goods	34.6	52.0	13.4
Capital goods	72.6	—	27.4
Durable consumer goods	78.3	—	21.7
Nondurable consumer goods	53.4	6.4	40.2
Commerce	7.0	—	93.0
Services	8.2	—	91.8

Source. Research of ADECIF, Rio de Janeiro, published in the *Jornal do Brazil,* April 21, 1970.

[a] Taking capital plus reserves into account.

The high profit capacity of the financial sector, typical of Brazilian capitalism's current stage of development, stimulated by the government's policies of fiscal incentives, gives this sector a key role in the control of domestic productive activities. This is why foreign capital has recently been penetrating and expanding through the international conglomerates, as for example in the case of DELTEC (Rockefeller), which today extends from livestock to the petrochemical industries. In the area of the productive sectors, foreign capital has been concentrating particularly on potentially promising export activities such as cattle, mining, and timber. Taking advantage of the facilities provided by national public works, such as the Trans-Amazonic Highway, as well as of the varied and extraordinary fiscal incentives, in association with the state and private national capital, they are in the process of initiating a new primary export model, a more viable formula for the integration of the Brazilian economy into modern international capitalism.

So, in spite of the "pragmatic" declarations of the regime with regard to its newfound nationalism, today more than in any previous period, foreign capital is at the center of the domestic economic process. Brazilian private capital is relegated to the role of a junior partner or a marginal participant in the advantages of the system. The state is in charge of guaranteeing infrastructural complementary investments and some basic inputs as well as dictating the laws and implementing the policies that will ensure cheap labor and social and political "peace."

NATURE AND CONCENTRATION OF THE MODEL

If one were to analyze the Brazilian economic model in depth, it could be argued that its "secret weapon," its essential formula, has been defined by two elements: first, the utilization of the idle industrial capacity "accumulated" during the 1962 to 1967 depression (and, as a matter of fact, during previous years) that permitted the subsequent relatively rapid expansion of income, and second, a substantial reduction of workers' and the backward middle sector's earnings in recent years. The second element permitted a concentration of the surplus generated by the already mentioned expansion (known as relative surplus value in Marxist terminology) in a systematic and even brutal fashion in the hands of foreign interests, the big national bourgeoisie, and some privileged intermediate sectors. For the attainment of this goal an immense repressive apparatus has been created.

From a historical viewpoint it could be affirmed that the "Brazilian Case" constitutes, in terms of its exploitation of the labor force, a duplication of the purest "decimonic capitalism," although, to be sure, it is complemented and modified by three key elements.

1. The monopolic-oligopolic structure.

2. The strong cooperation and participation of the state apparatus and its functions in the prevalent economic model.

3. The dominant and multifaceted role of international capital (such as accumulation of capital, control over decisions, and commercialization), which is what has shaped the markedly dependent nature of the model.

This combination, favorable for a few and devastating for the masses, was reinforced by a set of complementary measures, the most prominent of which was the creation of a complex finance mechanism unconditionally at the service of the process.

Let us see now, in more detail, some predominant aspects of the subject in question.

The massive financing of consumption of durable goods (especially the more expensive ones) was, of course, one of the basic preconditions for reactivating demand in the production branches of those goods. Obviously, this policy was based on and derived from the regressive redistribution of income previously mentioned. In addition, the compression, and not infrequently, the reduction of wages made possible a relative reduction in the government's running expenses. Through that reduction and an increase in revenues, and even in the public debt, the government was able to resume its high rate of investment. This was fundamental in activating demand for the industrial sector and developing complementary activities for the expansion of manufacturing.

In what refers to the utilization of idle capacity, this involved a decline in the capital-product relationship, which, together with the already noted evolution of salaries, guaranteed the generation of soaring corporation surpluses adequate to sustain a growing and conveniently diversified demand through the distribution of profits and huge salaries for the technocracy, as well as supporting the increased fiscal burden; the payment of high finance costs; and last, contributing, at least partially, to the realization of invest-ments in enterprises and in the "economic frontier" itself, as in the Amazons, for example.

THE PRECARIOUS MODEL. In spite of these and other factors, the dicta-torship has not been able to construct a scheme for a new cycle of expansion, which requires the generation and organization of new sources and stimuli for growth. Up to the present time it has done nothing but revitalize a scheme that from the structural point of view is only a continuation of the 1956 to 1961 cycle.

This is largely due to the fact that the concentrating and exclusivistic model of "consumerist" growth, carried to its ultimate consequences by the regime, has brought with it the aggravation of imbalances and disproportions among the various economic subsectors, which are scarcely compatible with a sustained rhythm of growth.

The drastic exclusion of certain social sectors from the benefits of the expansion has its counterpart, as we have seen, in the slight increase in the production of nondurable consumer goods. More recently, between 1968 and 1970, that sector's production has increased annually at a rate of barely over 2 percent, which is less than the rate of demographic growth and less than half the percentage of growth of the urban population.

For its part, the production of capital goods has grown at an annual rate of 6.9 percent (we may note in passing that that is one-fourth the rate of growth of durable consumer goods), decreasing its participation in the gross industrial product from 11.7 to 11 percent. On the other hand, the production of durable goods rose during the same period at a yearly rate of over 27 percent.

As can be seen, industrial dynamism is principally a result of the behavior of the durable consumer goods sector, as much because of its immediate effects as because of its swaying power over the other branches, especially those generating intermediary goods.

It seems unlikely that this scheme can be sustained. In effect, in order for industry—and consequently the urban economy—to avoid a slowdown in its progress, the demand for durable goods would have to continue to grow at a yearly rate of over 25 percent, which would only be possible if new impulse were given to the process of regressive redistribution of income. This would allow a new margin of increase and diversification of consumption. Nonethe-less, this option seems almost impossible since the vast majority of workers, after six years of having their wages confiscated, have reached a level of income close to that of subsistence. A new attempt at drastic compression would not only have limited economic results—in quantitative terms—but it would also be politically unfeasible.

A greater activation of loans to finance consumption also seems highly problematic, either because of the existing relative total or because of the limitations and contradictions within the financing sector itself.

As for durable goods, the "external solution" is at a dead end, at least as a principal way out. If there is any viable opportunity at all for Brazilian manufacturing abroad, it is in the area of nondurable consumer goods, or semielaborated products.

It is actually possible to identify three key elements capable of interrupting the dynamism of the recent growth and of provoking a crisis of uncertain proportions.

The first lies in the structural disproportions analyzed at the beginning of this section, including, as a matter of fact, the effects of the relative or absolute reduction of income for a large proportion of the population on the volume and composition of demand.

The second is a result of the character and behavior of one of the "weak links" of the system: the finance sector (which is and has been fundamentally important, as we have seen). The burden of its high costs, its tendency to become disconnected from the area of reality, and the unrestrained speculation that is a concomitant of its growth, are a true "time bomb," which, were it to explode, could multiply and extend the contradictions perceived in the sphere of reality.

The third aspect relates to a little-mentioned factor that daily becomes more important. We are referring to the international conjuncture. The well-known upheavals and evident depressive tendencies currently affecting the centers and interests of capitalism to which the "Brazilian Miracle" is umbilically tied (especially at the financial level), constitute a real and potential threat to its eventual survival.

ALTERNATIVES TO THE SYSTEM. The regime's principal escape route would be through a discovery of a sizable source of fresh impulse involving or implying the creation of activities with renewed dynamic potential, capable of counteracting the effects of a deterioration of capitalism's current motor force.

Apparently, the main path chosen by the regime has been that of a search for export market opportunities through strong incentives. They are based, on the one hand, on the "economic frontier": minerals, livestocks, timber, and so forth. On the other hand, they are connected to the industrial sector itself, attempting to achieve—especially in the lagging sectors such as textiles, clothing, and footwear—an improvement in competitivity and efficiency through an accelerated technological reorganization, with the principal objective of reaching the foreign market.

Without stopping to consider in depth the possible effects that the achievement of one or the other alternative could have on domestic development, which is a subject for a more thorough analysis, we will consider the actual probability of obtaining a foreign market adequate to both.

The rapid growth of Brazilian exports since 1968—responsible to a certain degree for the current hope of a foreign market—has been in great measure due to the expansive conditions of international capitalist trade (30 percent in the 1969 to 1970 period). As we have mentioned, these circumstances no longer exist. The U.S. restrictions on trade, which Delfin Netto has named as the main factor, are only one aspect of the problem. The repercussions and multiplying effects of those redistributions, and the measures taken by other central countries regarding trade and international finance, are what is truly essential.

With respect to manufactured goods, it is evident that those produced in Brazil will be affected, either by the obstacles placed in their course, or by the reduction in the volume of trade or the increase in international competition. As for this last, in spite of the current technological renovations— through the imports of equipment and techniques for those branches that the government seeks to develop for export purposes—it seems that Brazilian exports could hardly survive strong sustained competition, since the country has not even shown itself to be in conditions of creating or "recreating" technology.

In addition, the export of manufactured goods was responsible for more than 25 percent of the increase in Brazilian sales abroad since 1965. In spite of all the propaganda unleashed in relation to this, its total sum has barely surpassed the US$300 million mark in 1970, which is less than what was supplied in foreign reserves that year solely by the increase in the price of coffee in respect to the prices prevalent in the mid-1950s.[14]

In order to attain this modest result, the government accumulated such a conglomeration of incentives, exemptions, and direct and indirect subsidies to the export of manufactured goods that the prices of those articles abroad were, on the average, half of what they cost on the domestic market. Consequently, an improvement in competition in the field is hardly likely.[15]

Thus, faced with adverse external circumstances and limiting domestic conditions, the possibility of manufactured exports becoming a viable option for a new expansive cycle are extremely unlikely.

[14] Even this favorable circumstance is disappearing. In 1970, almost eleven and a half million sacks of coffee had been exported by August, at a price of US$622 million; in the same time period in 1971, the exports totaled 12 million sacks at a total of US$500 millions.

[15] By way of example, and without going into rigorous and exact detail, we may take the hypothetical example of the domestic and foreign price of a Volkswagen produced in Brazil. The domestic price of the standard model—1500 horsepower motor—is equivalent to US$2500. On the other hand, its FOB export value is slightly more than US-$1000, similar to that of the German model, in spite of the multitude of subsidies and exemptions that the national industry enjoys. A Brazilian liquid-blender also cost 50 percent less for the foreign importers. Nevertheless, it was estimated that the profits obtained on the exported blenders are 30 percent greater than those obtained by the sales of the same product on the domestic market (IPEA, *Exportaciones dinamicas brasilenas*, 1970, Rio de Janeiro). This is an indication of the true magnitude of a subsidy that has managed to reduce the sale price by half and increase the profit rate by 30 percent.

The only hope left, then, would be the development of primary or semi-elaborated exports: livestock, minerals, timber and even quasimanufactured goods, such as steel. In favorable foreign trade conditions, this scheme could have some relevance, since Brazil is in a condition to produce these items and is now a marginal exporter of those headings. Nevertheless, some doubt is justified—even under the best of circumstances—regarding their sway over the domestic economy and the opportunities that this would create for domestic investment. But it is almost unnecessary to reiterate that the international perspectives make the possibilities of obtaining even this modest contribution extremely doubtful.

In conclusion, it is enough to contrast an examination of the profound contradictions and flaws in the model—internal as well as external—with the mediocrity and limitations of the options that the regime is juggling with to arrive at the conclusion that the much-talked about "Brazilian Miracle" is probably arriving at a decisive crossroads, in which its true nature as an *economic and social fraud* might finally be exposed.

CONCLUSION: THE ECONOMIC RESULTS OF 1971: A CONFIRMATION OF RECENT TRENDS

This article was written at the end of October 1971, when the results of the Brazilian economy for 1971 were not yet known. The *provisional* data for 1971 were subsequently published in the magazine *Conjuntura Economica* (February 1972) of the Getulio Vargas Foundation (a semiofficial institution), as well as in various Brazilian newspapers and magazines.

The year 1971 has been considered extremely representative of the Brazilian economic explosion. For this reason we think it pertinent to make a brief analysis of the *content* of some data presented as characteristic of the progress of the economic "miracle." This analysis is compatible with and can even be adjusted in general terms to the observations and reasonings hitherto expressed, and in some fashion it helps to up-date them. According to the data published, three fundamental characteristics have prevailed in the economy's behavior in recent years: a high growth rate of the gross national product (11.3 percent); an increase in the foreign reserves (over US$500 million); and a rate of inflation of close to 20 percent.

THE STRUCTURE OF GROWTH

Let us examine the gross national product growth structure. Its most important element, the industrial product maintained the strong expansive rate of the previous years, increasing in real terms by 11.2 percent. In the same way as in recent years, this rate was maintained in great measure thanks to the impulse given by the branches of production of durable goods, and in spite of the bad performance in the nondurable goods sector, that is, clothing and food, so important to mass consumption.

Thus, the growth of production of cars doubled its already high average rate of 1964 to 1970, while the production of food declined by at least 0.3 percent in per capita terms, taking into account the 2.6 percent average annual growth rate of the population. It is interesting to note that the growth in the availability of certain items of internal consumption such as footwear and food products must have been even lower, as the exportation of shoes and industrialized meat increased noticeably during that year. In 1970 it was US$8.3 and US$10 million, respectively, and in 1971 it reached US$27 and US$35 million. (See Table 17.)

TABLE 17
1971: Increase in Production (in Percentages) in Respect to 1970

Leisure vehicles (units)	37
Household electrical appliances (units)	27
Household electronics (units)	18
Air conditioners (units)	75
Refrigerators (units)	30
Clothing and footwear	−0.68
Food products	2.3

Source. Durable consumer goods and food products: *Conjuntura Economica.*
Economic Consultants for the Ministry of the Treasury, cited in the newspaper *O Globo*, October 12, 1971, page 14, Rio de Janeiro.

Agricultural production has grown in real terms by about 14.8 percent. This high rate is explained principally by the increase in coffee production of more than 120 percent. Let us remember that the production of coffee in 1971 represented around 14 percent of the total agricultural production. The great increase in coffee production was fundamentally due to a recovery of production in regard to 1970, when it had declined by 41.2 percent. By excluding coffee, agricultural production decreased to a growth rate of less than 3 percent, and the rate of growth of the economy's gross national product falls from 11.3 percent to 9 percent. This all indicates that the high growth of agricultural production did not mean an increase in the domestically available food products and the agrarian per capita input. The following table helps to clarify the matter. (See Table 18.)

It is of equal interest to note that in spite of the fall in the production of some essential food articles for the masses—which of necessity implied a decline in per capita consumption—an increase in the exportation of some of these articles was allowed. This was the case for rice and corn, whose foreign sales increased in 1971 from 450 to 490 percent, in comparison to 1970, reaching US$7 and US$43 million respectively.

THE EXTERNAL SECTOR. The income from imports in 1971 grew by only 4 percent (FOB) in respect to 1970, in spite of the government's forecast

TABLE 18
Growth of the Real Agricultural and Livestock Products

Agriculture	14.8
Rice	−19.7
Potatoes	4.2
Coffee	120.6
Sugar Cane	0.0
Onions	−13.4
Beans	6.9
Corn	1.0
Wheat	11.5
Livestock production and derivates	4.3

Source. Getulio Vargas Foundation, *Conjuntura Economica,* Rio de Janeiro, February 1972.

promising a 14 percent increase. Given the high growth of imports (FOB), 28 percent, the first important deficit in the balance of trade since the take-over of the military regime was recorded: US$324 million. On the other hand, the deficit in the service sector (in areas such as transportation, tourism, remittance of profits, technical assistance, and royalties) grew by almost 20 percent to US$975 million. Consequently, the deficit in the running transactions equaled US$1,300 million, more than twice the 1970 deficit.

The net entry of foreign capital was so great that in spite of this deficit, a surplus in the balance of payments was recorded in the order of US$536 million, boosting the Brazilian reserves from US$1,187 million at the end of 1970 to US$1,723 million by the end of 1971. Because direct foreign investments barely reached US$100 million, it is obvious that the voluminous net entry of capital must have implied an increase in the foreign debt much greater than of the reserves. It is estimated that the Brazilian foreign debt grew from US$5,295 million at the end of 1970 to US$7,000 million at the end of 1971. This meant an increase of close to US$1,700 million, equal to more than three times the increase in reserves. *Between the end of 1967 and the end of 1971, for each dollar increase in the reserves, the foreign debt grew by US$2.4.*

In this way the fictitious character of the alleged external solidity of the economy is maintained and even reenforced. This implies an increase in the Brazilian economy's financial dependence on international capitalism.

It should also be noted that a kind of imbalance has taken shape, which, if it is not attenuated by the balance of trade, will tend to increase exponentially in the near future. If the current mode of development is maintained, and according to the government's projections, a high growth rate of the gross national product in 1972 to 1976 that will rectify the performance of

1968 to 1970 demands that the income from imports expand by 15 percent annually. It must also sustain the flow of foreign financing at the rate of US$1.5 billion per year. This would be necessary in order to reoutfit and technologically modernize the industrial economy through imports and simultaneously to cover the enormous and growing payments abroad for amortizations, interests, profits, technical assistance, and so on. Such prerequisites, at least in the area of exports, can hardly be met, as the 1971 results demonstrate. Apart from the difficulty of sustaining a high expansive rate of manufactured exports—whose soaring government subsidies even increased in 1971—the fact of their reduced participation in the total value of sales to foreign countries significantly limits their importance in the total income from exports—at least for the future years. In 1971, for example, the exporting of these articles grew by 17.6 percent, but the reduction of 3.4 percent in the value of exports of raw goods—which even now represent 71 percent of the total value of foreign sales—was enough to brake the total growth of income on exports.

The line of least resistance in overcoming the difficulties we have pointed out seems to be a search for greater foreign financing. This tends to aggravate —cumulatively and in the medium run—precisely those imbalances that it attenuates on a short-term basis. Similarly, it tends to create stimuli, facilities, and pressures to denationalize production activities and to "internationalize" the domestic economic policies.

Seen from a realistic angle, it is true that these imbalances seem eminently accountable given that it is a question of the circulation of capital within an international scheme in which the modern and dynamic sectors of the Brazilian economy are included. And as an integrated scheme, the fact that some of its components have levels of greater and growing indebtedness is not necessarily a rupture factor of the economic dynamism of these components.

It is also true that within this scheme, these components represent the weakest link, and their reaction to the upheavals that may eventually occur on an international scale is greater. Similarly, an economic policy of its kind depends in great measure on the confidence it inspires in the metropolis. This would explain the Brazilian government's enormous efforts in this direction.

INFLATION, WAGES, AND MONETARY POLICIES. The index of domestically available prices, considered the best indicator of inflation, grew by 21.4 percent in 1971, in comparison to 18.5 percent in 1970. Thus inflation has been kept at a more or less stable level throughout the last few years, notwithstanding certain variations in its different components (cost of living, wholesale prices, and construction costs). This is true despite the almost complete disappearance of those factors that the government's technocrats pointed out some years ago as responsible for inflation: the public deficit, wage policies, "demagoguery," and disorderly monetary policies. In 1971, the Treasury's cash deficit declined to 0.3 percent of the gross national product (in 1970 it was 0.4 percent), amply surpassed, furthermore, by the public debt, whose total was six times greater than the deficit's.

There was no significant slackening in the wage policies this year. In Guanabara, the minimum real wage measured in relation to the mean for the year (deflated on a monthly basis, using the index of cost of living of the Getulio Vargas Foundation), grew by 0.4 percent, the first increase since 1964 (see Table 6). In Sao Paulo, on the other hand, it decreased by 0.8 percent (calculations based on the cost of living index of DIEESE), partially nullifying the small increase obtained in 1970, which had been the first one since 1965 (see Table 5).

Lastly, the medium of payments rose by 32 percent; according to the adherents of the quantitative theory of currency, this was a rhythm compatible with the growth of the gross national product and of prices. The US$325 million (FOB) deficit in the balance of trade was a source of anguish for the quantitative adherents. It implies that appreciable quantities of goods entered the country in much greater amounts than those that left it. According to the quantitativists, this difference should act as a strong absorbent of liquidity and as an element of price control. Nevertheless, the rate of increase of prices surpassed that of 1970. This indicate how strong the inflationary pressures and the expansion of liquidity in the extrabanking market must have been, both of which in great measure were outside the control of the government's monetary policies. Another source of worry, noted on page 70 of the February 1972 issue of *Conjuntura Economica,* was that "the financial strategy for coffee which in previous years constituted an important source of non-inflationary resources reversed its trend, demanding a high amount of resources from the monetary authorities. . . . Also in 1972, the coffee account, which up to mid-1971 had served as an important and favorable element for the antiinflationary policies will now exercise an expansionist monetary effect." Mentioning that "some price indicators threatened to reverse their declining trends . . . unless an important compensatory effect occurs through an increase in the agricultural supply," the magazine concludes that "1972 will demand the implementation of a stricter monetary policy than that of previous years, in order to achieve the preservation of a slow down in the rise of prices. Along with this, it should be considered that the reduction in the cost of money, in accordance with the official emphasis, will act as a stimulant to loans, which will make the need for control over the primary issuance of money more relevant" (pp. 69–70).

Independently of the validity of the theoretical suppositions on which the arguments transcribed above are based, they plainly reveal a difficult situation in terms of the stabilization policy, given that, as we have said before, the system has its own mechanisms for creating liquidity that are outside the control of the government administration, capable of guaranteeing a necessary base for an increase in prices. Monetary restrictions and price controls would have to become extremely severe, which, nonetheless, would excessively restrict the level of economic activity.

INVESTMENTS. Apparently, the rhythm of total accumulation increased markedly in 1971 thanks to the continuing public investment program and under the influence of strong incentives and facilities for the acquisition and renewal of national and imported equipment, approved at the end of 1970. According to declarations from the Ministry of Planning, the importation plus the domestic manufacturing of equipment increased by 20 percent in 1971 in relation to 1970. These circumstances are not only a result of the public investments or stimuli and incentives, but of the general climate of optimism prevailing in some sectors regarding the future of the economy. The government does its best to reenforce this mood. Favorable expectations are so enormous that some automobile companies, who have recently been operating at a loss, are still planning and carrying out massive investments destined to increase and diversify their future production.

THE SOCIAL SITUATION. Finally, as indicated previously, the minimum real wage increased in Guanabara (0.4 percent) and decreased in Sao Paulo (−0.8 percent). More recent calculations by the DIEESE allow us to present Table 19, which brings the information presented in Table 7 up to date and which illustrates with some clarity the enduring nature of the acute deterioration of the buying power of wages for workers in late 1971.

With reference to the government's labor policies, it would also be pertinent to call attention to one other fact related to the problem of housing. In 1971, continuing a trend started in 1970, a noticeable deacceleration in the construction of smaller houses (buildings from one to three stories and four to nine stories high) was recorded. This is the area in which the National Housing Bank has its greatest activity: "The activity of construction of housnig destined for the lower income groups decreased. On the other hand, in those areas where private initiative has the greatest participation, destined for use by the higher income groups, and not necessarily for residential purposes, construction activity almost doubled in relation to the previous year." (*Conjuntura Economica*, February 1972, p. 32). As mentioned previously, the fundamental problem in the area of smaller houses was the low purchasing power of the working class, which was not sufficient to sustain an expansive rhythm in the construction of popular housing.

In October 1971, the government took a series of steps destined to give new impulse to the construction of housing under the financial supervision of the Banco Nacional de Vivienda (BNV)—National Housing Bank. Among other measures, some of which were designed to give the system greater flexibility, the most important ones revolved around a reduction in the cost of financing, in financing costs, and in the broadening of the financing margins, previously restricted to housing units of up to US$25,000. These are, in brief:

TABLE 19

Total Monthly Hours Necessary to Obtain a Survival Ration (Base: Minimum Wage in Sao Paulo)

Products	Quantity	December 1965[a]	December 1971
Meat	6.00 kg.	26 h., 24 min.	42 h., 42 min.
Milk	7.5 lts.	4 h., 15 min.	5 h., 22 min.
Beans	4.50 kg.	7 h., 15 min.	8 h., 19 min.
Rice	3.00 kg.	3 h., 45 min.	6 h., 03 min.
Wheat flour	1.50 kg.	2 h., 23 min.	2 h., 09 min.
Potatoes	6.00 kg.	7 h., 36 min.	4 h., 48 min.
Tomatoes	9.00 kg.	8 h., 24 min.	7 h., 48 min.
Bread	6.00 kg.	7 h., 48 min.	13 h., 30 min.
Coffee (powder)	600 grs.	46 min.	3 h., 23 min.
Bananas	7.5 dz.	4 h., 00 min.	3 h., 38 min.
Sugar	3.00 kg.	3 h., 48 min.	3 h., 03 min.
Butter	750 grs.	7 h., 19 min.	9 h., 23 min.
Lard	750 grs.	3 h., 44 min.	3 h., 18 min.
Total		87 h., 20 min.	113 h., 26 min.

Source. Products and quantity according to the Executive Decree No. 399 of April 30, 1938. Average price in the Sao Paulo Municipality, DIEESE.

[a] Note that in addition, December is a bad base year, since a significant reduction in the real minimum wage was already taking place (connected to the government's wage policy) as a consequence of the low readjustments that year and the recorded inflation rate.

1. The workers' accounts deposited in the BNV shall receive a real interest of up to 3 percent annually. The figure used to be of up to 6 percent, according to the worker's length of service in a given corporation. This reduction facilitates the decrease in the cost of financing for the BNV.

2. The workers shall be allowed to use the resources available in their accounts to pay for back loans or to buy houses through the BNV. Previously they had to wait five years before touching their account.

3. Similarly, workers shall be allowed to give written authorization to their employer to deduct a monthly quantity corresponding to the current installment payment on a loan made by the BNV to pay for their house.

4. Tax deductions shall be allowed on rents to all who have purchased apartment or office buildings through the BNV in an amount equivalent to 50 percent of the amount spent on the loan—with the corresponding monetary correction.

5. The purchasers of real-estate drafts shall be allowed a 30 percent deduction on their taxable rent income in exchange for a reduction from 8 percent to 6 percent in the interest received.

6. Last, a decree was modified that prohibited the BNV from financing any housing worth more than US$25,000. Financing is now permitted for an amount of up to US$50,000. In other words, if a house costs US$50,000, the BNV is allowed to finance up to 50 percent of it.

It is transparently clear that if the reforms that have been carried out manage to revitalize the area of private construction, they will do so in direct detriment or at least at the expense of the working classes and in benefit of the higher income groups. On the one hand, the workers' income will be decreased because of the reduced interest. On the other hand, the resources that they will be allowed to use were theirs to begin with and gave them interest. And, in regard to the measure that "allows" the worker to authorize his employer to deduct a quota from his monthly salary to pay for the BNV loan, this is nothing but a way of making the monthly payments obligatory, since from now on that authorization will probably be required prior to the purchase of any house.

On the other hand, the tax deductions allowed for income from rent will obviously benefit most those people with highest level of income. It is precisely those groups with the greatest income—who purchase the most costly houses, invest in real estate, and pay a significant amount of taxes—who will benefit from these allowances. It is equally obvious that the authorization to finance housing worth more than US$25,000 will involve an increase in the demand for financing from the BNV, and at the same time, will lead to changes in the BNV's makeup, which will benefit the upper-income groups.

In synthesis, a cursory analysis of some data and information regarding the behavior of the economy in 1971 clearly places in evidence the basic characteristics controlling the operation of the Brazilian economic model: an imbalanced growth of industry that relies on the manufacture of the more expensive durable consumer goods (such as automobiles); a feeble growth in the production of articles of great importance for the consumption of the masses; a deepening of the foreign financial disequilibrium; a persistent high level of inflation (20 percent a year); the prevalence of enormous optimism among investors promoted by extraordinary stimuli and incentives; and the continuation of a situation of social regression to which the majority of the population has been subjected.

Consequently, in 1971 the system does not seem to have changed its direction toward any satisfactory alternative that would lead to a solution of its external as well as internal contradictions and weaknesses. On the contrary, the economic policies of the government are fundamentally doing nothing but carrying the pattern of unbalanced and dependent capitalism to its ultimate consequences. Everything seems to indicate that this pattern will be perpetuated—at least until the indications of a fissure in the system become more apparent, through one of its weaker links.

2

Economic Dependency in a Modern Setting

5

James Petras & Thomas Cook | Dependency and the Industrial Bourgeoisie: Attitudes of Argentine Executives Toward Foreign Economic Investment and U.S. Policy

This is a study of Argentinian industrial executives and their attitudes toward foreign economic involvement in the Argentine economy and U.S. policy toward global and regional issues. The data base for the study consisted of interviews with 112 subjects. The analysis was conducted on three levels: (1) Argentine executives as a whole, (2) a comparison of executives of foreign versus national firms, and (3) an analysis of attitudes of executives, given three types of dependency—technological, financial, and commercial.

The results point toward favorable responses on the question of foreign economic involvement by both national and foreign executives. The dependency concept did not alter the basic findings—though on particular issues there were considerable differences between executives of national and foreign firms and between executives of dependent and nondependent firms.

For several years the concept of "dependency"[1] was used throughout Latin

---

[1] Theotonio Dos Santos defines dependence as:

"a situation in which the economy of certain countries is conditioned by the development and expansion of another economy to which the former is subjected. The relation of interdependence between two or more economies, and between these and world trade assumes the form of dependence when some countries (the dominant ones) can expand and can be self-starting, while other countries (the dependent ones) can do this only as a reflection of that expansion, which can have either a positive or negative effect on their immediate development."

America by scholars and leaders of varying political points of view and has only recently penetrated our academic iron curtain or wall. In 1965, a group of Latin American social scientists associated with the U.N. Latin American Social and Economic Planning Institute (ILPES) located in Santiago began discussing and circulating essays that attempted to discover the impact of external control over the economy on social and economic development. Going beyond previous work by Prebisch and the U.N. Economic Commission on Latin America, which focused primarily on the problem of the deterioration of terms of trade, these social scientists broadened the area of investigation to include all areas of foreign control or influence which could affect Latin American development. Out of these early discussions emerged impor-

---

See Theotonio Dos Santos, "The Structure of Dependence," *Readings in U.S. Imperialism,* K. T. Fann and Donald Hodges, eds. (Porter-Sargent, 1971), pp. 226. James Rosenau makes a distinction between "intervention" and "penetration." He defines intervention as an act involving the rejection of previously existing relationships between the intervening and target nation. Whether political, military or economic in nature, interventionary behavior has a "convention breaking character" and an "authority oriented nature." A "penetrated" political system, according to Rosenau, is one in which intervention into the socioeconomic and political processes is made in order to affect the allocation of values and the attainment of goals. See James N. Rosenau, "The Concept of Intervention," *Journal of International Affairs XXII,* No. 2 (1968), p. 167.

We consider dependency a condition in which the growth or expansion of a firm or country is contingent upon the need to import capital products or techniques over which it has little or no control; because the society lacks the ability to substitute other products, sources or funds or techniques, and because it lacks the internal capacity or drive to innovate or create. An autonomous country depends *primarily* on the mobilization of internal resources and has the capacity to choose the source of its external inputs.

Dependency is a *condition*—a *product* of historical and contemporary international relations. It expresses an asymmetric relationship between two or more countries: the dependent and the dominant country. In our time, dependency is the product of external penetration sometimes fostered by or facilitated by external intervention.

Dominant Country			
Stage 1	Stage 2	Stage 3	Stage 4
Expansion	Intervention	Penetration	= Dependent Country

The fact that a developing country needs to import machinery or technology does not necessarily make it a "dependent" country; what is crucial is the type of political regime which makes the decision on what to import (the global political context), the criteria used in the selection of imports, and the relationship between the current imports and the overall future development project. The decision to import technology by a working class socialist regime is directed toward maximizing social benefits through increases in production, creating the economic and scientific basis for the emergence of indigenous sources of innovation that will, in the future at least, partially surpass the need to import technology. Importation of technology in this context is a transitional phenomenon, a temporary dependence toward relative autonomy. In nonsocialist or dependent capitalist societies, importation of technology (or capital) creates a relatively stable group of institutions and elites that serve as permanent transmission belts for external penetration, independent of local needs. The decisions on selection and use of technology are based on the mutual interests of foreign and domestic elites—on the basis of private profits not social needs. The domestic elites, dependent on external sources, accept foreign control over technology and research and feel little need to build the basis to develop their own.

tant essays by Cardoso and Faletto, Quijano, Kaplan, and others.[2] Outside of establishment channels, the concept of dependency received a great deal of visibility through Gunder Frank's essays and writings and later the essays of Theotonio Dos Santos.[3] In 1968, Petras and Zeitlin published a reader focusing on the problem of Latin American dependence.[4] The discussion broadened; new books and monographs appeared and, finally, an "official panel" of the American Political Science Association was discussing the concept. "Dependency" has finally arrived.

Consistent with the pronouncements of national political leaders since the formulation of the Monroe Doctrine, U.S. social scientists have, as an article of faith, accepted the notion of a natural harmony of interest between the Americas. All the cliches about the "New World against the Old," and "our common destiny or "heritage" have permeated the writing of our most renowned scholars and naturally have influenced their interpretation of the history of U.S. Latin American relations.[5] The underlying theme has been that of benign influence. Policies not so obviously benign (such as the landing of Marines) were ascribed to mutual misunderstanding, errors of judgment, and particular political personalities (such as Teddy Roosevelt). Nevertheless, the problems of U.S.-Latin American relations could not be exorcised by the revelations of U.S. writers of textbooks on Latin America. One could still go on claiming that nationalism was a fear of foreigners, that anti-Yankeeism was a Communist ploy, that anti-imperialism was really anti-Americanism, that "moderate" nationalism (a euphemism for collaboration with U.S. investors) was healthy and "extremist" nationalism (noncollaboration with U.S. investors) was pathological but the Dominicans knew who controlled their political life, as the Chileans and Peruvians knew who sent their mineral profit earnings out of the country.

[2] An excellent collection of essays edited by Jose Matos Mar, *La dominacion de America Latina* (Lima: Moncloa, 1968) contains essays by Fernando H. Cardoso and Enzo Faletto, *"Dependencia y desarrollo en America Latina;"* Osvaldo Sunkel, *"Political nacional de desarrollo y dependencia externa;"* Celso Furtado, *"La hegemonia de los Estados Unidos y el futuro de America Latina."* Also see Anibal Quijano, *"Dependencia, cambio social y urbanizacion en Latino-America,"* Cuadernos de Desarrollo Urbano Regional, Marzo 1968, pp. 3–48; Marcos Kaplan, *"Estado, dependencia externo y desarrollo en America Latina,"* Estudios Internacionales, II, No. 2 (Julio-Septembre 1968), pp. 179–213.

[3] Probably Frank's single most influential work was his *Capitalism and Underdevelopment in Latin America* (New York: Monthly Review Press, 1967); two books by T. Dos Santos, *El nuevo caracter de la dependencia* (Cuadernos del Centro de Estudios Socioeconomics No. 10), U. de Chile, 1968; and *Dependencia y Cambio Social* (Cuadernos de CESO No. II, 1970).

[4] James F. Petras and Maurice Zeitlin, *Latin America: Reform or Revolution* (Fawcett, 1968).

[5] Among the many titles we need cite only typical cases.

A. A. Berle, *Latin America: Diplomacy and Reality* (New York: Harper and Row, 1962).

Lincoln Gordon, *A New Deal For Latin America: The Alliance For Progress* (Cambridge, Mass.: Harvard University Press, 1963).

Edwin Lieuwen, *U. S. Policy in Latin America* (Praeger, 1965).

As long as the Cold War held the noncommunist world together, the harmony of interest position was tolerated by the rest of the world; not necessarily believing it, many writers felt it convenient not to challenge the myth. With the disintegration of the Cold War alliance, and as the U.S. involvement in Vietnam graphically illustrated the negative effects of a U.S. presence, an increasing number of scholars began to challenge the position that U.S. global ambitions were compatible with the interests of the underdeveloped countries. U.S. social scientists holding fast to past dogmas were perceived as irrelevant at best and propagandists at worse.

Within the United States beginning in the middle 1960s (especially among younger scholars), the accepted assumptions began to be challenged.[6] The position of the United States as a world power was viewed from the point of view of the "recipient countries"—the problems posed by foreign investment were no longer viewed in terms of the "risks" to the investor but from the point of view of the development needs of the "recipient" country. Foreign investment was viewed not as "capital for development" but as a vehicle for denationalizing the economy and depleting financial and economic resources.

The initial discussion and debate on dependency focused on global issues (that is, foreign investment and nationalization). Historical and theoretical discussions and interpretations of the impact of external forces on underdevelopment tended to dominate the discussion. Classificatory schemes were constructed to categorize the different types of dependencies—and a stage theory was elaborated to account for the changes in the forms of dependence. Changes in the forms of dependence were traced to the dynamic changes in the imperialist center: the decision of foreign investors to transfer their funds from the "agro-mineral" to the manufacturing sector.[7]

While the discussion utilizing the concept of dependence has advanced our understanding of the impact of the United States on Latin American underdevelopment, little work has been done that attempts to link the notion of external dependence *with the internal class structure*. We need to examine the internal linkage that *permits* foreign forces to penetrate a country and create a dependent situation. More specifically, this involves an examination of the relationship between external investors and social classes within a country. Only a study of the historical pattern of economic development and the class structure of *each* Latin American country will allow us to under-

[6] See the essays in *Imperialism and Underdevelopment*, edited by Robert Rhodes (Monthly Review Press, 1970); also, Fann and Hodges, *Readings in U.S. Imperialism* (Porter Sargent Publishers, 1970).

[7] The continuing discussion on dependency can be seen in Anibal Quijano, *Redefinicion de la dependencia y proceso de marginalizacion en America Latina* (Santiago, 1970); Francisco Weffort, 'Notas sobre la 'Teoria de la dependencia': Teoria de clase o ideologia nacional?" and Fernando H. Cardoso, "Teoria de la dependencia o analisis de situaciones conceretas de dependencia?" in *Revista Latinoamericana de Ciencia Politica* (Diciembre 1970), 1, No. 3, pp. 389–401 and 402–415. See also Susanne Bodenheimer, "Dependency and Imperialism: The Roots of Latin American Underdevelopment," *Politics and Society* (May 1971), pp. 327–358.

stand how dependency is inserted into that society.[8] For example, although Argentina and Guatemala are dependent countries, the patterns of dependency are vastly different and a "general thoery of dependency" tells us little of significance concerning the specific social forces or polices that impede or facilitate the emergence of a dependent state. A theory of dependence should be grounded in a series of historical and empirical studies that examine the pattern of development and the behavior of strategic social classes regarding external penetration. Research on dependency can no longer rely upon strictly qualitative approaches and stimulating but discursive essays.[9]

THE ARGENTINE INDUSTRIAL EXECUTIVE AND DEPENDENCE

Argentina is probably the most industrialized of the dependent countries in the Third World. The dual nature of dependence *and* industrialization requires an approach different from that of dependent countries which are primarily agro-mineral exporters. The industrial sector in Argentina accounts for a higher proportion of the gross national product (GNP), and employs a higher proportion of the economically active population than any other country in Latin America.[10]

The industrialization effort of Argentina began at the turn of the nineteenth century and was greatly accelerated during the 1930s and 1940s.[11] During the worldwide depression of the 1930s, the decline in Argentine agrarian exports and the country's incapacity to import manufactured goods forced some sectors of the landed and financial oligarchy to transfer their investments toward industry—joining the immigrant capitalists who were largely confined to the industrial sector. World War II and the restrictions imposed by the war effort limited Argentina's ability to import industrial goods, thus providing entrepreneurs with an opportunity to develop national industries. In the initial postwar period the Peronist government provided national industry with protection from the flood of foreign industrial goods. The Peronist policies included loans, subsidies, tax relief, and protective tariffs to foster a national private industrial complex. The populist-income redistribution policies produced a large consumer market, especially in the Greater Buenos Aires area. Subsequent to the overthrow of Peron—in fact, during the last years of his government—the nationalist measures were watered

[8] Some of these issues are discussed in the Weffort—Cardoso exchange cited in footnote 7.

[9] For an example of an analytic case study of dependency see Anibal Quijano, *Nationalism and Capitalism in Peru: A Study in Neo Imperialism* (Monthly Review, July-August 1971).

[10] See Ernesto Leclau, "Argentine-Imperialist Strategy and the May Crises," *New Left Review*, No. 62 (July-August 1970), pp. 3–21.

[11] Some of the discussion in this section draws on the essays in *Fichas, 1*, No. 1, April 1964 (Buenos Aires).

down or eliminated. Foreign investors were attracted toward the large and lucrative Buenos Aires consumer market. Foreign investors concentrated on the manufacturing sectors—especially the production of durable consumer goods—either buying into (and eventually controlling) existing enterprises, or creating new firms. Thus, within the manufacturing sector, side by side—and in many cases in "joint ventures"—there has emerged an Argentine and foreign industrial elite.

In our discussion of dependency we will focus on three areas: the attitudes of Argentine executives (both foreign and domestic firms) toward foreign penetration; a comparison of the attitudes of executives of foreign firms to executives of national firms toward foreign penetration; and a comparison of the attitudes of executives of national dependent and nondependent firms to the same issue.

METHOD

Our study was directed at the largest modern industrial firms. We selected the 150 largest firms on the basis of the number of employees employed and the sales in the previous year. In order to "weight" the factor of modernity we devised a formula in which "sales" received twice the unit weight of employees.[12] Hence our selection formula reads:

Where E = Number of employees
S = Sales for the year
N = Total
N = 2S(E)

Within each firm we selected the highest executive officers. Where possible, we interviewed Presidents; if they were unavailable we interviewed members of the board of directors and executives. In addition, we sought out and interviewed the Presidents of committees of branches of industry established by the leading industrialists' association, Union Industrial Argentina (UIA). The breakdown of our population was the following:

President of firm	11.6%
Directors	17.9
Executives	57.1
President of Industrial Committees	12.5
N	112[13]

[12] By weighing sales, we gave more emphasis to technologically advanced firms that employ, in some cases, fewer workers, such as the petroleum industry. The coefficient expression 2S(E) was arbitrarily chosen.
[13] Only one respondent failed to answer the question.

In our analysis we have 112 interviews.

Our original universe included 150 firms.[14] Interviews were begun in January 1971 and completed July 1, 1971. The interviews were conducted by experienced Argentine interviewers. Letters of introduction explained the nature of the project, the source of financial assistance of the Project Director (Ford Foundation), and the use of the research findings. The classification of firms into national/foreign was based on two criteria: (1) a panel of economists of CONADE[15] identified foreign and national firms, and (2) we further refined our identification by including a question on the presence or absence of foreign investment in their firm. We included only those national firms having no foreign investments. We ended up with executives from 47 national and 41 foreign firms.[16] These two groups comprise the respondents for the second step of our analysis: our comparison of executives of foreign to national firms.

In the third part of our study, we differentiated among national firms distinguishing between dependent and nondependent firms to test the executive responses on a battery of questions dealing with foreign involvement in the economy and U.S. policy. We used three variables[17] to differentiate dependent from nondependent national firms: (1) technology, (2) imports, and (3) type of banks from which they obtain loans.

Technology is one of the major inputs making industries competitive in the modern world. The ability of a firm to develop or secure new techniques of production is a crucial determinant of its ability to stay alive. Since control of technology is a vital aspect in the development and growth of a modern industrial enterprise it is an important dimension to differentiate dependent and nondependent national firms.

Finance and banking provide us with another vital component in the operations of a modern corporation. Loans and financing are crucial to the expansion and survival of industrial corporate enterprises.

Foreign imports or purchases provide us with another dimension of dependence. The origins of products necessary for industrial development allow us to differentiate between those firms that depend largely on external as opposed to internal sources.

We have devised a series of questions to deal wtih varying aspects of dependence: they are divided into questions dealing with general foreign

[14] Almost 33 percent of the executives of the firms (45 out of 150) refused to be interviewed on the issues of dependence and foreign participation in Argentine economic development. The problems of doing empirical research with elites will be discussed in a later publication.

[15] CONADE is the National Development Council largely in charge of Government research and planning in economic development.

[16] Foreign firms were those identified as foreign by CONADE and who stated that they had foreign investment in their operation.

[17] In our more extensive analysis we will consider several other sources of foreign dependence including advertising, consulting, research, and purchases.

involvement in the economy, with specific U.S. policy, and with Argentine governmental policies. The three parts involve:

1. Questions that deal with foreign involvement in the Argentine economy.

2. Questions that deal with U.S. global, regional, and development policies.

3. Questions that deal with the Argentine government's policy toward foreign involvement.

These three dimensions will allow us to analyze the attitudes towards economic and political dependence, as well as to get some notion of Argentine policy outlooks among executives.

The following discussion focuses on the three major sets of hypotheses.

1. Argentine industrial executives tend to favor foreign participation in the Argentine economy.[18]

1a. Argentine industrial executives would tend to favor U.S. and Argentine government policies that facilitate foreign penetration of the economy.

2. Industrial executives of foreign firms will be more favorable toward the questions posed under hypotheses 1, 1a than executives of national firms.

3. Differences within the response patterns of national executive group will be a function of difference in levels of dependency (that is, the more dependent the firm, the more favorable the response).

3a. The effect of dependency upon the responses of national executives will depend upon the proximity of the dependency measure to their own particular position in the firm.

Each of the above hypotheses will be examined sequentially in the following discussion.

THE ARGENTINE EXECUTIVE—AN OVERVIEW

Most Argentine industrial executives have upper and upper middle class backgrounds—46.4 percent are sons of businessmen, executives, industrialists, or landowners and 28.6 percent are sons of professionals. Only 13.4 percent are from the petty-bourgeoisie (small business and artisans); less than 8.1 percent are from the working class and peasantry. Most executives are recruited from the same class background—although not necessarily from the same sector of the economy. There appears to be considerable *horizontal* mobility

---

[18] The Argentine writer, Gustavo Polit (pseudonym for Milciades Pena who tragically committed suicide in 1966) once wrote, ". . . all sectors of the industrialists and capitalists need and aspire for association with foreign capital; no objective basis exists to hinder native industrialists from forming connections with international capital. But there do exist countless conflicts and disagreements in connection with the terms and conditions involved in establishing the relationship." James Petras and Maurice Zeitlin, *Latin America: Reform or Revolution* (New York: Fawcett, 1968), p. 424.

but little *vertical* mobility. Most executives have at least some university education (79.5 percent), most attend either a commercial secondary school (34.8 percent) or private preparatory school (27.7 percent) in preparation for their industrial careers. Most began as employees (40.2 percent) or professionals (29.5 percent), a small minority began at the top as owners or executives (11.6 percent). However most executives of these giant firms held similar important positions prior to their current position (67.9 percent). The modal age of the executives is between 46 and 50 years, although the modal age at which they arrived at their present job is 36 to 40 years. Most firms were corporations rather than family firms (90.2 percent). Approximately 34 percent of the executives received a portion of the profits of the firm while 58.9 percent claimed otherwise. About one-sixth of the executives held positions in two or more other firms, 24 percent held a position in one other firm while 58.9 percent were participants in only one firm. Over one-fourth held positions in agro-banking and/or financial institutions. Over one-fifth have held public office—about 8 percent had been ministers, cabinet advisers, or ministerial subsecretaries.

In summary, the industrial executives come from the economic elite and attend the better schools, leading to university education. They move rapidly up the hierarchical ladder to the top posts in the economy. A sizeable minority extend their reach into government and other sectors of the economy, increasing their potential influence and power over the development of the economy and political decision making. The attitudes of Argentine industrial executives have ramifications and implications for the whole society. The position taken by the executives on an issue such as foreign involvement in Argentine development will probably be reflected in national political decisions.

ATTITUDES TOWARD FOREIGN ECONOMIC INVOLVEMENT

The overwhelming majority (96.4 percent) of executives favor foreign participation in industry. This almost unanimous support drops off somewhat in regard to foreign participation in banking (73.3 percent) yet it still remains very high. High proportions of Argentine executives also favor foreign participation in research centers (87.5 percent) and in the development of technology (92.9 percent). If we now turn from foreign firm participation in the economy to foreign *individual* participation we find that 83.9 percent of Argentine executives favor foreign ownership, 76.8 percent favor foreigners in executive positions, and 83.9 percent favor foreigners in technical positions. Overall, we can say that Argentine executives are hardly militant nationalists.

Thus, preliminary analysis points toward acceptance of our first hypothesis —Argentine industrial executives tend to favor foreign participation in the economy.

ARGENTINE EXECUTIVES AND U.S. POLICY

A majority or more Argentine executives support U.S. policy toward Western Europe (85.7 percent), the socialist bloc (60.7 percent), underdeveloped countries (70.5 percent), inter-American commerce (58.9 percent), loans and credits in the inter-American system (76.8 percent), internal security (73.2 percent), Argentine development (71.4 percent), and leadership in the inter-American system (75.9 percent). U.S. policy only obtained a bare majority support of Argentine executives in two issue areas: U.S. policy toward intervention[19] (51.8 percent) and U.S. policy toward Chile (54.5 percent). However, only in the area of intervention was there a substantial proportion opposed (43.8 percent).[20] While the industrial executives were generally favorable to U.S. policies, the *degree* of their support varied from issue to issue. If we consider the "extremes," those who responded as "favorable" or "unfavorable" (eliminating the "moderate" negative and positive responses) we find that the United States receives over 50 percent "strong" support only in its policies to Western Europe and as leader in the inter-American system. Only one-third to one-half of the respondents "strongly" favored U.S. policy toward internal security (46.4 percent), toward socialist countries (39.3 percent), and toward underdeveloped countries (35.7 percent). Only one-third to one-fifth of the respondents strongly favor U.S. policy toward loans and credits (31.3 percent), and Argentine development (30.4 percent), Chile (24.1 percent), commerce (26.8 percent), and intervention (22.3 percent).

On those issues directly related to the economic interests and political future of Argentine corporate interests (commerce, loans, Argentine development) the executives are less intensely favorable to U.S. policy than they are to U.S. global policies or regional leadership or hegemony.

In terms of external financing almost all Argentine executives perceive international and U.S. agency loans as contributing to the development of the country. Furthermore, Argentine executives favor few or no controls on profit remittance (80.4 percent), and a majority believes that state guarantees should be provided to foreign investment (59.8 percent). All but one of the 112 respondents believe foreign investment has a role to play in development. Opposition to U.S. economic policy was generalized only on the issue of "tied" loans: 81.2 percent of the executives responded unfavorably. However, Argentine executives were divided on the issue of the *form* in which foreign investment should participate. Over one-third (37.5 percent) stated that foreign capital should participate with few or no restrictions, a smaller proportion (29.5 percent) favored "mixed" and "equal" participation with

---

[19] By changing the wording from "intervention" to "internal security" support for U. S. policy jumped 24 percent!

[20] On U.S. policy toward Chile there was a high proportion (25 percent) of "no responses" and "don't know."

Argentine corporations, over one-fifth favored mixed enterprises in which Argentines would predominate (21.5 percent); and a little over one-tenth (10.7 percent) believed that foreign participation should be limited to loans, credits and licensing agreements.

In summary most Argentine industrial executives favored development through external dependence and collaboration; but the *degree* of support of U.S. policies varied according to the *salience* of U.S. policy to Argentine economic interests. Moreover, the Argentine executives were divided over the terms of dependency—between those who favored a laissez faire policy that opened the country to unrestrained foreign penetration and those who sought to limit and control foreign investment competition with national industries and to direct foreign investment toward national development goals.[21] Hence our second and third hypotheses have been validated.

The division among the executives on the role of foreign investment suggests that there may be two types of *dependent* outlooks: (1) the *colonial enclave executive* is totally identified with the foreign investor community; and (2) the *developmental integrationist* who wishes to regulate the behavior of foreign investment in order to integrate it with national development. Both styles of collaborative behavior begin with the common acceptance of foreign dependence but diverge when it comes to defining the terms of dependency and the implementation of specific policies.

COMPARING ATTITUDES OF EXECUTIVES OF NATIONAL AND FOREIGN FIRMS

One possible explanation for the large measure of support for foreign participation in the Argentine economy and U.S. policy among executives is the presence of a substantial proportion of foreign firms. Employed by corporations linked to U.S. or European multinational corporations, and supported by their governments, executives of foreign corporations would tend to support foreign involvement in the economy. Because U.S. investments predominate among foreign investment in Argentina, one would expect that the executives of foreign firms would likely support U.S. policies. How about executives of national firms? Would they differ from their counterparts in foreign firms?

[21] As Gustavo Polit pointed out:

". . . unity (between Argentine industrialists and international capital) does not mean identity of interests; and it is certain that there are irritations and clashes between the industrial capitalists and foreign capital. The source of these conflicts, however, is not the desire of the industrialists to abolish foreign control over the Argentinian economy, but their determination to raise custom barriers against foreign competition. This is the response of the Argentinian industrialists, together with the foreign companies which have invested capital in the industry of Argentina, when confronted with foreign industrialists who insist on exporting, not capital, but goods that compete with local industry. Their anti-imperialist struggle has never gone beyond this."
Polit, p. 430, cited in footnote 18.

FINDINGS

Comparing the responses of the national/foreign executives on a favor/oppose basis we find that a *clear majority of executives of both groups support foreign involvement in the Argentine economy and U.S. policies* except on the question of the U.S. policy toward intervention—where only a slight majority (51 percent) of the "national executives"[22] support U.S. policy, 63.4 percent of the foreign executives supported it. In general we find that differentiating between national and foreign firms does not alter the pro-foreign, pro-U.S. results that we found among Argentine executives as a whole.[23]

Nevertheless, a closer look does show that the *proportion* of national executives as opposed to foreign executives who support U.S. policy differs according to the issue under consideration. This is the case if we examine the degree of support of foreign involvement in the economy. In the area of foreign participation in the economy, considering only the extremes,[24] a significantly smaller proportion of national executives "strongly" favors foreign participation in industry and banking. In the areas of research and in the development of technology, the differences between national and foreign executives are very small—though the trend of the responses is in the hypothesized direction (less support of foreign involvement among national executives than among foreign executives). Relative to foreigners occupying positions in industry, a substantially smaller proportion of national executives (46.8 percent) than foreign executives (78 percent) express strong support of foreign ownership. On the issue of foreigners in executive positions, the differences between the national and foreign executives are smaller though in the same general direction: 40.4 percent of the national executives strongly favor foreigners as opposed to 61 percent of the foreign executives. There are minor differences on the participation of foreigners in technical positions.

It appears that where foreign firms may represent a threat to national firms either in direct competition in the industrial area or indirectly through their control of banks and hence credits the national executives tend to be *less favorable* than the executives of foreign firms. Similarly, when it comes to considering the presence of foreigners in the firm who may *displace* Argentine executives or owners, the executives of national firms show less favorable responses than the executives of foreign firms.

The proportion of executives of foreign firms who strongly favored foreign

[22] We will refer to the execusives of national firms as "national executives" or "nationals" and executives of foreign firms as "foreign executives" or "foreign," though all the executives interviewed were Argentine nationals.

[23] For display of the preliminary results see Tables 1 *a* and *b* in the Appendix.

[24] The responses were coded on a four-point Likert scale as "favorable," "moderately favorable," "moderately opposed," "opposed." The extremes were defined as those falling in the "favorable"—"opposed" categories.

involvement in ownership was 78 percent, in industry 97.6 percent, in banks 70.7 percent but only 61 percent when it came to foreigners in executive posts. Apparently even for this group there is a limit or cut-off point in their nonnationalism. Argentine executives employed by foreign firms differed slightly from the executives of national firms when it came to the question of foreigners occupying *executive* positions in industrial firms. While executives of foreign firms may not feel threatened by the extension or maintenance of foreign ownership or control, they may be uneasy over the possibility that they could be displaced at the executive level. National executives (some of whom are company presidents, others who may aspire to ownership) may feel the threat of displacement at the ownership as well as the executive level. However, national or foreign excutives may not feel as strong a threat in the areas of technology and research.

On the questions dealing with U.S. policy we find almost *no* difference between national and foreign executives on the "extreme" position responses except in the areas of policy related to U.S. leadership in the inter-American system and Chile. In both cases a greater portion of the executives of foreign firms were strongly favorable. There may be two sets of contradictory factors operating among the national executives: one group may oppose U.S. policy because it limits Argentina's efforts to broaden its commercial outlets and another group may oppose U.S. policy as being too soft on communism.

In the policy areas most relevant to Latin American and Argentine economic development and political independence the differences in extreme positive responses between the national and foreign executives are insignificant. On the negative side, considering the "extreme" responses alone, we find that national executives differ from foreign executives in four issue areas: U.S. policy toward intervention, Argentine development, U.S. leadership, and loans and credits. In all four areas a substantially greater percentage of national executives express opposition than foreign executives.

If we consider the ranking of issues according to the favorable responses (considering only the positive extreme) expressed by the two groups, we find some interesting results. (see Table on next page)

Within the category of foreign involvement in the economy, foreign firm participation in industry ranked first among foreign executives while among the nationals it ranked third. The *ranking* differences among the other choices were only slightly different. While executives of national and foreign firms approve of foreign penetration of the research and technology development areas they diverge somewhat concerning the relative merits of a foreign presence in industry. Although the rank ordering of favorable responses of both groups to U.S. policy is quite similar, the national executives differed substantially from the foreign executives in their assessment of the contribution of U.S. loans and credits to development (70.7 percent for foreigns to 53.2 percent for the nationals) though over 50 percent of both groups favored U.S. policy.

Attitudes of Foreign and National Executives toward Foreign Involvement and U.S. Policy

	Rank Order	Extreme Percent Positive
Foreign Executives		
Foreign involvement		
Foreign firms in industry	1	97.6
Foreign firms in technology	2	87.8
Foreign firms in research	3	85.4
Foreigners in industry	4	78
Foreigners in technical positions	4	78
U.S. policy		
U.S. leadership	1	68.3
West Europe	1	68.4
Internal security in Western hemisphere	2	56.1
National Executives		
Foreign involvement		
Foreign firms in technology	1	87.2
Foreign firms in research	2	76.6
Foreign firms in industry	3	72.3
Foreigners in technical positions	4	68.1
U.S. Policy		
West Europe	1	53.2
U.S. leadership	2	46.8
Internal security	2	46.8

From the above discussion it is clear that executives of national firms, as well as executives of foreign firms, have accepted foreign penetration and Argentine dependence. A question remains however regarding the *terms* of dependence. Do executives of national firms perceive dependent relationships between themselves and foreign investors and the United States different from executives of foreign firms? We can identify two types of dependent outlooks, the integration-developmentalist and the enclave-colonialist. We will consider three issues in discussing the terms of dependence:

1. The issue of tied loans.[25]

2. Profit remittances.

3. State guarantees of foreign investment.

The colonial-enclave-dependent outlook would tend to accept tied loans,

[25] On the question of tied loans the four possible responses were coded "approve," "critical approval," "mildly disapprove," "disapprove." The extremes are "approve" and "disapprove." On the question of profit remittance the possible responses vary between "no controls," and "strong controls."

few or no controls on profit remittances and state guarantees of foreign investment; the integration-developmental-dependent outlook would reject tied loans, favor strong controls of profit remittances and oppose state guarantees of foreign investment.

In comparing the foreign to the national executives, we find that both tend toward the colonial-enclave type of dependent outlook on two of the three measures: on profit remittances over 70 percent of the nationals and over 90 percent of the foreign executives favor few or no controls. On state guarantees of foreign investment, 66 percent of the nationals and 56 percent of the foreigns are favorable.[26] However, both groups express opposition to "tied loans"—an obvious case of excessive exploitation that even the Rockefeller Report recognized.

Despite the pervasiveness of the colonial-enclave outlook among both groups there were significant differences between the two groups on the *degree* of support of colonial-enclave dependency. Considering only the "extremes" we find that only 4.3 percent of the nationals approve tied loans compared to 12.2 percent foreign executives. On the negative extreme, 61.7 percent of the nationals disapprove while only 48.8 percent of the executives of foreign firms disapprove. On the issue of profit remittances, 10.6 percent of the nationals favor "no controls" compared to 36.6 percent of the foreign executives. At the other extreme, 25.5 percent of the executives employed in national firms favored strong controls compared to 4.9 percent of the foreign executives. The executives from the national firms tend to be more receptive to mild types of regulation and control over foreign investment while the Argentine executives of foreign firms tend to identify more with the interests of the home office of the corporation than with the development needs of the nation. The problem of decapitalization of the economy caused by the flight of profits appears to be of more concern to the national-executives than the foreign executives. National executives are more likely than foreign executives to favor measures that attempt to harness foreign investment to national development—though this group appears to be a small proportion of the total of national executives.

The division on the issue of profit remittances between national executives who favor some or strong controls (85.1 percent) and foreign executives (63.4 percent) should not however distract us from the fact that both national and foreign executives believe that foreign investment has a role to play in development. Over 90 percent of the nationals and foreign executives agreed that foreign investment had a role to play in development. The differences between nationals and executives are essentially over whether there should be no controls or few controls. Neither of these two positions is likely to pose serious constraints on U.S. economic involvement and hardly likely to lead to any serious political conflicts between the United States and Argentina.

26 For a display of the preliminary results see Tables 2 *a* and *b* in the Appendix.

A point at issue among Argentine executives seems to concern the *terms of dependency*, more specifically, the relationship between the Argentine industrial bourgeoisie and the foreign industrial bourgeoisie: the terms of collaboration and/or subordination. Discussions of "joint ventures" fail to reveal the balance of forces within international corporate agreements. The problem is to determine the specific aspects of dependency; we need to differentiate the forms of joint collaboration and then compare the national and foreign executives to see if there are any variations in their behavior.

In an open-ended question we asked our interviewees to state the form in which foreign investment should participate in development.[27] We were able to group the responses in four general categories:

1. Few or no conditions on foreign investments' participation in the economy.

2. Equal participation with Argentine firms in mixed enterprises.

3. Predominance of Argentine firms in mixed enterprises.

4. Limit foreign investors to providing loans, credits and/or licensing agreements.

We will refer to it (1) as the liberal position, (2) as the neoliberal position, (3) as the national-dependent position and (4) as the neodependent position. As we move from the liberal to the neodependent position it is clear that the forms of dependency have changed—the situation has become more complex and the presence of the foreign investor is perhaps less visible, however important it may still be.

The modal response of the executives of the foreign form falls in the "liberal" category (46.3 percent), while the modal response of the national executives falls in the neoliberal category (34.1 percent). The foreign executives tend to favor the unrestricted penetration of foreign capital much more so than national executives, who, while favoring foreign participation, hope that it will not displace them. Thus, while there may be a weak nationalistic sentiment—as evidenced by their endorsement of foreign participation in the economy—there is a strong sense of identification with their *position* and the need to bargain to prevent excess external encroachment. The politics of the national executives is much more complex than the foreign executives: the nationals open the door to foreign investment and at the same time guard against losing all control—not an easy task considering that they are dealing with giant multinational corporations with support from their governments and international financial institutions. The unevenness of the contest may help to explain why over twice as many national executives (17.1 percent) as foreign executives (7.3 percent) favor the neodependent model with its emphasis on loans, and licensing agreements. The threat of loss of control through these forms of dependence is less apparent and perhaps less immediate.

[27] For a display of the preliminary results see Table 3 in the Appendix.

It is clear that executives from foreign and national firms favor collaboration with foreign investors and endorse governmental policies that facilitate foreign penetration. The special problem that executives of national firms face—the possible expansion of the foreign firm that leads to their displacement—causes them to be somewhat more prudent: foreign penetration is permitted on condition that the nationals retain a piece of the action, even if it be in a subordinate position.

ATTITUDES OF EXECUTIVES OF NATIONAL DEPENDENTS AND NONDEPENDENT FIRMS

In our discussion of executives of national firms we assumed that ownership or investment separated the national from the foreign firms. As we have seen, however, a high proportion of executives of national and foreign firms favored foreign participation in the economy and supported U.S. policies and hegemony in the hemisphere. However, it is well known that there are numerous other activities that link firms in the underdeveloped countries to the developed countries: technology, licensing agreements, purchases, financial loans and credits, advertising, consulting, and so on. In this section we separate national firms on the basis of three dimensions of dependence: technology, purchases, and bank financing. Our national firms are then divided into three groups: "dependent," "partially dependent" and "nondependent." A dependent firm could be one whose technology originates outside of the country, who receives loans from foreign banks, or who purchases over 30 percent of its goods outside of the country. A partially dependent firm is one whose technology originates in Argentina and abroad, who receives loans from both national and foreign banks, or who purchases between 11 and 30 percent of its goods abroad. A nondependent firm uses technology that originates in Argentina, borrows exclusively from national banks, and purchases less than 10 percent of its goods abroad. We considered the attitudes of both groups across a broad range of 24 questions, (potential components of the dependency concept dealing with political, economic, and technical issues) to determine if this core group of nondependent nationals would differ from the dependent nationals, and, in general, to see if there is a nationalist core among industrial executives.

TECHNOLOGICAL DEPENDENCE AND NONDEPENDENCE

Our first group, separated on the basis of technological dependence, created a problem: only 4.9 percent of our national firms were *not* dependent. The rest were either totally or partially dependent on foreign sources for technology. Almost all Argentine owned industrial enterprises are linked to foreign firms through their technological dependence. The proforeign, pro-U.S. outlooks of the national enterprises *might* be largely a function of their technological dependence.

Given the small number (two) of nondependent firms, we confined our analysis and discussion to dependent and partially dependent firms.[28] Of the 24 issues of dependency that we considered, on only two issues did a majority of the executives of the partially dependent firms answer negatively to foreign participation or U.S. policy. Fifty-four percent of the partial dependents[29] opposed U.S. policy toward intervention and all opposed "tied loans." The two issues on which a majority of dependents were opposed were the issue of U.S. policy toward intervention and tied loans. The policy issues where there appeared to be a substantive difference between partially dependents and dependents were U.S. policy to Western Europe and U.S. policy to Chile.[30] On the issues of foreign participtaion in the economy, the proportions of partially dependents favoring foreign participation ranged from 69.2 to 100 percent depending on the issue except on the issue of foreign participation in banking. With the dependents, the proportion favoring ranged from 65.4 to 100 percent. On U.S. policy (excluding the issue of "intervention"), the proportion of partially dependents responding favorably ranged from 53.8 to 100 percent. On U.S. policy (excluding Chile and intervention), the proportion of dependents responding favorably ranged from 50 to 73.1 percent. If there were any "trends" it appeared that the proportion of dependents who *opposed* U.S. policy was somewhat higher than the partially dependents. Nonetheless, the overall findings suggest that the distinction between partially dependent and dependent fail to reveal any clear cut differences with the previous pattern favoring foreign penetration and U.S. policy.

FINANCIAL DEPENDENCE AND NONDEPENDENCE

The next component of dependency that we consider is financial.[31] Beginning in the post-Peronist period but especially after 1966, foreign banks accelerated their penetration of the Argentine financial system. European and U.S. banks created branch offices all over Argentina and proceeded to take over nationally owned banks. The control of Argentine savings provided U.S. investors with an excellent opportunity to maximize earnings by risking Argentine funds. The Argentine banking system thus became another victim of external control and another aspect of foreign dependency. As seen earlier, even considering the high proportion of nationals with proforeign and pro-U.S. outlooks, there was more opposition on the issue of foreign control of banking than on most other issues.

[28] See Tables 4 *a* and *b* in the appendix for the preliminary results.
[29] We will refer to executives of national "dependent," "partially dependent" and "nondependent" firms as "dependents," "partially dependents" and "nondependents."
[30] A disproportionate number of respondents did not respond or have information and therefore account for the low percentages.
[31] For preliminary results see Tables 5 *a* and *b* in the Appendix.

In our group of national firms, the proportion of firms who borrowed only from foreign banks was 5 percent. However, the proportion that was partially dependent on foreign banks was 47.5 percent compared to 47.5 percent that borrowed only from national banks. A greater proportion of the firms were financially dependent on foreign finances than were not—suggesting another link between the formally "national" firm and foreign enterprises—thus providing additional evidence to buttress the notion that the national firms (because they are linked to the outside) favor policies that permit foreign penetration and U.S. hegemony.

Examining the responses of the partially dependent and the non-dependent, we find both have substantial majorities favorable to foreign involvement and U.S. policy except on the issue of U.S. intervention and tied loans. On the former issues, 57.9 percent of the partially dependent favored U.S. policy against 42.1 percent; while 36.8 percent of the nondependent favored and 63.2 percent opposed. On two other issues there were substantial differences in the *pattern* of responses (that is, where one group responds positively and the other negatively): U.S. policy to Argentine development and to Chile. Both groups opposed tied loans: partially dependent (84.2 percent) and nondependent (84.2 percent).

Comparing the differences between partially dependent to nondependent we find a pattern on the issues concerned with *foreign participation* and on *U.S. policy*. The nondependent are more likely to oppose foreign participation than the dependent: in eight issue areas the nondependent exceeded dependent on four issues, and in two areas they were equal. On 10 of the 11 policy issues a higher proportion of nondependents opposed U.S. policy. This suggests that opposition is more likely to emerge on specific aspects of U.S. policy from the groups that are not financially bound to U.S. financial institutions.

IMPORT DEPENDENCY AND NONDEPENDENCY[32]

Almost half (47 percent) of Argentine firms *are* dependent on foreign imports. The growth of industry in Argentina has not eliminated external dependency but has changed the nature of dependency: from importers of finished goods to importers of capital goods and technology. The large scale foreign enterprises that have moved into Argentina have not created new enterprises capable of exporting goods and competing on the international market. Rather, they have established firms within Argentina that form part of the market for U.S. industrial exports. These foreign firms within Argentina capitalize on the protective barriers to keep out foreign competition and have taken over a substantial part of the national market. Even where they

[32] See Tables 6 *a* and *b* in the Appendix for display of preliminary results on import dependence.

have not formed subsidiaries, the Argentine customers of U.S. and European industrial exporters serve as the political clients of foreign export groups.

We will compare two types, the nondependents and the dependents,[33] to see if there are any differences between their responses and previous groups in terms of favorableness to foreign penetration and U.S. policy.

In the area of foreign participation, a substantial majority of nondependent and dependent executives favor foreign penetration except on the issue of foreign control of banks and foreigners in executive positions. The nondependents divide with 50 percent in favor and 44.4 percent opposed (among the dependents, 72.7 percent favor foreign banks and 81.8 percent favor foreign executives in industry). In the area of U.S. policy, a substantial majority of dependents are favorable on all questions except intervention, tied loans and inter-American commerce. The nondependents have a similar pattern of response: a high percentage of opposition toward U.S. policy on tied loans (94.4), intervention (55.6), and inter-American commerce. It should be kept in mind however that these are specific policy differences; on global questions dealing with U.S. leadership (83.3 percent) and state guarantees of foreign investmen: (77.8 percent), the nondependents responded favorably. The opposition emerged within the framework of dependency— perhaps seeking to adjust particular types of relationships.

Comparing the executives of dependent import firms to the executives of nondependent firms, we find that on seven of the eight questions (on one question the same proportion responded positively) dealing with foreign economic penetration, the dependent group had a higher proportion of favorable responses. In the area of U.S. policy, consistent differences between the two groups are not anywhere as clear-cut as they were on economic issues.

Among nondependents, opposition to economic penetration appears to be limited to specific areas: banks and takeover of executive positions. This suggests that *fear of displacement rather than dependency* may be the factor underlying the occasional conflicts that emerge between the United States and Argentina, and between foreign business and Argentina firms. Specific differences between foreign and Argentine elites, however, are within a generally harmonious framework based on a convergence on basic political-economic questions—the acceptance of U.S. political leadership in the hemisphere and foreign investment in Argentine development.

External dependence is *not* an external phenomenon: it has its roots in the attitudes and behavior of almost all Argentine industrial executives. The Argentine executives seem to perceive foreign entrepreneurship as necessary to Argentine development. Substantial majorities of national industrial executives accept foreign control as perhaps the necessary price for survival and possible growth. Foreign firms, products and techniques are reference points to which Argentine executives turn. The Argentine executives are more involved in the world of the multinational corporation than they are interested

[33] The number of partial dependents is too small to consider.

in attempting to mobilize internal resources for development. Thus, in the multitude of day-to-day policy choices confronting Argentine industrial executives, there need be no person or group representing U.S. interests on the premises to keep watch. Rather, the imperial presence is incorporated into the political culture of a dependent Argentina.

CONCLUSION

In conclusion we might reexamine the hypotheses stated on page 153 with our evaluation of their acceptance.

1. Argentine industrial executives tend to favor foreign participation in the Argentine economy.

1a. Argentine industrial executives would tend to favor U.S. and Argentine government policies that facilitate foreign penetration of the economy.

Finding: The results support the hypotheses.

2. Industrial executives of foreign firms will be more favorable toward the questions posed under hypotheses 1 and 1a than executives of national firms.

Finding: With a few exceptions, as noted in the discussion, the response patterns of the national executives were essentially the same as that of foreign executives.

3. Differences within the response patterns of national executives will be a function of differences in levels of dependency.

Finding: Our analysis suggests that the response patterns of national executives were not a function of dependency level. While there were noted exceptions, the pattern evidenced in step two of the analysis was not altered by the introduction of "dependency level" as a control variable.

Given the conditions under which the industrial executives exist and the particular circumstances in which industrialization is taking place in Argentina, they are not likely to play a dynamic role in their country's development. Analyzing the situation in Argentina, we find that the assumption of conflict between national and foreign industrialists that might lead the former to play a nationalist-developmentalist role is incorrect. Foreign and national socioeconomic elites have been intertwined with each other either through financial, technological-economic, political, and/or ideological links.

In Argentina large industrial enterprises are not really national. They are controlled or influenced by foreign capital directly through investments or indirectly through the export of technology and goods as well as through financial levers. National capital is integrated into a dependent relationship with foreign capital. This interconnection of interests makes the industrial executives a major conduit for external penetration. A nondependent economic policy and an independent foreign policy must be based on other social forces and probably another social system.

TABLE 1a

Nationals

Issue	Favorable	Mod Favorable	Mod Oppose	Oppose
Attitudes Toward Foreign Involvement—Argentina (Percent)				
1. Foreign firms in industry	72.3	21.3	2.1	2.1
2. Foreign firms in banks	42.6	17.0	25.5	8.5
3. Foreign firms in research	76.6	6.4	6.4	0
4. Foreign firms in developmental technology	87.2	4.3	6.4	0
5. Foreign firms in ownership	46.8	27.7	12.8	8.5
6. Foreigners in executive positions	40.4	29.8	23.8	4.3
7. Foreigners in technical positions	68.1	8.5	12.8	8.5
U.S. Policy				
1. Western Europe	53.2	25.5	10.6	2.1
2. Socialist bloc countries	40.4	19.1	12.8	6.4
3. Underdeveloped countries	36.2	34	19	10.6
4. Inter-American commerce	23.4	34	25.5	17
5. Loans/credits	29.8	42.6	17	10.6
6. Internal security in western hemisphere	46.8	21.3	17	12.8
7. Intervention	25.5	25.5	25.5	23.4
8. Argentine development	27.4	38.3	19.1	12.8
9. Chile	14.9	36.2	10.6	10.6
10. Leadership in inter-American system (North America)	46.8	28.9	8.9	12.8
	Totally Agree	Mild/ Agree	Mild/ Disagree	Disagree
	53.2	40.4	6.4	0

Foreign

Issue	Favorable	Mod Favorable	Mod Oppose	Oppose
Attitudes Toward Foreign Involvement (Percent)				
1. Foreign firms in industry	97.6	2.4	0	0
2. Foreign firms in banks	70.7	22.0	2.4	4.9
3. Foreign firms in research	85.4	9.8	2.4	2.4
4. Foreign firms in developmental technology	87.8	9.8	0	0
5. Foreign firms in ownership	78	17.1	2.4	2.4
6. Foreigners in executive positions	61	26.8	7.3	4.9
7. Foreigners in technological positions	78	14.6	7.3	0
U.S. Policy				
1. Western Europe	63.4	31.7	4.9	0
2. Socialist bloc countries	36.6	24.4	19.5	2.4
3. Underdeveloped countries	41.5	24.4	17.1	14.6
4. Inter-American commerce	34.1	29.3	19.5	17.1
5. Loans-credits	36.6	53.7	7.3	2.4
6. Internal security in western hemisphere	56.1	24.4	9.8	4.9
7. Intervention	26.8	36.6	22	9.8
8. Argentine development	36.6	48.8	7.3	4.9
9. Chile	31.7	31.7	12.2	7.3
10. Leadership in inter-American system (North America)	68.3	14.6	12.2	4.9
	Totally Agree	Mild/Agree	Mild/Disagree	Disagree
11. U.S. loan/credit agencies aid development	70.7	26.8	0	2.4

TABLE 2a
Integration versus Enclave (Percent)

Issue	Nationals $N = 47$			
	Approve	Approve with Criticism	Disapprove Mildly	Disapprove
1. Tied loans	4.3	3.5	25.5	61.7
	No Control	Few Control	Strong Control	Not Allow
2. Profit remittances	10.6	59.6	25.5	0
3. State guarantee of foreign investment	Yes 66	No 27.7		

TABLE 2b
Integration versus Enclave (Percent)

Issue	Foreign $N = 41$			
	Approve	Approve with Criticism	Disapprove Mildly	Disapprove
1. Tied loans	12.2	14.6	22	48.8
	No Control	Few Control	Strong Control	Not Allow
2. Profit remittances	36.6	58.5	4.9	0
3. State guarantee of foreign investment	Yes 56.1	No 39		

TABLE 3
Preferred form of foreign investment (Percent)
$N = 88$

Classification	Foreign	National
Liberal	46.3	34
Neoliberal	29.2	34.1
Dependent national	14.6	14.9
Neodependent	7.3	17.1

TABLE 4a
Dependency Analysis Technology

Issue	Dependent (N=26)				Partially Dependent (N=13)				Nondependent (N=2)			
	% Favor	(N)	% Oppose	(N)	% Favor	(N)	% Oppose	(N)	% Favor	(N)	% Oppose	(N)
a. 1. Firms in industry	100	(26)	0		84.6	(11)	7.7	(1)	50	(1)	50	(1)
2. Firms in banks	73.1	(19)	23.1	(6)	38.5	(5)	46.2	(6)	0		100	(2)
3. Firms in research	96.2	(25)	3.8	(1)	69.2	(9)	7.7	(1)	50	(1)	50	(1)
4. Firms in development technology	96.2	(25)	3.8	(1)	84.6	(11)	0		50	(1)	50	(1)
5. Ownership	65.4	(17)	30.8	(8)	84.6	(11)	7.7	(1)	50	(1)	50	(1)
6. Executive positions	65.4	(17)	34.6	(9)	69.2	(9)	23.1	(3)	50	(1)	50	(1)
7. Technical positions	76.9	(20)	23.1	(6)	69.2	(9)	23.1	(3)	50	(1)	50	(1)
8. Foreign investment in development	100	(26)	0		92.3	(12)	7.7	(1)	100	(2)	0	

(continued)

TABLE 4a (*continued*)
Dependency Analysis Technology

Issue	Dependent (N = 26)				Partially Dependent (N = 13)				Nondependent (N = 2)			
	% Favor	(N)	% Oppose	(N)	% Favor	(N)	% Oppose	(N)	% Favor	(N)	% Oppose	(N)
b. U.S. Policy												
1. Western Europe	65.4	(17)	19.2	(5)	92.3	(12)	7.7	(1)	100	(2)	0	
2. Socialist bloc	50.0	(13)	23.1	(6)	61.5	(8)	23.1	(3)	100	(2)	0	
3. Underdeveloped countries	65.4	(17)	34.6	(9)	69.2	(9)	30.8	(4)	50	(1)	50	(1)
4. Inter-American commerce	57.7	(15)	42.3	(11)	53.8	(7)	46.2	(6)	0		100	(2)
5. Loans and credits	73.1	(19)	26.9	(7)	69.2	(9)	30.8	(4)	50	(1)	50	(1)
6. Internal security	65.4	(17)	30.8	(8)	61.5	(8)	38.5	(5)	50	(1)	50	(1)
7. Intervention	50.0	(13)	50.	(13)	46.2	(6)	53.8	(7)			100	(2)
8. Argentine development	69.2	(18)	30.8	(8)	61.5	(8)	38.5	(5)			100	(2)
9. Chile	34.6	(9)	26.9	(7)	61.5	(8)	7.7	(1)	50	(1)	50	(1)
10. North American leadership in inter-American system	73.1	(19)	23.1	(6)	61.5	(8)	30.8	(4)	100	(2)	0	

TABLE 4b
Dependency Analysis
Dependency Measure
1. Technology

	Dependent (N=26)		Partially Dependent (N=13)		Nondependent (N=2)	
	% Favor	% Oppose	% Favor	% Oppose	% Favor	% Oppose
Tied	15.4 (4)	84.6 (22)	0	100 (13)	0	100 (2)
State guarantee of foreign investment	73.1 (19)	19.2 (5)	61.5 (8)	30.8 (4)	50 (1)	50 (1)

	Dependent (N=26)				Partially Dependent (N=13)				Nondependent (N=2)			
	No Control	Few Control	Strong Control	Prohibit Control	No Control	Few Control	Strong Control	Prohibit Control	No Control	Few Control	Strong Control	Prohibit Control
Profit Remittances	15.4 (4)	61.5 (16)	18.2 (5)	0 0	7.7 (1)	53.8 (7)	30.8 (4)	0 0	0 0	0 0	100 (2)	0 0

TABLE 5a
Dependency Analysis: Finance

Issue	Dependent (N=)				Partially Dependent (N=19)				Nondependent (N=19)			
	% Favor	(N)	% Oppose	(N)	% Favor	(N)	% Oppose	(N)	% Favor	(N)	% Oppose	(N)
a. 1. Firms in industry	50	(1)	50	(1)	94.7	(18)	5.3	(1)	94.7	(18)	0	(0)
2. Firms in banks	50	(1)	50	(1)	63.2	(12)	36.8	(7)	57.9	(11)	31.6	(6)
3. Firms in research	50	(1)	50	(1)	84.2	(16)	0	(0)	84.2	(16)	10.5	(2)
4. Firms in development technology	50	(1)	50	(1)	100	(19)	0	(0)	84.2	(16)	10.5	(2)
5. Ownership	50	(1)	50	(1)	63.2	(12)	36.8	(7)	78.9	(15)	5.3	(1)
6. Executive positions	50	(1)	50	(1)	68.4	(13)	31.6	(6)	47.4	(9)	31.6	(6)
7. Technical positions	0	(0)	100	(2)	89.5	(17)	10.5	(2)	63.2	(12)	26.3	(5)
8. Foreign investment in development	100	(2)	0	(0)	100	(19)	0	(0)	100	(19)	0	(0)

(continued)

TABLE 5a (*continued*)
Dependency Analysis: Finance

Issue	Dependent (N=)				Partially Dependent (N=19)				Nondependent (N=19)			
	% Favor	(N)	% Oppose	(N)	% Favor	(N)	% Oppose	(N)	% Favor	(N)	% Oppose	(N)
b. U.S. Policy												
1. Western Europe	50	(1)	0	(0)	84.2	(16)	10.5	(2)	68.4	(13)	21.1	(4)
2. Socialist bloc	50	(1)	0	(0)	63.2	(12)	10.5	(2)	57.9	(11)	31.6	(6)
3. Underdeveloped countries	50	(1)	50	(1)	84.2	(16)	15.8	(3)	52.6	(10)	47.4	(9)
4. Inter-American commerce	50	(1)	50	(1)	57.9	(11)	42.1	(8)	52.6	(10)	47.4	(9)
5. Loans and credits	50	(1)	50	(1)	84.2	(16)	15.8	(3)	57.9	(11)	36.8	(7)
6. Internal security	100	(2)	0	(0)	68.4	(13)	31.6	(6)	52.6	(10)	26.3	(5)
7. Intervention	50	(1)	50	(1)	57.9	(11)	42.1	(8)	36.8	(7)	63.2	(12)
8. Argentine development	50	(1)	50	(1)	78.9	(15)	15.8	(3)	47.4	(9)	52.6	(10)
9. Chile	50	(1)	0	(1)	57.9	(11)	21.1	(4)	42.1	(8)	31.6	(6)
10. North American leadership in inter-American system	100	(2)	0	(0)	94.7	(18)	5.3	(1)	52.6	(10)	42.1	(8)

TABLE 5b
Dependency Analysis
Measure
2. Financial

	Dependent (N=26)		Partially Dependent (N=13)		Nondependent (N=2)	
	% Favor	% Oppose	% Favor	% Oppose	% Favor	% Oppose
Tied loans	0 (0)	100 (2)	15.8 (3)	84.2 (16)	10.5 (2)	84.2 (16)
State guarantee of foreign investment	100 (2)	0 (0)	73.7 (14)	26.3 (5)	57.9 (11)	21.1 (4)
	1	2 3 4	1	2 3 4	1	2 3 4
Profit Remittances	(0) 0	(1) 50 (1) 50	(3) 15.8	(12) 63.2 (4) 21.0	(2) 10.5	(8) 42.1 (7) 3.68

Note: 1 = No control
2 = Few control
3 = Strong control
4 = Prohibit

TABLE 6a
Dependency Analysis: Imports

Issue	Dependent (N=11)				Partially Dependent (N=5)				Nondependent (N=18)			
	% Favor	(N)	% Oppose	(N)	% Favor	(N)	% Oppose	(N)	% Favor	(N)	% Oppose	(N)
a. 1. Firms in industry	100	(11)	0	(0)	100	(5)	0	(0)	83.3	(15)	11.1	(2)
2. Firms in banks	72.7	(8)	27.3	(3)	40	(2)	60	(3)	50	(9)	44.4	(8)
3. Firms in research	100	(11)	0	(0)	60	(3)	20	(1)	77.8	(14)	11.1	(2)
4. Firms in development technology	100	(11)	0	(0)	80	(4)	20	(1)	83.3	(15)	11.1	(2)
5. Ownership	90.9	(10)	9.1	(1)	60	(3)	40	(2)	66.7	(12)	27.8	(5)
6. Executive positions	81.8	(9)	18.2	(2)	80	(4)	20	(1)	50	(9)	44.4	(8)
7. Technical positions	90.9	(10)	9.1	(1)	80	(4)	20	(1)	55.6	(10)	38.9	(7)
8. Foreign investment in development	100	(11)	0	(0)	100	(5)	0	(0)	100	(18)	0	(0)

(continued)

TABLE 6a (continued)
Dependency Analysis Import

Issue	Dependent (N=11)				Partially Dependent (N=5)				Nondependent (N=18)			
	% Favor	(N)	% Oppose	(N)	% Favor	(N)	% Oppose	(N)	% Favor	(N)	% Oppose	(N)
b. U.S. Policy												
1. Western Europe	81.8	(9)	9.1	(1)	60	(3)	40	(2)	77.8	(14)	11.1	(2)
2. Socialist bloc	72.7	(8)	9.1	(1)	40	(2)	60	(3)	61.1	(11)	22.2	(4)
3. Underdeveloped countries	63.6	(7)	36.4	(4)	40	(2)	60	(3)	72.2	(13)	22.2	(4)
4. Inter-American commerce	36.4	(4)	54.5	(6)	40	(2)	60	(3)	50	(9)	50.0	(9)
5. Loans and credits	72.7	(8)	27.3	(3)	80	(4)	20	(1)	61.1	(11)	38.9	(7)
6. Internal security	72.7	(8)	27.3	(3)	100	(4)	0		55.6	(10)	44.4	(6)
7. Intervention	45.5	(5)	54.5	(6)	40	(2)	60	(3)	44.4	(8)	55.6	(10)
8. Argentine development	63.6	(7)	36.4	(4)	20	(1)	60	(3)	66.7	(12)	33.3	(6)
9. Chile	45.5	(5)	9.1	(1)	60	(3)	20	(1)	50	(9)	33.3	(6)
10. North American leadership in inter-Americas	63.6	(7)	36.4	(4)	40	(2)	60	(3)	83.3	(15)	16.7	(3)

TABLE 6b
Dependency Analysis

Measure Imports	Dependent (N=11)		Partially Dependent (N=5)		Nondependent (N=18)	
	% Favor	% Oppose	% Favor	% Oppose	% Favor	% Oppose
Tied loans	9.1 (1)	90.9 (10)	20 (1)	80 (4)	5.6 (1)	94.4 (17)
State guarantee of foreign investment	81.8 (9)	0 (0)	20 (1)	80 (4)	77.8 (14)	16.7 (3)
	1 2	4 3	1 2	4 3	1 2	4 3
Profit Remittances	(9) 81.8 (0) 0	(2) 18.2 0	(3) 60 (1) 20	(1) 20 0	(8) 44.4 (2) 11.1	(7) 38.9 0

Note: 1 = No control
2 = Few control
3 = Strong control
4 = Prohibit

6

James Petras & Thomas Cook | Politics in a Nondemocratic State: the Argentine Industrial Elite

This chapter focuses on the behavior of a relatively small, elite group in an authoritarian political setting: Argentina. In 1966 the elected government of President Illia was overthrown by General Juan Carlos Ongania and a military dictatorship was established: the congress was dismissed, elections were abolished, parties were dissolved, speech and press censorship was instituted, and the right of assembly was severely curtailed. Trade unions were intervened, substantially reducing their autonomy from the state, and the army was used to break strikes while the police arrested trade union leaders. The end result was the creation of a nondemocratic state that, however, was intended by its makers to offer a more adequate form of representation modeled on the corporatist ideal.

The corporate idea of nondemocratic representation largely rested on the notion that direct consultation between the executive (the military elite) and the "producers" (the entrepreneurial elite) would result in the most beneficial policies for the country as a whole. Initially at least many industrialists, and even segments of the Peronist-led trade union bureaucracy, responded favorably to the coup and its corporatist appeals or at least acquiesced in the overthrow of Illia. Throughout the four years of the Ongania military regime (1966 to 1970), and during the subsequent military governments, the public image of the government was that of a repressive regime hostile toward the demands of the lower classes and sympathetic to big business interests, especially foreign business. One of the issues that we explore in this paper is whether business executives perceived the military dictatorship as representative of their interests and whether they perceived themselves as having access to government policy-making circles.

Based on interviews with Argentine industrial executives conducted during the military government of Levingston and, later, Lanusse (September 1970 to June 1971), the authors describe and analyze responses of the executives toward several components of political action: direct versus indirect political action, political routes to problem solving, political efficacy, and finally, the extent to which industrialists differentiate between political events having broad (that is, industry-wide) as opposed to narrow (that is, firm-specific) consequences.[1]

Our objective in this chapter is to gain insight into the following questions of political concern: (1) the forms of political activity characteristic of the Argentine executive; (2) the routes to problem solving utilized by Argentine executives in terms of their respective firms and on an industry-wide basis; (3) the types of issue areas that the executives feel they are most successful in influencing political decision-making; and (4) how executives' perceptions of political divisions affecting the wider society are influenced by their narrower personal interests. In other words, our objective is to understand the extent to which industrialists differentiate between regime policies that may have beneficial consequences for their particular firms but not necessarily for society as a whole.

Recent Argentine political history provides us with a variety of different types of regimes that especially lend themselves to comparative study. Between 1945 and 1955 Argentine was ruled by a nationalist-populist regime under the leadership of Juan Peron; between 1956 and 1966, conservative military regimes alternated with moderate radical parliamentary governments; and from 1966 to 1970, Argentina was ruled by a corporatist-oriented military dictatorship. By comparing industrialists' perceptions toward past and present Argentine political experiences (that include a variety of regimes and policies) we may be able to untangle some of the seeming incongruities in the behavior of the Argentine political system. What may, for example, appear as irrational on the macropolitical level may, in fact, mask the rational behavior of particular subsystem groups pursuing their individual self-interests (that is, suboptimization).

---

[1] The literature discussing industrialization and the role of industrialists in the Argentine economic and political system is numerous but uneven in quality. See John Freels, *El Sector Industrial en la Politica Nacional* (Editorial Universitaria de Buenos Aires: Buenos Aires, 1970) ; Thomas R. Fillol, *Social Factors in Economic Development: The Argentine Case* (Cambridge, The MIT Press, 1961) ; Thomas C. Cochran and Ruben E. Reina, *Entrepreneurship in Argentine Culture* (University of Pennsylvania Press, Philadelphia, 1962) ; Jose Luis Imaz, *Los Que Mandan* (EUDEBA: Buenos Aires, 1969) ; Mario S. Brodersohn, *Estrategias de industrializacion para la Argentina* (Editorial del Instituto: Buenos Aires, 1970) ; Ismael Vinas and Eugenio Gastiazoro, *Economia y dependencia* (Carlos Perez, editor: Buenos Aires, 1968) ; Adolfo Dorfman, *Historia de la industria Argentina* (Solar/Hachette: Buenos Aires, 1970).

In the final section of the paper we will compare the responses of foreign and national executives. Continuing previous research, we will assess the extent to which conclusions reached concerning the Argentine executive in general are modified when we control for the fact that a respondent is an executive official of a foreign as opposed to a nationally owned firm.[2]

As background for discussion of the questions posed at the outset of this chapter, we will present a demographic portrait of the respondents in our study. As will be seen, they represent a distinct subset of the general Argentine population.

A POLITICAL PROFILE OF ARGENTINE INDUSTRIAL EXECUTIVES

Although almost half (48 percent) of the executives interviewed could be classified as single-sector participants (that is, limited to firm and/or industry-specific activity), a substantial segment (35 percent) are involved in a multisector web of economic activity; commerce, finance, agriculture, real estate and insurance. The extent of multisector activity suggests the presence of a core of individuals with economy-wide perceptions, interests, and activities that extend beyond the operations of the particular firms in which they are employed. One possible effect of the multisector core is that they may form a network of overlapping group memberships that could serve as a bridge between economic isolates (single-sector participants) linking their varied interests to form a single, homogeneous class outlook. As the following discussion will point out, this type of multisector activity is not limited to strictly economic concerns.

In the area of overt political activity, approximately one-fifth (21.4 percent) of the executives occupied public office. This low proportion suggests that most executives prefer to occupy a less-visible role relative to political activity. Among the more overt political activists, the pattern of officeholding is fairly clear cut; they tend to concentrate at the upper levels of the political hierarchy: 37.5 percent were ministers, cabinet advisers, or ministerial sub-secretaries. Few held low level or local public offices, and none were members of Parliament. Overt congressional activity apparently held less appeal as a political activity than higher level executive positions. This may be a result of the relative weakness of local government and congress in comparison with the powers available to executive authorities. In any event, it is apparent that, while most executives "specialize"in economic activities, there is a substantial number who, by their direct political participation, provide a potential level for the exertion of influence upon the political system.

On a less visible basis, the majority of executives are active within their respective industrialists' associations. Almost two-thirds (63.4 percent) are members of an associaion and more than half (56.3) claim to have held office

---

[2] See our preceding essay for a discussion of our methodology.

in the association or attended meetings. The differential participation in "private-economic" as opposed to "public-political" office suggests that most industrialists may view political activity from the perspective of their particular industrial enterprise. Thus, they may be more concerned with improving the position of their firm within their industry over and against any interest in fashioning a national economic policy that accommodates a variety of competing and potentially conflicting economic sectors.

While the preceding data provide some insight into points of *potential* access to decision making (that is, through public office or association membership), it provides only a partial insight into the *actual* decision-making process. The latter question is more directly addressed through data which focus on the actual routes to problem solving, that executives follow in seeking solutions at both the firm and industry-wide level. It is the difference between the potential and the actual routes to problem solving that is our central concern.

ROUTES TO PROBLEM SOLVING

In this analysis, the "routes to problem solving" are defined in terms of individuals or groups that may serve as a vehicle for the executive to seek a solution to a problem confronting either his firm or his industry.[3] The data in Table 1 refer to the frequency with which alternative routes were utilized in problem-solving situations. In cases involving either the firm or the industry, a clear pattern of interaction is evidenced.

Industrial executives facing problems within the *firm* are more likely to turn to their industrial association or public officials than to follow any other route to resolve problems. As Part A of Table 1 indicates, almost one-half (46.4 percent) of the executives frequently contact industrial associations when they have problems to solve. The next most frequent route to problem solving utilized by industrial executives is public officials (27.7 percent). Contrary to popular notions, the clergy and military are not viewed as influential or capable of solving the kinds of problems that face industrialists. In both instances, the respondents indicate almost no interaction with these groups in problem-solving situations. The same can be said relative to political leaders and political parties. This latter finding is, however, not surprising given the nature of the existing governmental system in Argentina. Within the present authoritarian context, bureaucratic and associational politics appear to be the major routes to problem solving. It is interesting to note in this regard that less than 10 percent of the industrialists frequently

---

[3] The questions asked the respondents were as follows:

1. FIRM. "In the daily operations of your firm, when there are problems that require outside assistance, do you contact (alternatives presented in Table 1a)?"
2. INDUSTRY. "When the industry to which your firm is related faces problems that it cannot resolve internally, do you contact (alternatives presented in Table 1b)?"

TABLE 1

Routes to Problem Solving in Firm and Industry (in Percent)

Route to Problem Solving	a. Degree of Interaction: Firm		
	Great Deal	Seldom	Never
Trade Unions	9.8	35.7	50.9
Entrepreneurial associations	46.4	37.5	13.4
Political leaders	0.9	11.6	83.0
Political parties	0.9	4.5	90.2
Military	2.7	12.5	81.3
Clergy	0	3.6	90.2
Public officials	27.7	33.9	33.9
Other	10.7	5.4	19.6

Route to Problem Solving	b. Degree of Interaction: Industry		
	Great Deal	Seldom	Never
Trade Unions	6.3	33.9	38.4
Entrepreneurial associations	45.5	19.6	13.4
Political leaders	1.8	14.3	62.5
Political parties	0.9	6.3	69.6
Military	3.6	11.6	62.5
Clergy	0.9	1.8	75.9
Public officials	36.6	20.5	22.3
Other	7.1	4.5	17.0

contact the trade unions when the firm has any problems. This may be the result of the closer relationships and common economic interests that industrialists have with their industrial colleagues ("class solidarity"). The industrialists' long term effort to form a cooperative labor movement led by management-oriented labor leaders apparently has been successful only in a limited number of cases.

The results reported in Part B of Table 1 show a strikingly similar pattern when the question is directed toward problem solving at the industry-wide level. In fact, when the alternative routes are ranked with respect to the "Great Deal" response option, a comparison of the ranks under parts A and B results in a perfect rank-order correlation.[4] Albeit there are some discrepancies when the "seldom" and "never" responses are compared, the conclusions reached vis-a-vis problem solving at the industry level mirror those

[4] We used Kendall's rank-order correlation coefficient (TAU), corrected for ties, as our measure of agreement between ranks. See Hubert M. Blalock, Jr., *Social Statistics* (New York: cGraw-Hill Book Company, 1960), pp. 319–321.

discussed with respect to the firm. In both cases, there appear to be two distinct possibilities for problem solving.

1. A two-step process, whereby industrialists come together in their association to form a consensual body followed by the exertion of associational pressure upon the government.

2. Direct access to public officials, using personal influence to obtain favorable policy decisions.

The data suggest that these two general approaches are applicable at both the firm and industry-wide level. Given these general options, the next logical question concerns the extent to which the political activity of the executives is effective in producing desired policy decisions (such as providing solutions to problems). That is, how do the executives perceive their political effectiveness relative to specific policy areas?

POLITICAL EFFICACY AND PUBLIC POLICY

As the foregoing discussion has pointed out, industrialists have been active in their associations and, to a lesser degree, involved in politics. The question is how effective do the industrialists believe their activities have been in shaping public policy? The modal response of the industrial elite in the six issue areas that were probed (taxes, public works, government subsidies, labor laws, protection of property, and protection of national industry) was partial or moderate success (see Table 2). Overwhelming majorities in all issue areas

TABLE 2
(in Percent)

	Efficacy		
Issue Area	Success	Partial or Moderate Success	Failure
Taxes	3.6	66.1	25.9
Public works	19.6	67.0	6.3
Subsidies	8.0	62.5	13.4
Labor laws	16.1	54.5	22.3
Protect property	33.0	54.5	6.3
Protect national industry	25.9	63.4	4.5

felt that industrialists' campaigns to shape public policy in these key areas had been completely successful or partially successful.[5] Only in two issue

---

[5] For an alternative viewpoint see John Freels, op. cit., p. 130. The reader will note that our data focus on specific issue areas while Freels discusses efficacy in a nonspecific context.

areas—taxes (25.9 percent) and labors laws (22.3 percent)—did one find over one-fifth of the industrialists claiming that their campaigns were complete failures. The areas in which the *smallest* percentage of industrialists felt that their campaigns were failures were public works (6.3 percent), protection of private property (6.3 percent), and protection of national industry (4.5 percent), issues that affect the very survival as well as growth of the private sector. At the other extreme, the issue areas in which complete success was perceived in substantial proportion were protection of private property (33 percent), protection of national industry (25.9 percent), and public works (19.6 percent). The industrialists felt that they had been fairly effective in influencing government policy, especially in those areas affecting the foundations or basic principles of their economic enterprises, and somewhat less influential in shaping policy in the areas of labor-management relations.

Despite (or perhaps because of) the military dictatorship, the industrial elite has had few problems in influencing policy in crucial issue areas. The absence of parties, elections, and congress is more than counterweighted by the existence of industrial associations and accessible public officials. The industrialists, however, have not been able to contain the powerful trade-union movement, the General Confederation of Labor (CGT) and its capacity to launch militant general strikes. Neither the military nor the industrialists have been capable of imposing the kind of "labor peace" which their counterparts in Brazil have achieved. On the contrary, the massive labor uprisings in the interior, the frequent general strikes, and the growing sympathy among labor rank and file for revolutionary socialist labor leaders and urban guerrillas has generated much concern among the industrialists as well as the military—threatening their economic as well as political hegemony.[6] While the industrialists have been rather effective in influencing public policy, the government has become increasingly ineffective in controlling the labor force. The growth of mass disaffection and the need to channel it into less abrasive channels and not elite disaffection with the military per se is behind the moves by the government to return the parties to legality and to call elections. It may be for the same reasons that the industrial executives, while praising the Brazilian experience, find it necessary in Argentina to call for elections rather than risk a civil war.

ROLE OF GOVERNMENT AND POLITICAL REPRESENTATION

Government-promoted industrialization was a prominent factor in Argentine economic development, especially in the post-World War II period. When the Argentine executives were asked to identify the most favorable period for the development of industries, the first choice of the industrialists was the

---

[6] For a discussion of the major urban uprising in Cordoba, see "Otro Mayo Argentino" Cuadernos de Marcha, No. 27, Julio, 1969 (Uruguay); Francisco Delich, *Crisis y protesta social Cordoba, Mayo de 1969* (Ediciones Signos: Buenos Aires, 1970); for a discussion of the growth of nationalism see *Panorama*, May 18–24, 1971.

Peronist period of 1945 to 1955—the period during which the state was most active in the promotion of industry (see Table 3). Despite the opposition of the economic elite toward the Peronist government, especially the large industrial enterprises, their perception of political reality was not clouded by their personal preferences. Hence, while most perceived the period of 1945 to 1955 as the most favorable for the development of industries, a substantial plurality of industrialists (41.1 percent) perceived the Ongania dictatorship (1966 to 1970) as the most favorable to their particular firm. In other words, the industrialists clearly distinguish between state policies favorable to industry and policies favoring particularistic interests—suggesting a substantial degree of political sophistication and rationality.[7]

TABLE 3
Industrial Development and Political Regime (in Percent)

Unit of Analysis	Prior to 1945	1945– 1955	1956– 1958	1958– 1962	1963– 1966	1966– 1970	All Periods are same	Other Combi- ations
Industry	11.6	29.5	3.6	14.3	2.7	22.3	2.7	10.7
Firm	9.8	8.9	3.6	16.1	5.4	41.1	5.4	6.3

The question: "In which period did industry (or your firm) benefit most?"

When assessing their relationship to the state or, more specifically, the role of government in economic development, the industrial elite reject both the laissez-faire liberal view of government as well as the heavily statist or "socialist" approach. Over half the respondents favored an "involved state, selective intervention to aid private firms" as compared to less than 10 percent (8.9 percent) who preferred a government confined to playing the role of merely maintaining order and 1.8 percent who favored the state's owning and directing basic industries. As other studies have shown, the Latin American industrialists are for public "welfare" when it favors their class interests.[8] The liberal rhetoric—the noninterventionist state—is mainly directed against governmental programs that redistribute income to the working and salaried classes.

Given the substantial role that the industrial elite assigns to government in the economy, it is important to determine whether the industrial elite felt adequately represented in the government. Despite the rightist proelite image of the government, almost two-thirds (64.3 percent) of the industrialists did not feel adequately represented in the government, and less than one-fourth

[7] For an alternative viewpoint stressing non-rational behavior see Thomas C. Cochran and Ruben Reina, *Entrepreneurship in Argentine Culture* (Philadelphia: University of Pennsylvania Press, 1962).

[8] Fernando H. Cardoso, "The Industrial Elite," in Seymour Martin Lipset and Aldo Solari (eds.), *Elites in Latin America* (New York: Oxford University Press, 1967), pp. 94–114.

(22.3 percent) felt adequately represented. This suggests that while the military during the Ongania presidency was originally perceived as favorable to industry, the subsequent period of political and social instability apparently had a negative impact on the industrialists' perceptions. In followup questions attempting to explore the possible reasons for this perception, the responses appear somewhat contradictory: the most common response (33.9 percent) to the question of why the industrialists were not represented was that citizens had no voice or vote. When asked under what circumstances they would feel represented in the government the overwhelming majority (62.5 percent) preferred political parties and a congress. Thus, it would appear that the industrial elite are alienated democrats, opposed to a military dictatorship and favoring a representative democracy. This, however, is too simple a viewpoint. The commitment to democratic forms of representation must be set against recent political experiences in Argentina and Brazil. As we pointed out earlier, the industrial elite perceived the military dictatorship of 1966 to 1970 as having the most favorable economic policies in terms of their firm. This proauthoritarian political posture is underscored by the favorable responses of the executives toward the current Brazilian politicoeconomic experience. Two-thirds were completely favorable or favorable with some criticism. Only 10.7 percent completely rejected the Brazilian dictatorship's political-economic approach—hardly an indication of great democratic commitment. One possible explanation is that the Argentine industrialists, while preferring a stable elitist "developmental" dictatorship such as they had in Argentina between 1966 and 1970, and as exists in Brazil presently, would accept a parliamentary democracy over an *unstable* dictatorship under attack from the trade unions and the urban guerrillas and unable to meet the industrialists' needs.

FOREIGN VERSUS NATIONAL EXECUTIVES: AN OVERVIEW

The classification of firms into national and foreign was based on two main criteria: (1) identification by a panel of economists (CONADE)[9] of foreign/ national firms; and (2) responses to a question concerning the presence or absence of foreign investment in their firm. Foreign firms were those identified as foreign by CONADE and which stated that they had foreign investment in their firm. In this final step we obtained 47 national and 41 foreign firms (87.5 percent of the 112 respondents contained in the preceding analysis).

Table 4 compares in summary form the major background factors of national and foreign executives. As can be seen, they are quite similar in their background characteristics. Both came from middle or upper class backgrounds although a higher percentage of nationals[9] were sons of professionals. In terms of education, a higher percentage of foreigns[9] attended private

[9] "Nationals" refers to executives employed by national firms and "foreigns" refers to executives employed by foreign controlled firms.

TABLE 4

Foreign versus National Executives: An Overview (Percent)

	Nationals	Foreigns
Sons of businessmen, executives, industrialists, or landowners	46.8	41.5
Sons of professionals	25.5	36.6
Sons of small businessmen and artisans	6.4	4.9
From working class and peasantry	2.1	2.4
Private prep school	19.1	29.3
Some university education	72.3	87.8
From commercial secondary school	36.2	29.3
Began as employees	42.6	41.5
Began as professionals	23.4	31.7
Began as owners	12.8	7.3
Previous positions were important	66.0	68.3
Modal ages	46 to 50 yrs	41 to 45 yrs
Modal age arriving at present job	36 to 40 yrs	41 to 45 yrs

preparatory school and received some university education, while the nationals were slightly more likely to have attended a commercial secondary school. Both, however, have tended to have at least some university education. For both entry into the firm began at the employee level, though a substantial proportion began at the professional level. Slightly more nationals began as owners (12.8 percent) than did the foreign (7.3 percent). Subclassifying for nationals and foreigns does not alter greatly the conclusions we presented regarding the Argentine executive as a whole; vis-à-vis their general background characteristics.

POLITICAL ACTIVITY: FOREIGN VERSUS NATIONALS

Table 5 makes clear that the modal tendency for both groups is informal political activity. Less than 25 percent in both groups have held a political office of any kind. When, however, we analyze the distributions of offices *within* the group of officeholders (past and present) a substantial difference between the two groups is evident. Almost three times (55.4 percent) as many foreign officeholders as nationals (19.7 percent) have held positions as either ministers, cabinet advisors, or ministerial subsecretaries. Although both groups tend towards indirect political activity, among those who have held office, the foreign executive participates at a higher level.

If one accepts the assumption that access to high political office is positively correlated with influence over public policy, then the presence of a higher

TABLE 5
Political Activity: Foreign versus National (Percent)

	National	Foreign
Have held public office	21.3	22
Public office held		
Minister	2.1	4.9
Cabinet advisor	0.0	4.9
Subsecretary	2.1	2.4
Employee	4.3	2.4
Local government	2.1	0.0
Professional (industrial advisor)	8.5	2.4
Public enterprise official	2.1	4.9
No position	76.6	78.0

proportion of foreign employed executives in high government posts suggests that they may wield somewhat more influence over government policy than their national counterparts. In order to assess the credibility of this assumption, we repeated the analysis of routes to problem solving, controlling for foreign and national firms.

ROUTES TO PROBLEM SOLVING: FOREIGN VERSUS NATIONAL

A comparison of the two groups in parts A and B of Table 6 reveals several distinct patterns. Although both groups rely upon the industrial associations when confronted with problems endemic to the firm, they are not in agreement relative to alternative routes to problem solving. National executives rely almost exclusively upon the industrial associations (51.8 percent) with only minor reference to interaction with public officials (17 percent). Foreign executives, while citing the industrial association as the primary route (46.3 percent), place much more emphasis upon interaction with public officials. Thirty-nine percent cite public officials as a viable route to problem solving when the firm is involved.

Table 6, part B indicates a clearer differentiation between nationals and foreign executives concerning problems that have industry-wide implications. In this comparison, nationals were consistent in their responses with the majority (51.1 percent), citing the industrial association as the main route to problem solving vis-à-vis industry-wide problems. Less than one-third cite public officials as a likely alternative route. Conversely, foreign executives cite public officials as the most viable route to problem solving (41.5 percent), and cite the industrial association as the most likely alternative—a clear reversal of their response to problem solving when it affects the firm. Thus,

TABLE 6
Routes to Problem Solving in Firm and Industry (in Percent)

a. Degree of Interaction: Firm

Route to Problem Solving	Great Deal		Seldom		Never	
	Nationals	Foreigns	Nationals	Foreigns	Nationals	Foreigns
Trade unions	8.5	9.8	40.4	36.6	48.9	51.2
Entrepreneurial associations	51.1	46.3	40.4	34.1	6.4	19.5
Political leaders	2.1	0.0	10.6	9.8	85.1	85.4
Political parties	2.1	0.0	2.1	4.9	93.6	90.2
Military	4.3	2.4	8.5	17.1	85.1	78.0
Clergy	0.0	0.0	0.0	7.3	93.6	87.8
Public officials	17.0	39.0	42.6	34.1	38.3	26.8
Other	12.8	9.8	8.5	2.4	19.1	14.6

b. Degree of Interaction: Industry

Route to Problem Solving	Great Deal		Seldom		Never	
	Nationals	Foreigns	Nationals	Foreigns	Nationals	Foreigns
Trade unions	6.4	2.4	36.2	31.7	31.9	43.9
Entrepreneurial associations	55.3	31.7	8.5	31.7	10.6	14.6
Political leaders	2.1	2.4	14.9	12.2	57.4	63.4
Political parties	2.1	0.0	4.3	9.8	66.0	65.9
Military	4.3	2.4	12.8	14.6	57.4	58.5
Clergy	0.0	2.4	2.1	2.4	72.3	73.2
Public officials	31.9	41.5	21.3	19.5	21.3	19.5
Other	10.6	4.9	6.4	4.9	17.0	7.3

while the nationals rely upon the industrial associations for solving problems at both the firm and industry-wide levels, the foreign executives clearly distinguish between the two levels, citing interaction with public officials as the most effective way of dealing with industry-wide problems. It should be pointed out, however, that consistent with the previous analysis, neither of the two groups emphasize interaction with political leaders, political parties, the military, or clergy as important routes to problem solving at either the firm or industry-wide level.

Our initial discussion suggested two possible approaches to problem solving—one involving interest articulation through associational groups, the other involving direct influence of public officials. In our breakdown of national and foreign industrial executives we found that contrasting political styles were associated with different industrial subgroups. Specifically, the foreign executives tended toward direct contact with public officials while the nationals tended to work through the industrial associations.

One determinant of different political styles might be located in our previous discussion of differential participation in the higher echelons of government. The greater frequency of interchange between foreign executives and higher government officials may lead to greater contact and interchange of views concerning matters affecting the interests of the foreign industrial community. This suggests that foreign firms may adopt the strategy of recruiting executives from among the more politically active segments of the managerial class.

When we extend the analysis to the question of specific issue areas where the respondents felt most effective (that is, have been the most successful in influencing policy), there are also distinct differences between the two groups. Table 7 summarizes these results. Looking only at the extreme categories of "success" and "failure," the nationals indicate their greatest success in the area of protecting property (34 percent), followed by public works (27.7 percent). Their greatest perceived failure is in the area of taxation (21.3 percent). While the foreign executives share the negative perception in taxation (24.4 percent), they express an equally negative perception of their influence in the area of labor laws. Contrary to the nationals, they feel that they have been most successful in efforts to protect national industry (31.7 percent); nearly double the percentage that expressed this same view among the nationals.

Even though these differences exist, it should be noted that the modal response of both groups was the perception of total or partial success in affecting policy across the set of issue areas. According to our data, national executives are no more or less effective in policy areas than the foreign executives despite the differing political routes chosen to influence policy.

Comparative analysis does point out, however, that the distinction between foreign and national firms reveals a certain amount of intra-executive group variance towards questions of political efficacy.

TABLE 7
Efficacy (in Percent)

Issue Areas	Success		Partial or Moderate Success		Failure	
	Nationals	Foreigns	Nationals	Foreigns	Nationals	Foreigns
Taxes	4.3	4.9	74.5	63.4	21.3	24.4
Public works	27.7	14.6	65.9	68.3	4.3	7.3
Subsidies	8.5	12.2	63.9	56.1	12.8	12.2
Labor laws	17.0	14.6	63.8	46.4	19.1	24.4
Protect property	34.0	19.5	55.3	68.3	10.6	2.4
Protect national industry	17.0	31.7	72.3	56.1	8.5	0.0

ROLE OF GOVERNMENT AND POLITICAL REPRESENTATION: FOREIGN VERSUS NATIONAL EXECUTIVES

In our initial analysis of industrialists, we found that the modal tendency was to regard the nationalist-Peronist period (1945 to 1955) as the most favorable for the *development of industry*. When, however, we refined our analysis to separate national and foreign executives, we found that the modal tendency for nationals was still the 1945 to 1955 period, but for the foreign executives it was the 1966 to 1970 period. The national and the foreign executives have the same modal tendency regarding the most propitious time for the development of their firms (the 1966 to 1970 period). This suggests that while differing over their interpretation of the historic role of Peronism and the Peronist promotion of industry, these differences have appeared to be less important regarding contemporary Argentine industrial development. Both groups share a high regard for the liberal economic policies of the Ongania military regime in promoting the growth of their firms.

The two groups of executives share a similar view of the role of government in economic development. A near majority (48.9 percent) of the nationals and a clear majority (56.1 percent) of the foreigns favor an "involved state, selective intervention to aid private firms." The other two alternatives, "maintaining order" and "state ownership of private industry," did not have much support.

POLITICAL REPRESENTATION AND INDUSTRIALISTS

The conclusions reached in our previous analysis of industrialists' attitudes toward representation were not altered: a majority of both national and foreign industrialists did not feel adequately represented. While both groups share the feeling of inadequate representation, they differ markedly in their choice of alternatives; about 70 percent of the nationals prefer the institutions of parliamentary democracy compared to less than 45 percent of the foreign executives. Conversely, the foreign executives felt a greater affinity for the authoritarian-corporatist modal of government which characterizes Brazil than did the national executives: almost two-thirds of the foreign executives favored the Brazilian approach as opposed to 40 percent of the nationals. None of the foreign executives completely rejected the Brazilian approach compared to six percent of the nationals.[10]

CONCLUSION

Nondemocratic forms of representation evoke substantial support from the industrial elite over the short run especially as a bulwark of private property.

---

[10] To probe this last point, we asked those who felt inadequately represented to cite their reasons. Over one fifth of the nationals (21.3 percent) stated that the "military are incompetent to develop economic policies"—only 2.4 percent of the foreign executives expressed this viewpoint.

TABLE 8
Industrial Development and Political Regime (in Percent)

Unit of Analysis		Prior to 1945	1945–1955	1956–1958	1958–1962	1963–1966	1966–1970	All periods the same	Other Combinations
Industry	Nationals	12.8	29.8	2.1	14.9	0.0	21.3	6.4	12.8
	Foreigns	14.6	14.6	4.9	12.2	7.3	31.7	0.0	12.2
Firm	Nationals	6.4	4.3	2.1	25.5	6.4	36.2	10.6	4.3
	Foreigns	12.2	7.3	7.3	9.8	4.9	51.2	2.4	4.9

Certain negative effects of nondemocratic rule, however, appeared to have precipitated a decline of support among the industrial elite: social unrest and political instability coupled with inflation led to the "de-legitimization" of the regime. The regimes failure to develop successful economic and social policies crystallized strong mass opposition. The result was the disaffection of the regime. The regime's failure to develop successful economic and social for new political formulas which would bring about a modicum of political security without making serious inroads on private property.[11] The quest for security and development however has not uniformly led toward support of parliamentary politics. Substantial sectors of the industral elite, especially executives of foreign firms, are impressed by the ultraauthoritarian Brazilian developmental model. One executive euphorically described Brazil as an "industrial palace." Nondemocratic forms of representation appear acceptable to the industrial elite as long as they effectively perform the practical tasks of social control and government promotion of industrial opportunities. The notion of the economic elites as upholders of democratic values against the irrational and antidemocratic demands of the masses hardly fits with our discussion of Argentine industrialists. Their concerns are primarily socio-economic policy; different forms of political representation are considered in relationship with their perceived capacity to meet the specific needs of the industrial elite. The notion that private enterprise is a necessary prerequisite for democracy is largely unfounded.

The critical considerations for the industrialists are less "ideological"— less concerned with parliamentary democracy per se—and more often directed toward the issues of effective rule and accessibility. This "pragmatic" outlook suggests that for Argentine industrialists political forms of representation are variable, depending on their capacity to generate the types of policy outputs favoring their economic interests.

In times of stress and class conflict the problematic nature of political institutions can lead to rapid shifts toward, as well as away from, nondemocratic forms of representation. In present circumstances the industrial elites, as well as their antagonists among the industrial working class, may choose non-democratic forms of representation (corporatist regimes in one case and the "dictatorship of the proletariat" in the other) as the most effective means for securing their basic interests. In raising the issue of nondemocratic representation, we are pointing to the need for more empirical research in an area that is too often clouded by purely normative and ideological pronouncements.

---

[11] The corporatist Ongania regime was eventually replaced and the current "President," General Lanusse, has legalized the nonrevolutionary political parties and promised elections for March 1973.

3

The United States
and Latin America

7

James Petras & Robert LaPorte, Jr. | U.S. Response to Economic Nationalism in Chile

INTRODUCTION: THE WORLD CONTEXT OF ECONOMIC NATIONALISM

Economic nationalism is not a new topic in international affairs. Its oldest manifestation might be the first tariff barrier established to protect a particular nation's industry. In fact, an explanation of the rise of U.S. nationalism would include the desires of postindependence American capitalists to restrain and limit "outsider" influence over colonial American markets and resources. Hamilton's "Report on the Subject of Manufactures" was directed at promoting U.S. industrial expansion by limiting the presence of foreign industrial products from the more "advanced" European countries.

Similarly, what is considered to be a modern manifestation of economic nationalism—the nationalization and expropriation of foreign commercial/industrial holdings—is a predictable pattern of behavior with several longstanding precedents among developing countries. The measures adopted by the Soviet and Mexican revolutionary governments between the two world wars are the best known of several examples.

Since World War II, Third World nations have been concerned with the problem of control over the decisions affecting their political and economic destinies. Conflicts and problems have arisen because of the growth of complex technology and the monopolization by the industrialized nations of technology, managerial expertise and capital to exploit natural resources. Third

World leaders have come to perceive their partnership with multinational corporations as an asymmetrical relationship that has not been beneficial. Some officials feel that no exploitation of natural resources is better than foreign exploitation.

It is the intent of this work to examine economic nationalism in Latin America, with particular emphasis on Chile. The purpose is to ascertain the effects of economic nationalism on the foreign policy of the hemisphere's most powerful nation, the United States. The reaction of the United States to the Chilean decision to control all major foreign economic enterprises will condition future U.S.-Chilean relations. U.S. policies affecting Chile will have broad implications regarding U.S.-Latin American relations in the 1970s as well as the direction and scope of economic nationalism in Latin America. The critical nature of U.S.-Chilean relations is undeniable. U.S. policy statements and measures suggest that the problem is not based on transitory or peripheral issues. The spillover effects of the U.S. reaction will be felt in the capitals of almost all Latin American nations, whether or not they wish to be drawn into the conflict.

The problem of U.S.-Chilean relations can best be understood by examining it from several complementary perspectives. Under the following set of assumptions we proceed with our discussion.

1. To understand economic nationalism in Chile, the issue must be placed in the wider context of political developments in the rest of Latin America.

2. The sources of U.S. policy regarding the Chilean case are varied, in some cases reinforcing, in others conflicting with each other.

3. United States policy options are considered within a cost-benefit analysis framework with ideological, Cold War overtones, and decisions are not the result of irrational, misinformed, or misunderstood individuals.

4. The direction of U.S.-Chilean relations has broader implications for hemispheric relations in the 1970s.[1]

ECONOMIC NATIONALISM IN LATIN AMERICA AND CHILE

INTRODUCTION TO THE PROBLEM AND ISSUES. The decolonization process which was part of the 19th century revolutionary movements of Latin America was largely concerned with political independence not economic nationalism. Tariff barriers were nonexistent, partly because of the laissez-faire outlook of the dominant agrocommercial elite. Manifestations of

[1] Data for this article were derived from a number of sources, including unstructured interviews with U.S. Department of State, Treasury, and Agency for International Development officials; Congressional (Senate and House) officials; special reports and documents from the Department of State, A.I.D., Department of Treasury, Inter-American Development Bank, World Bank, Export-Import Bank, Congressional hearings and reports; and content analysis of both U.S. and Chilean newspapers and journals.

economic nationalism were sporadic and confined to particular countries such as Paraguay, which failed to sustain them. It was not until the twentieth century that Latin America witnessed large-scale nationalizations and expropriations of foreign holdings as part of the revolutionary experience of Mexico—a set of actions that triggered an extremely hostile reaction in the United States. Apart from Mexican experience, only one other Latin American country, Cuba, has dared to invoke the wrath of the United States by nationalizing major holdings, resulting in U.S.-imposed economic sanctions throughout the hemisphere. The historical examples of the Mexican and Cuban experiences are the reference points in viewing contemporary Latin American economic nationalism.

Economic nationalism may be defined as a process by which a particular political system attempts to assert public or private control over economic resource exploitation within its geographical boundaries. It is a process of substituting national for foreign or multinational economic control of domestic resources.[2] As such it takes many forms, depending upon the resource base of the particular political system as well as the intensity of commitment and political purpose of the political leadership. Internal policies or the ideological posture assumed toward internal issues may have played a role but have not been the major variables influencing nationalistic actions that can be illustrated by recent Latin American experiences. A great variety of regimes with differing approaches to internal problems have adopted nationalist measures. The modernizing Peruvian junta nationalized the International Petroleum Corporation (IPC) in 1968. The conservative Ecuadorian government seized U.S. fishing boats that violated its 200 mile limit (an action to exert control over maritime resources). The rightist as well as the populist Bolivian juntas (under Ovando, and later Torres) nationalized Gulf Corporation assets (1969) and a number of other U.S. owned mining enterprises. In Colombia, Rojas Pinilla running on a militant nationalist-populist platform swept the capital city of Bogota and only lost by a narrow 50,000 votes, largely reported from isolated rural areas and purportedly of questionable validity. As a result, rightist President Pastrana has signed the Andean pact restricting foreign investment. In Argentina, the Peronist labor unions have pressured the military to adopt nationalist policies (buy Argentine campaigns, takeover of the Swift packing house, abstention on the China question in the United Nations, friendship agreements with the Allende government and so on). In addition, the Andean countries have signed an investment code which purports to restrict areas and terms of foreign investment. The probusiness Social Christian COPEI government of Venezuela has passed a law leading to the gradual expropriation of all major

[2] This definition is purposively broad to include *all* economic activity and resources, although our principal concern is with *newer forms* of nationalism (for example, nationalization and expropriation of foreign economic holdings) as opposed to *older forms* (e.g., tariff establishment, commercial regulations, and taxation policies).

oil resources and has forced the major oil companies operating in Venezuela to accept more government control.[3] The recent measures taken by the social-ist government of Chile in nationalizing the Anaconda and Kennecott mining properties emerge from, and are, a logical extension of a pattern followed throughout the region by regimes with significant social, political, and economic differences from the Chilean government. Rather than view the Chilean government's policies in terms of sinister ideological moves engi-neered by "the Marxists," the Chilean government's action should be seen as part of the region's response to deep-seated national needs to better direct and control national resources. Nationalism in Latin America today does not reflect the action of a single nation; it is a Latin American phenomenon with both short and long range impact and implications for the international economy and the industrialized nations of both East and West.

The Chilean decision to nationalize U.S. property is the most recent direct confrontation with U.S. business interests and the most significant challenge to U.S. policy since the Cuban revolution. What happens to U.S.-Chilean relations as a result of the struggle over the Chilean copper industry will have repercussions for U.S.-Latin American relations during the rest of the decade. The Chilean situation can be viewed as a "test" of U.S. commitment in defending U.S. investors or as an "opportunity" to develop a new set of relationships with nations in Latin America as well as the rest of the world. U.S.-Chilean relations provide a convenient means by which to view the continuation of an expansionist policy or the development of a postimperial foreign policy.

PRE-ALLENDE CHILE AND THE UNITED STATES. During the Alliance for Progress, the United States had presented Chile as a "showcase" country —an example of what the Latin countries could do with U.S. technical and economic assistance.[4] Up to the end of the 1960s, Chile had the distinction of receiving the most U.S. aid per capita of any country in Latin America.[5] The rhetoric of the Chilean Christian Democratic government fit in nicely with the Alliance and its stated goal of a "democratic alternative" to Cuban-style development; Frei, then President, spoke of a "revolution in liberty." The Chilean example was to become an important propaganda weapon in

[3] It should be noted that Venezuela is not alone in this action since other members of OPEC (Organization of Petroleum Exporting Countries) are now beginning to dictate terms to oil companies rather than vice versa (see "Venezuela says Oil Concerns Want Imposed Price Settlement," New York Times, February 12, 1971; and "Oil Nations Seeking Role in Companies," New York Times, November 3, 1971; and "Six Persian Gulf Oil Nations Win Price Increase at Geneva Talks," New York Times, January 27, 1972.

[4] For a comprehensive, critical discussion and analysis of U.S. assistance to Chile, both pre-Alliance and for the first few years of the Alliance, see U.S. Congress, Senate Sub-committee on Foreign Aid Expenditures, Committee on Government Operations, U.S. Foreign Aid in Action: A Case Study, 89th Congress, 2nd Session, 1966, better known as the Gruening Report.

[5] Ibid.

U.S. efforts to wed Latin America to the effort to stem the spread of "Castro-communism."[6]

From the immediate post-World War II period through the Frei Administration (which ended in November 1970), political and economic relations between the United States and Chile were cordial and friendly, even though occasional tensions developed between the Chilean government and U.S. business interests. During this period of collaboration with the United States, Chile accumulated a debt to both U.S. public agencies (A.I.D. and the Export-Import Bank), and "international" banks IBRD and IDB—whose operating capital and loan assessment procedures are both scrutinized and controlled by the United States), of $2.23 billion.[7] This huge external debt coupled with the control of the vital copper industry by U.S. firms created a certain degree of tension and uneasiness in domestic Chilean politics even during the pre-Allende period. It was obvious to some observers that repayment of this debt would put a severe strain on Chile's development effort and divert needed resources out of the country. The Frei government was mortgaging the future for the sake of immediate political good will—which was not forthcoming in any case.

THE ALLENDE PERIOD AND THE UNITED STATES. With the election of Dr. Salvador Allende Gossens as President of Chile in September 1970, Chilean-U.S. relations entered a new phase. Almost all experienced political observers in Chile were aware of the fact that the United States was hostile to Allende. During the Presidential elections, the U.S. Ambassador preferred the rightist Alessandri but could have lived with the Christian Democrat Tomic. Hostility toward the new President was evident not only in the behavior of U.S. officials in Chile but also in the liberal press in the United States.[8]

U.S. rejection of the democratically elected Allende government has taken several forms, from public snubs to economic sanctions, all directed at expressing U.S. displeasure.

Another instance of symbolic opposition to the new regime in Chile is the general tone of U.S. statements that might be termed "fear mongering." By this we mean the use of various labels and symbols such as "communist-inspired" in reference to Allende's political philosophy and programs which,

[6] The attitude of U.S. policy makers, businessmen and academicians toward the Chilean Christian Democratic government during the 1960s is best expressed in a *Look* magazine editor's flowery and inaccurate account. See: Leonard Gross, *The Last Best Hope: Eduardo Frei and Chilean Democracy* (New York: Random House, 1967).

[7] This includes all sources. The total U.S. public debt is $960 million. While U.S. private debt is $64 million, total Chilean debt to the United States is around $1.024 billion. See: U.S. House of Representatives, Subcommittee on Inter-American Affairs, "Recent Developments in Chile," October 1971, Hearing, October 15, 1971, 92nd Congress, 1st Session, pp. 7–9.

[8] A *New York Times* editorial of September 6, 1970 contended that Allende's election was "a heavy blow at liberal democracy."

after many years of the Cold War, arouse certain images in the minds of both North and South Americans. The U.S. administration and press have chosen to play up and distort the Communist Party support of the Allende regime and to emphasize the Chilean President's Marxist credentials rather than his long-term commitment to democratic, electoral policies and support for humanitarian and social welfare causes. The image of Allende, developed and cultivated by various public and private statements, is one of a potential Communist dictator eager to employ authoritarian tactics to eliminate democracy in Chile.[9]

U.S. REACTION: ECONOMIC AND POLITICAL PRESSURES. President Nixon and other policy makers have repeatedly stated that the U.S. objective was to "have the kind of relationship with the Chilean government that it is prepared to have with us."[10] Charles Meyers, Assistant Secretary of State for Inter-American Affairs, has emphatically insisted that the U.S. government has taken a neutral position, refraining from any hostile acts. As has already been discussed above, U.S. policy makers have taken a number of symbolic measures indicating their opposition and hostility to the Allende government. More direct and serious actions have been taken to underscore U.S. displeasure toward Chile's democratically elected President. Short of an economic blockade, a number of economic measures designed to pressure the Chilean government have been adopted; thus far, U.S. policy makers have avoided the more extreme policies adopted vis-à-vis Cuba, that is, freezing of assets and other massive global pressures.

Economic pressure on Chile has taken the form of cutting U.S. and "international" lines of credit to the Allende government. Two examples of this response present themselves. Chile's small-loan application to the Export-Import Bank for the purchase of commercial passenger aircraft from Boeing (a U.S. firm) to be used for Chilean National Airlines was denied. As a result, the United States has forced Chile to consider alternative European producers, perhaps a minor inconvenience. United States representatives within the Inter-American Development Bank, reacting to threats to reduce or withhold U.S. funds to IDB because of its willingness to listen to Chilean requests for development loan funding, have "delayed" Chilean requests (which has the same effect as an overt denial). United States A.I.D. funds have not been either requested or suggested in the case of Chile since the end of the Frei regime.[11]

[9] According to the *New York Times*, "U.S. diplomats have officially cautioned Chilean officials . . . that the Government's plan to nationalize . . . could seriously damage relations between the two countries." February 3, 1971.

[10] State of the World Message of 1971.

[11] United States A.I.D. loans to Chile amounted to around $500 million with no new funds in the pipeline according to U.S. A.I.D. officials. According to an A.I.D. official, "the A.I.D. program under Frei was going down at the end—a mutual thing." Interview No. 1, U.S. A.I.D., October 20, 1971.

While cutting off loans and credits, U.S. officials insistently demand payments on loans accumulated by previous Chilean governments. The aim of U.S. policy makers is to pressure the Chilean government to meet U.S. corporate compensation demands.[12]

A third form of U.S. pressure on the Allende regime has been in the area of diplomatic relations between the United States and other Latin nations. This can be seen in U.S. relations with Chile's two neighbors, Peru and Bolivia. United States relations with Peru have improved considerably during 1971 with State Department officials' attributing the "change" to a shift in Peruvian politics from a nationalist to a more "open" position regarding foreign investment.[13] According to one State Department official, Peru was a "dirty word" two years ago; now that has changed. In Bolivia, the United States now has a new rightist regime that owes its existence in part to U.S. Air Force personnel who "aided" Colonel Hugo Banzer and his associates.[14] This regime can be counted upon to facilitate U.S. policy toward Chile. With Brazil the United States enjoys an almost "model" relationship.[15] Brazil considers Chile's experiment with democratic socialism to be a "threat" to its own aspirations for regional hegemony. Thus, the Brazilian government is actively supporting U.S. efforts to diplomatically "isolate" Chile in Latin America. Given Chile's dependence on meat and grain imports from Argentina,[16] a successful blockade in Latin America can have economic as well as political consequences over the short and long run.

THE COPPER ISSUE. The U.S. dispute with Chile over the copper issue must be viewed within this hostile atmosphere of U.S.-Chilean relations. The copper issue itself is not new—the Frei government felt compelled to begin to "Chileanize" copper—and the idea of nationalization of copper was no surprise to U.S. policy makers. Furthermore, the notion of uncompensated expropriation has precedent in other Latin contexts.[17] The reaction of the U.S. government toward Chile can best be understood through a discussion and analysis of the attitudes of congressmen, State Department and other Administration officials as well as policy advisers.

[12] Or, as one nationally syndicated column put it, ". . . keep Chile's feet to the fire." See Evans and Novak, "Rocky May Get State Department," *The Washington Post*, February 7, 1972.

[13] Interviews with U.S. Department of State officials, October 1971, Washington, D.C. This "change", however, did not mean a moderation in the Peruvian position regarding the I.P.C. case. The United States is permitting Peru to do what it will not allow Chile to do—namely, to expropriate without compensation.

[14] See *The Washington Post* reports of the coup on August 23 and 24, 1971.

[15] Interviews with U.S. Department of State officials, October 1971.

[16] Argentina's dependence upon the U.S.-controlled international financial institutions is revealed in the concessions that they made to receive an IMF loan in February 1972.

[17] The case of the I.P.C. in Peru, the land expropriations in Mexico and Bolivia.

SOURCES OF PRESENT U.S. POLICY TOWARD CHILE: THE INPUTS

An adequate description and analysis of U.S. policy requires an examination of several participating groups that directly and indirectly affect the decision-making process. These include two executive agencies (Treasury and State); the Congress (Senate and House committees and subcommittees and individual members); the "international" banks—including the Inter-American Development Bank (IDB), and the International Bank for Reconstruction and Development (the World Bank or IBRD); and the United States-owned institutions (the Export-Import Bank or EX-IM Bank).[18] The actions of the Chilean government must be considered part of the policy process since its behavior (both policy initiatives as well as its responses to U.S. policies trigger, in turn, further U.S. actions). In addition, the policy inputs of the U.S. business community—the individual firms (commercial and financial, as well as extractive and manufacturing) who do business or have financial investment or other economic ties with Chile or other Latin American countries—have very important consequences for U.S. policy. The Council on Foreign Affairs is included here since its input may be regarded as an informal expression of U.S. elite attitudes and opinions. These domestic and foreign, public and private organizations and personnel constitute the institutional framework for analysis.

THE U.S. DEPARTMENT OF STATE. On October 13, 1971, Secretary of State William P. Rogers stated:

> The Controller General of Chile announced his findings on October 11 that no compensation would be paid for the U.S. copper mining investments expropriated on July 16 except for modest amounts in the cases of two smaller properties.
>
> The United States Government is deeply disappointed and disturbed at this serious departure from accepted standards of international law. Under established principles of international law, the expropriation must be accompanied by reasonable provision for payment of just compensation. The United States had made clear to the Government of Chile its hope that a solution could be found on a reasonable and pragmatic basis consistent with international law.
>
> It appears that the major factor in the Controller General's decision with respect to the larger producers was the determination of September 28 of alleged "excess profits." The unprecedented retroactive application of the excess profits concept, which was not obligatory under the expropriation legislation adopted by the Chilean Congress, is particularly disquieting. The U.S. companies which are affected by this determination of the Chilean Government earned their profits in Chile in accordance

[18] The Export-Import Bank is directly controlled by the Treasury Department.

with Chilean law and under specific contractual agreements made directly with the Government of Chile. The excess profits deductions punish the companies today for acts that were legal and approved by the Government of Chile at the time. No claim is being made that these excess profits deductions are based on violations of Chilean law. This retroactive determination has serious implications for the rule of law.

Should Chile fail to meet its international obligations, it could jeopardize flows of private funds and erode the base of support for foreign assistance, with possible adverse effects on other developing countries. The course of action which the Chilean Government appears to have chosen, therefore, could have an adverse effect on the international development process.

The United States hopes that the Government of Chile, in accordance with its obligations under international law will give further careful consideration to this matter.[19]

This statement which has become the official policy of the Department of State is an explicit endorsement of the position of the U.S. copper companies. The State Department's claim that it holds a "position of moderation" is hardly convincing.[20] This policy statement also obliquely refers to and warns against other countries following the Chilean example.[21] This was the first officially stated concern not so much about Chilean actions per se but about action that might be taken against all U.S. business holdings in Latin America.[22] Thus, the statement is clearly directed not only at Chile's ability to garner U.S. public and private loans and investment, but is also directed toward other Third World countries. By wielding the weapon of economic sanctions and exhibiting the capacity to manipulate international financial funds, the United States can, in the Secretary's words, produce an "adverse effect on the international development process."

Despite the blunt language and obvious threats explicitly stated, officials continued to argue that the State Department is the voice of reason and moderation between both Chile and U.S. decision makers. As one official stated, "We have been pressing for our views on foreign investment (i.e.) the right of expropriation with just compensation."[23] Officials imply that there are others in the Executive Branch who were much more "hard-nosed" or

[19] For an official analysis of this statement, see the testimony of Assistant Secretary of State Charles A. Meyer before the House Subcommittee on Inter-American Affairs, "Recent Developments in Chile, October 1971," pp. 2–5 and 12–13, cited in footnote 7. In response to Congressman Gross' (R-Iowa) question as to whether Secretary Rogers' statement was "moderate or hard," Assistant Secretary Meyer replied "moderate."

[20] Interviews with U.S. Department of State Officials, October 1971.

[21] The notion that change in one country will have an automatic multiplier impact in other countries is referred to as the "ripple effect"; in other contexts it was called the "domino theory," and earlier the "demonstration effect."

[22] See the section on the input of U.S. business to U.S. policy toward Chile.

[23] Interview No. 2, U.S. Department of State, October 20, 1971.

advocated a harder line to the President.[24] In attempting to preempt the position of the hard-liners, the moderates . . . adopt virtually the same position, expressed, perhaps, in softer terms.

The State Department's influence over Administration decisions affecting Latin American affairs appears to have been considerable prior to the elevation of Secretary of the Treasury John Connally in the Nixon Administration with the advent of the New Economic Policy program.[25] Until the Chilean "crisis" developed, Latin America was a low-priority area in the eyes of most officials in the Nixon administration. Apparently the Nixon administration was fairly satisfied with the configuration of regimes in Latin America, in part the product of the Johnson administration.[26] The nationalization of U.S.-owned copper interests in Chile coincided with a shift in the Nixon administration decision-making structure. A major part of the responsibility for Latin American policy was shifted from the State Department to the Treasury Department and Secretary Connally. To the outsider it appeared that State and Treasury were making independent policy contributions; nevertheless, it appears that even statements by Rogers were agreed upon by Connally and the Treasury officials.[27]

Until the end of 1972 State Department officials continued to regard the Chilean situation under Allende differently from Cuba in the early 1960s. One official compared Chile under Allende with Argentina under Peron. According to this view, Chilean economic nationalism was an expression of the periodic nationalism that has "plagued" Latin America and U.S.-Latin American relations in the past. Allende's marxism, however, did not cause too much consternation among State Department officials. As one official reported:

> In general, it doesn't make much difference having a Marxist in Chile. I don't have ideological problems with having a Marxist in power. [He was] freely elected, therefore, [we are] absolutely enjoined from making any sort of judgment . . . [I] hope we can keep our shirts on and continue diplomatic pressure on Allende, stating fairly over and over our position. . . .[28]

In other words, while legal forms of opposition exist and while the United States can effectively apply "diplomatic pressures," U.S. officials do not feel that irreversible changes will be brought about. Not all the officials inter-

---

[24] *Ibid.* This official stated that the Department of Treasury and the Department of State have emphasized "different points of view," with Connally taking the "harder line."

[25] For example, it appears that the State Department was influential in shaping Nixon's flexible approach to Peru and of preventing the use of the Hickenlooper Amendment and sugar quota revisions.

[26] As one State Department official remarked, "above Meyer (Assistant Secretary of State for Inter-American Affairs), nobody (in the Nixon Administration) could care less about Latin America." Interview No. 4, U.S. Department of State, October 20, 1971.

[27] One U.S. A.I.D. official stated, "I wouldn't want to say that Connally's statement was harsher than Rogers, but Meyer's statement is not a pure State Department statement. Treasury was in agreement." Interview No. 1, U.S. A.I.D., October 20, 1971.

[28] Interview No. 7, U.S. Department of State, October 21, 1971.

viewed agree in their evaluations of present and future prospects for Chile, Allende, or U.S.-Chilean relations. Privately, officials express a range of attitudes toward all three subjects. For example, one State Department official perceived Allende as a pragmatist rather than a radical ideologue in regard to his handling of the copper conflict:

On the copper issue, Allende had to appease the more radical elements in his own party who helped him get elected. Nationalization was a foregone conclusion; [it] couldn't have been avoided. What if Chile [does not compensate]? Might be a convenient excuse for Allende to prolong an immediate balance of payments crisis if he didn't have to pay compensation for U.S. debts. As far as the debt to the rest of the world, I would think that he would want to maintain some appearance of international respectability.[29]

Another official stressed the distinct methods and goals of Chilean Communists and Socialists from their counterparts in other parts of the world:

Allende is not a Castro. Forces within Chile react in different ways. The Communists do not want Chile to become a client of Soviet assistance. The Socialists don't want to be in bed with the Soviet Union . . . Chileans to a man hate the copper companies. . . .[30]

On the other hand, some officials stress the ideological incompatibility between Chile and the United States:

I am pessimistic about Chile. I see a gradual deterioration in relationships with Santiago which is permanent in nature. . . . Chilean ideological nationalism is not compatible with U.S. interests. . . .[31]

There is considerable "identification" (among some State Department officials) with U.S. private investors:

Chile is clearly negative on U.S. investment. If I was an investor, I wouldn't touch Chile with a ten foot pole. A country that shows itself willing to rewrite rules ex post facto . . . [is] indicative of a general mentality to treat outsiders particularly arbitrarily. Colombia and Venezuela [are] diametrically opposed to Chile. Domestically, it is a Czechoslovakian 1947 situation in Chile.[32]

This tendency to view Chile in traditional Cold War terms and the attempt to draw on emotion-laden analogies from the past suggest that at least some sectors of the State Department have changed little over time. The negative appraisal of some State Department officials is not shared by others. They reject the idea that the United States should "write off" Chile as a result of the nationalization of copper. As one official stated:

[29] Interview No. 2, U.S. Department of State, October 20, 1971.
[30] Interview No. 4, U.S. Department of State, October 20, 1971.
[31] Interview No. 11, U.S. Department of State, October 21, 1971.
[32] Interview No. 3, U.S. Department of State, October 20, 1971.

. . . If [the U.S.] is hurt badly in terms of having to reimburse on guarantees [OPIC guarantees to U.S. business expropriated in Latin America], we may well say that if you want [U.S. business] to invest it is your business. . . .[33]

As we shall see, however, this "hands-off" viewpoint carries little weight in policy-making circles. The input of the State Department to the making of U.S. policy toward Chile under Allende has not been great. By their own admission, State Department officials claim that other executive department officials have "the ear of the President" and that the State Department has not been frequently consulted in events since the copper nationalization crisis. The attitude and opinion of State Department officials, although varied, does come together regarding the relative contribution of the Department to the making of U.S. policy:

Connally is the President's principal spokesman, the architect of our New Economic Policy. I would rather not centralize the conflict theme around Connally, but I would say that we [State and Treasury] have always had conflicting views.[34]

It is interesting to notice the historical parallel between Chilean and the Cuban situations regarding the formation of U.S. policy making. In defining and implementing the U.S. position toward Cuba in the early years of the revolution, according to retired Ambassador Philip W. Bonsal, the Treasury Department under Secretary Robert Anderson also "called the shots" in U.S.-Cuban relations prior to the break.[35] In fact, as the Ambassador to Cuba, Bonsal found out secondhand what U.S. policy would be toward Cuba:

My visitor (a U.S. oil company executive) went on to tell me that on the previous day representatives of the two American (oil) companies . . . had been summoned to the office of the Secretary of the Treasury, Robert Anderson, and had been informed by the Secretary that a refusal to accede to the Cuban government's request would be in accord with the policy of the United States government toward Cuba and that the companies would not incur any penalties under American antitrust laws should they take a joint stand in this matter . . . What we were doing was to present a situation to the Cuban revolutionaries and their presumable, then reluctant, Russian friends which involved the fate of the Cuban government. . . .[36]

The U.S. decision to encourage U.S. firms to refuse to refine Soviet crude oil in order to topple the Cuban government was a decision taken outside of the State Department. Similarly, the decision to cut the Cuban sugar quota was not an action suggested by the State Department. According to Bonsal, the

[33] Interview No. 10, U.S. Department of State, October 21, 1971.
[34] Ibid.
[35] Philip W. Bonsal, *Cuba, Castro and the United States* (Pittsburgh: University of Pittsburgh Press, 1971).
[36] Ibid., pp. 149–150.

Department of Treasury and the Secretary of the Treasury made the major decisions shaping U.S. policy toward postrevolutionary Cuba. In 1971, State Department officials suggested that U.S. policy toward Chile was being handled in the same manner as the Cuban situation a decade ago.

THE U.S. DEPARTMENT OF THE TREASURY. It appears that the decisions as well as the decision makers in the U.S. Department of the Treasury are more closely linked to U.S. corporate and business interests than is the Department of State. In any case, Treasury is more likely to articulate and defend U.S. private economic interests than are other agencies within the Executive Branch. This is all the more significant in light of the above observations that, in critical moments involving conflicts between U.S. private interests and Latin nationalist governments, it is Treasury that emerges as the spokesman of U.S. policy.

The *National Journal* quotes a "ranking Treasury official" as saying: "The time has come when we must assert our own interests—economic as well as political."[37]

The Secretary of Treasury in a fit of anger apparently blurted out a similar position.

> . . . the United States can afford to be tough with Latin Americans because we have no friends left there any more. . . .[38]

According to the *Business Week* writer who interviewed Connally:

> The Secretary is especially miffed when foreign nations expropriate U.S. assets. Under his orders, U.S. representatives have taken to abstaining from votes on World Bank and other loans to expropriating countries, and Connally is forcing the reopening of debate at top levels on what U.S. policy should be. He is particularly bitter about Latin American hostility toward U.S. investment. . . .[39]

[37] Mark L. Chadwin, "Foreign Policy Report: Nixon Administration Debates New Position Paper on Latin America," *National Journal*, Part I, January 15, 1972, p. 97.

[38] "Connally's Hard Sell Against Inflation," *Business Week* (July 10, 1971), pp. 62–66. It is interesting to note the reaction of Connally supporters in the Treasury Department to this widely circulated quotation: "Connally told us he didn't make the statement about the U.S. having no friends and we believe him. Anyway, the *supposed* statement was *only* reported in the *New York Times*." Interview No. 9, U.S. Department of the Treasury, October 21, 1971. Our italics.

[39] Ibid. Connally's close ties with business associates with substantial business links with Latin America as well as his own corporate and banking activities have shaped his "personsal" decisions. One of the last areas of conflict between the United States and Peru concerns Brown and Root Overseas Inc. who secured a multimillion dollar contract to build roads from U.S. A.I.D. and the Peruvian government. As a result of mismanagement, the Peruvian government suspended the contract and payment to Brown and Root. Connally's backing of Brown and Root may be the result of the substantial financial contributions Connally received from the corporation and its lobbyist for his gubernatorial campaigns. Connally sits on the board of at least one Texas-based bank with a director of Brown and Root. See General Accounting Office Report, "Allegations of Mismanagement of a Peruvian Highway Project Financed with U.S. Assistance Funds," Washington, D.C., December 2, 1971; see also David Welsh, "Building Lyndon Johnson," *Ramparts*, 7 (10), p. 108, and *The Texas Observer*, October 4, 1968 and January 8, 1969.

The point is not that Connally is merely "hostile" to Latin efforts to nation-alize U.S. firms but that he is in a position to influence basic policy decisions. As the *New York Times* points out:

> . . . Mr. Connally, as Treasury Secretary, wields immense influence on U.S. lending policies in Latin America . . . Mr. Connally is said to believe that his policy of 'deterrence'—cracking down on Chile—may frighten off other possible expropriating countries.[40]

What has emerged publicly, then, is a business-oriented Secretary of the Treasury who has not been reticent about expressing opposition toward Latin American nationalist leadership and the Chilean leadership in particular. Once policy has been defined through Connally's initiative, the State Depart-ment has moved toward the more extreme position, shedding its reservations and "flexibility."

The input of the Treasury Department to Executive policy making regard-ing U.S.-Chilean relations does not end with Connally's access to the Presi-dent. Treasury Department officials claimed Department control over other public institutions (the Export-Import Bank, the World Bank, the Interna-tional Monetary Fund, and the Inter-American Development Bank) in carry-ing out their anti-Chilean position:

> . . . Treasury is having an input (to U.S. foreign policy) that it hasn't had in the past. The National Advisory Council passes [on] credit programs, Export-Import Bank loans, [the] whole range of Federal Government financial activities abroad. Connally [has an] increasing input in finan-cial aspects which other agencies sometimes tend to play down. Execu-tive Directors of the IMF and the World Bank are both under the Secretary of Treasury so we have a considerable punch in both of those . . .[41] [On the Export-Import loan refusal to Chile]. We pulled a hard line on Chile . . . We recognize the right of any sovereign government to expropriate, but we insist that international obligations [i.e., prompt, adequate, effective compensation for nationalized properties] be met.[42]

[40] "We Don't Have Any Friends Anyway," *The New York Times*, August 15, 1971. This article also discussed the conflict between Connally and Rogers concerning U.S. policy toward Chile and Latin America.

[41] As the *New York Times* noted ". . . the Treasury's semi-secret orders to its men in the international lending agencies—the World Bank, the Inter-American Development Bank, the Export-Import Bank and other institutions—to grant no further loans to expropriating countries assumed *a priori* that the governments in question will not pay fair and prompt compensation. Until now the World Bank has continued lending to a country that nationalizes private assets so long as it appears ready to pay fair compen-sation within reasonable time." See Ibid.

[42] Interview No. 9, Office of the Assistant Secretary for International Affairs, U.S. Department of the Treasury, October 21, 1971. It is interesting to note that the individual interviewed here felt that "prompt" payment was "one to two years, but would vary from case to case," and that in the case of Peru's nationalization of the IPC, "Might say we are being gentle with Peru" in that no compensation has even been agreed upon in almost four years. The historical precedents on time payments for settlements (Mexican oil, for example) were apparently unknown to these officials. This was not the case with State Department officials.

Treasury control over the international public lending agencies was claimed by the Treasury officials interviewed and substantiated by State Department officials.

> I assume quite strongly that the Treasury did play a role in the decision of the Export-Import Bank not to [lend funds to] sell planes to Chile. . . .[43]

In short, the Treasury position and input to policy regarding Chile has been to exert as much pressure on Allende as possible. The strategy of outside influence (the denial of direct loans, credits, and aid) has been directed to force a favorable settlement for U.S. business interests. Equally important has been the action taken to isolate Chile by increasing the "external" costs, thus discouraging other Latin nations from following the Chilean example.

THE U.S. CONGRESS. The range of Congressional opinions concerning U.S.-Chilean relations and the copper issue appears to parallel the diversity of opinions and attitudes in the State and Treasury Departments. Congressional "hardliners," "moderates," and a few "liberals" are present in the hearings and Congressional activities concerning U.S.-Chilean relations. Up through the early part of 1972, no House position existed. Individual Congressional members presented their positions and indicated their pleasure or displeasure over U.S. policy on an individual basis. Neither House nor Senate leadership has enunciated a specific policy toward Chile. Congressional activity has taken shape through Committee hearings and reports and through the efforts of individual Congressmen.[44] The differences between the Senate and House membership on this issue are sufficient to warrant a separate discussion and analysis.

THE SENATE. An interesting facet of the Chilean copper crisis has been the extent to which some Senate liberals have responded in a very unliberal fashion. Senator Javits of New York has been especially hostile to economic nationalism not only in Chile but in other Latin American countries as well. At the same time he has been one of the most outspoken defenders of foreign investors. On May 10, 1971, Javits vehemently defended foreign investment:

> The role of private foreign investment in Latin America is one of the most pressing questions of the day, and one that must move toward resolution. It is a primary area where the lack of a logical coherent policy works to the detriment of Latin American growth objectievs. This "no policy" approach or "highly restrictive policy" approach—such as

---

[43] Interview No. 10, U.S. Department of State, October 21, 1971.
[44] Hence, we relied upon such materials as the *Congressional Record*, hearings and reports of various House and Senate Subcommittees, and interviews with Congressional staff and personnel.

the one just developed by the countries of the Andean group[45]— not only impedes foreign capital flows, but also *threatens to exacerbate the economic and political relationships between the United States and Latin America.*[46]

Earlier, while the Chilean Congress was debating the amendment to nationalize the copper industry, Javits attacked the amendment as follows:

> . . . the proposed amendment to the Chilean constitution now pending, if passed in its present form, may serve to isolate Chile from the inter-American system and *weaken decisively Chile's close links with the economic system of the Western Hemisphere.*
>
> The pending constitutional amendment would expropriate only American interests. The amendment, as drafted, apparently is a case of outright discrimination. In addition, it states that payment would be over 30 years with an interest rate of 3 percent per annum. These *highly inadequate payment terms hardly constitute prompt, adequate and effective payment . . . Clearly, this amendment is bad legislation with serious international repercussions as well as with far-reaching repercussions for future capital flows into Chile and for continued Chilean economic development.*[47]

As the Senator who has most outspokenly supported the multinational, U.S.-based corporations, Javits represents the view that American capital should not be infringed upon even when foreign political leadership has a democratically based consensus to limit exploitation of national resources by these corporations. The Javits position exposes the marginal differences that exist between conservative and liberal U.S. political leadership on a key foreign policy issue. Javits' stand is indicative of the inflexible Congressional posture—a position corresponding closely to that advocated by the major copper corporations.[48]

Other, more identifiably conservative Senators chose different means of expressing their hostility toward Chilean and Latin American economic nationalism. That the positions, attitudes, and techniques they advocate are meant to intimidate the Chileans is amply illustrated in the Senate debate over the U.S. contributions to the Inter-American Development Bank Fund in

---

[45] He is referring to the mild Andean Code for foreign investment—a rather flexible document that attempts to restrict foreign investment in certain critical economic sectors, that is, heavy industry, mining, and so on; certainly not a device to gravely threaten U.S. investors. Javits apparently interprets it in this fashion, however.

[46] "A New Policy for the Americas," *Congressional Record, 117* (67), May 10, 1971. Our italics.

[47] Senator Jacob K. Javits, "OPIC, New Hope for U.S. Participation in the Second Development Decade," Address to the International Management Division of the American Association, New York City, February 1, 1971. Our italics.

[48] As the latter portion of this section reveals, the Javits corporate position was the one adopted by the Nixon Administration.

October 1971.[49] Senator Byrd (I-Virginia) opened the debate by arguing that American taxpayers should no longer support the "giveaway programs that the Federal Government has engaged in over the last 25 years."[50] Senator Dominick (R-Colorado) wanted to be assured that U.S. control of the Bank would prevent loans going to Chile:

Senator Dominick: "Am I correct that at the insistence of the directors of this Bank, these loans could be given . . . to Chile . . .?

Senator Fulbright (D-Arkansas): "No, nothing in the act would restrict it."

Senator Byrd: "There is nothing in the act that would restrict the directors of that Bank from making loans to Chile, though Chile has just expropriated American property and refused to pay the owners of the property . . . Yet these funds, to answer the question of the Senator from Colorado, could be used for Chile."

Senator Fulbright: "Let me make it clear, we have 40 percent of the votes, and it requires a two-thirds vote to approve a loan. The United States can positively prevent anything out of this bill going to Chile, if that is what the Senator has in mind."

Senator Dominick: "Does the Senator from Arkansas or the Senator from Virginia have any idea whether the people we have on that board with this 40 percent voting right would veto such a loan?"

Senator Fulbright: "I would certainly think they would. On the question of the Bank itself, . . . we have a 40 percent voting right and would veto any aid to Chile.[51]

Not satisfied with the assurance that the United States could successfully block any loan to Chile through the two thirds rue ol IDB loans, Senator Brock (R-Tennessee) proposed an amendment to this bill,[52] that would direct:

U.S. Governors and U.S. Executive Directors of the international financial institutions for which U.S. financial contributions are authorized by this act or any person acting for them shall vote against any loans, grants, guarantee or any utilization of the funds of the institution for the benefit of any country which:

(1) has nationalized or expropriated or seized ownership or control of property owned by any United States citizen or by any corporation, partnership, or association which has substantial beneficial ownership by United States citizens, or

[49] See "Contributions to the Inter-American Development Bank Fund for Special Operations," Congressional Record-Senate, 92nd Congress, 1st Session, *117* (156), October 19, 1971, pp. S16580–S16584.
[50] Ibid.
[51] Ibid.
[52] "S.748 to authorize payment and appropriation of the second and third installments of the U.S. contributions to the Fund for Special Operations of the Inter-American Development Bank."

(2) has taken steps to repudiate or nullify existing contracts or agreements with any United States citizen or any corporation partnership, or association which has substantial beneficial ownership by United States citizens, or

(3) has imposed or enforced discriminatory taxes or other exactions, or restrictive maintenance or operational conditions, or has taken other actions, which have the effect of nationalizing, expropriating, or otherwise seizing ownership or control of property so owned;[53]

Because the amendment was so general and all-inclusive it was rejected.

It was clear from this debate, however, that conservative and liberal opinion was united in the desire to take all actions necessary in support of U.S. business interests. The key question was not whether a probusiness policy was to be adopted but to select the measures that would be most *effective*. Hence, we find Senator Fulbright (a moderate, often liberal spokesman on most foreign policy issues) raising this issue of effectiveness in arguing against the Brock amendment:

Senator Fulbright: "I agree with the objection that we should not have our investments expropriated. We should protect them and do everything reasonable to protect them. I do not think this procedure will be effective and I know it would be very offensive to some countries to whom it is likely to apply just as a matter of their own dignity and their own self-respect. However, I do not think it does anything substantive to the existing law.[54]

The left-wing liberals in the Senate approached the Chilean situation from a different standpoint. Senators Church and Kennedy have expressed opinions and attitudes quite different from the bipartisan liberal-moderate-conservative coalition that dominated the Senate on this issue. One of Senator Church's assistants summed up U.S. policy in the following terms:

[Toward] Any government oriented toward change in a democratic context [in Latin America] we get up tight and provoked. When the real history of U.S. relations with the Allende regime is written, the theme will be provocation . . . [U.S. strategy dictates] . . . need to control Chile . . . We won't get our way and we will pack up our marbles . . . [telling the Chileans] if you don't work with big business, then screw you guys. . . . We will try to get a new government [in Chile]. Maybe a new Frei government. We cannot stand Allende. It won't be through military intervention. It will be through a political upset.[55]

[53] "Contributions to the Inter-American Development Bank Fund for Special Operations," cited in footnote 52.
[54] Ibid.
[55] Interview with a member of Senator Church's staff, October 20, 1971, Washington, D.C. This individual went on so say:
"Chile is a country with a democratic framework. With Allende's election, we (the U.S. Government) seem to be disturbed by his party affiliation. But that is a Chilean decision not a North American one. Who are we to tell the Chilean people what kind of government they should have?"

His conclusions as to U.S. objectives were borne out in the public statement of presidential advisor Herbert Klein when he remarked after a trip to several Latin American countries, "We found that the Allende government in Chile was not going to last long."[56]

Kennedy's position is close to that of Church. Both Senators agree that the current government of Chile was "a decision of the Chilean people" and that the copper issue is "a matter between the companies (Anaconda and Kennecott) and the Chilean government" and not an issue in which the U.S. government should interject itself.[57]

Kennedy has publicly gone on record in support of the present Chilean government:

> A wise Administration policy would have recognized that the Chilean experiment in socialism had been decided by the people of Chile in an election far more democratic than the charade we saw last week in Vietnam. But the Administration response was brusque and frigid, colored by its attachment to the ideology of the Cold War. We can never know whether a more sensitive policy toward Chile might have helped to avoid the expropriation decision, which we learned of today . . . We should halt the tendency to identify U.S. Government interests with the interests of U.S. private investment. Private investment must come to terms with a changed environment, an environment dominated by the force of nationalism. If that occurs, there can be benefits to both country and corporation . . . Finally, we should acknowledge wide political diversity in Latin America. There must be an awareness that a Chilean experiment in socialism is in the end a Chilean decision.[58]

The "hands-off Chile" position of both Church and Kennedy, however, represents a small minority in the Senate and, for that matter, in Congress as a whole. Most senators of both parties who have spoken on this issue take the position that the Chilean expropriation of U.S. copper corporations is a "threat" to U.S. public interests and that the U.S. government must undertake all steps to ensure that these actions do not become habit-forming in other Latin American or Third World nations.

THE HOUSE. House attitudes and opinions, as a body and individually, reflect a high degree of unanimity regarding the policy the United States should adopt toward Latin American governments (such as the Chilean government) that challenge private U.S. business interests in their countries. Given the importance of the committee structure of the House, the attitudes and opinions of members of the two House committees most involved in

---

[56] See "Klein Sees Brief Rule by Allende," *Washington Post*, December 2, 1971.

[57] Interview with a member of Senator Kennedy's staff, October 20, 1971, Washington, D.C.

[58] Senator Edward Kennedy in an address to the Chicago Council on Foreign Relations, October 12, 1971.

Latin American policy determination—the Committee on Foreign Affairs and the Committee on Banking and Currency—demand the greatest attention. The most important hearings in the House to date have been organized by the Inter-American Affairs Subcommittee of the Committee on Foreign Affairs. We will focus principally on the activities of this subcommittee.[59]

According to one staff member, the position of the majority of members of the Inter-American Affairs Subcommittee is "moderate"—a position and role that has "counseled moderation" to both the Treasury and State Departments as well as to other members of Congress.[60] It has attempted, also, to preach "moderation" to the government of Chile so that Chile would not become a victim of economic "repercussions" that would certainly occur if Chile did not change its compensation policy.[61] The difficulty with this descripiton lies in what is meant by "moderate," as opposed to "immoderate." An examination of the recent hearing on U.S.-Chilean relations, reveals that the Chairman of the Subcommittee is "hopeful" as well as "disturbed" by the nationalization of copper.[62] Opening the hearing, Chairman Fascell stated:

> Despite the election of a Marxist President pledged to expropriate various U.S. businesses, many Americans, myself included, have remained hopeful that despite divergent internal policies the United States and Chile could continue their constructive partnership within the inter-American system.[63]

However, he went on to say that the hearing was being conducted because of recent Chilean events,[64] which he described as "most disturbing. . . ."[65] There was no hard and fast *initial* position but it appeared that as Chilean nationalism increased in momentum this ambivalence shifted to a more negative reaction.

The hearing includes testimony and memoranda from leading Executive Branch officials involved in U.S.-Latin American relations, including Charles A. Meyers, Assistant Secretary of State for Inter-American Affairs, Marshall T. Mays, General Counsel for the Overseas Private Investment Corporation (OPIC), Walter C. Sauer, Vice-Chairman and First Vice President of the

---

[59] The Inter-American Affairs Subcommittee chaired by Representative Dante B. Fascell, D–Florida. Although the attitudes of the members of the Committee on Banking and Currency are less well known, there are indications that these Congressmen do agree on a hardline, retaliatory position toward those countries which expropriate U.S. firms. One staff member of the Committee was quoted as saying "[this] is one of the few areas where you find unanimity in our committee." See Mark L. Chadwin, cited in footnote 40, pp. 97–107.

[60] Interview with staff member, Committee on Foreign Affairs, October 21, 1971.

[61] Ibid.

[62] "Recent Developments in Chile," cited in footnote 7.

[63] Ibid., p. 1.

[64] He referred to the Comptroller General of Chile's decision, announced on October 11, 1971, of no compensation for the expropriation of the Anaconda and Kennecott properties.

[65] "Recent Developments in Chile," p. 1, cited in footnote 7.

Export-Import Bank of the United States, and John W. Fisher, Director of the Office of Bolivian-Chilean Affairs, Bureau of Inter-American Affairs, Department of State. For the most part, the testimony of Administration officials was directed toward defending the hostile Nixon position toward economic nationalism in Latin America and Chile with terse and/or ambiguous responses to Congressional queries. The exchange between Secretary Meyer and Congressional hardliner Gross (R-Iowa) furthermore suggests that there are voices in the Congress who would substitute more severe non-economic pressures on Chile:

Mr. Gross: "All right. So we have done pretty well by the Chileans, haven't we?"

Mr. Meyer: "I think very."

Mr. Gross: "Very well, indeed, and yet Secretary of State Rogers at this late juncture in this affair issues a very moderate statement, doesn't he?"

Mr. Meyer: "Yes sir."

Mr. Gross: "I think it is time for the State Department, the inhabitants of Foggy Bottom, to get hard nosed about something. Too long, Mr. Secretary, have we played dollar diplomacy around the world and we are still at it in Chile. Ready to sweeten the pot again, I suspect. I wouldn't be surprised to read the newspapers tomorrow and find we have extended them some more credit."[66]

The general drift of the House Subcommittee was that harsher measures should be adopted pressuring for a favorable compensation settlement. The Congressmen, far from being concerned with parochial economic interests, were concerned with all U.S. private investments and the possible impact of Chilean policy. Congressional interest was tied to the "ripple effect" enunciated in Secretary of State Rogers' statement of October 13 (cited earlier):

Mr. Fascell: "Mr. Secretary, I am curious about the U.S. concern about the 'ripple effect.' I know I, myself, have expressed that kind of concern. Yet it seems with other cases in other countries that matters are beginning to work themselves out or at least there seems to be a reasonable opportunity to work themselves out. Is our concern with respect to the 'ripple effect' only because of the seeming risk of economic nationalism in Latin America as a general proposition, or do we have some other specific fear in mind?"

Mr. Meyer: "No, the general rise of economic nationalism is a concern quite obviously, Mr. Chairman, and for the definition of the 'ripple effect,' I would add as follows: There is, as you well know, a tendency in all of the years that I have been associated with the hemisphere to attribute to 20 plus countries a characterstic or an action taken by one. My feeling of the 'ripple effect,' which I think the Secretary implied in his statement, was it can develop

---

[66] Ibid., pp. 14–15.

within our country sort of an attitude of an additional pox on all our houses."

Mr. Fascell: "You are talking about the 'ripple effect' in the United States more than you are in [Latin America].

Mr. Meyer: "Yes."[67]

Another problem that concerned subcommittee members was U.S. government payments to expropriated companies through OPIC, an issue that raised the ire of some Representatives:

Mr. Gross: "Are the newspaper reports correct that if you have to meet these obligations that OPIC will be bankrupt?"

Mr. Mays: "I don't think bankrupt is the proper term to apply to a government corporation, Mr. Gross. We do not have adequate reserves to pay claims in excess of $200 million, in which case we would ask the Office of Management and Budget for an approval to request an appropriation to pay these claims."

Mr. Gross: "In other words, you then would be coming to Congress for another $150 million or what?"

Mr. Mays: "We don't know what the amount would be at this time but under those circumstances of complete confiscation without compensation of honoring of debt obligations, we would have to come to the Congress."

Mr. Gross: "But you would be coming to Congress for a sweetener?"

Mr. Mays: "For appropriations to pay claims backed by the full faith and credit of the United States, Mr. Gross."

Mr. Gross: "To get yourselves back in business again, right?"

Mr. Mays: "To meet these obligations."

Mr. Gross: "And it will be a real cold day in hell before I vote to nick the taxpayers for more money to underwrite you in situations of this kind."[68]

Along with a growing mood of hostility and frustration over the failure to hold back nationalism, some U.S. Congressmen have turned against the very corporations they are so angrily defending, as Congressman Gross's intemperate outburst against insurance payments suggests.

Perhaps the final measure of House attitude toward Chile and Latin American nationalism can be seen in the House version of the bills to fund the international lending agencies for 1972 to 1974. The total authorization was for $1.96 billion for the World Bank, the Inter-American Development Bank, and the Asian Development Bank. The Senate approved the same dollar total; however, House amendments have forced a House-Senate conference

[67] Ibid., p. 18.
[68] Ibid., pp. 21–22.

to resolve the differences.[69] The House amendments to the three bills "require U.S. representatives on the banks to vote against loans to any nation that expropriated American property without just compensation."[70] These amendments were very similar to the defeated Brock-sponsored amendment to the Senate bill.

THE "INTERNATIONAL" BANKS

"Aid" has never been an unconditional transfer of financial resources. Usually the conditions attached to aid are clearly and directly intended to serve the interests of the governments providing it . . . *Aid from the World Bank is not* . . . *available to countries which nationalize foreign-owned assets without compensation*, which fail to repay their debts or in which there are claims on behalf of foreign investors which the Bank considers should be settled. *Aid is, in general, available to countries whose internal political arrangements, foreign policy alignments, treatment of foreign private investment*, debt-servicing record, export policies, and so on, *are considered desirable, or at least acceptable, by the countries or institutions* providing aid, and which *do not appear to threaten their interests.*[71]

Hayter's demythification of the "international" nature of international public lending agencies lies at the heart of the policy input of these institutions to U.S.-Chilean relations.

The role and nature of the international lending agencies had been discussed during the Senate debate over additional funding for both the World Bank and IDB; similarly, the House discussed similar issues in its debate over similar funding proposals.[72] What emerged was an assessment of the

[69] See "House Votes $1.96 Billion Aid to Developing Nations," *The Washington Post*, February 2, 1972.

[70] Ibid. The *Post* writer concluded, "This provision was aimed especially at Chile . . . The relatively easy passage seemed surprising in view of the fact that the House traditionally has been very hostile to bilateral foreign aid controlled by the U.S. and even more so to multilateral aid where other nations have a say in who is to get the loans." Perhaps, certain Congressmen viewed the amendments as a means of retaliation for expropriations, making passage of the bills a hardnosed approach to economic nationalism.

[71] Teresa Hayter, *Aid As Imperialism* (Baltimore Penguin Books, Inc., 1971), pp. 15–17. Our italics. In this fascinating expose 'of the politics of international lending institutions' decision making, Ms. Hayter successfully illustrates how politics and U.S. government policy rather than the merits of loan applications influence these decisions. Hayter examines the following operations: IMF, IBRD, USAID, IDB, and the Inter-American Committee for the Alliance for Progress (CIAP).

[72] Senator Church in a Senate speech after the debate rejecting the foreign aid bill described the U.S. foreign aid program as a "grotesque" money tree sheltering foreign investments of our biggest corporations and furnishing aid and comfort to repressive governments all over the world," *New York Times*, October 31, 1971, p. 27. In the same vein, Senator Fulbright described U.S. foreign aid as a form of "welfare imperialism." Fulbright went on to point out that, "This has been part of the policy of preservation of the status quo, the prevention of any change in so many countries that need change," *New York Times*, November 1, 1971, p. 9.

World Bank and the Inter-American Development Bank as transmission belts of U.S. policy. Congressional control through appropriations coupled with U.S. representation in sufficient numbers on the Boards of Directors of both institutions insures that loans to countries out of favor with the United States will not be granted. The U.S. representatives on the Inter-American Development Bank, the Executive Director of the World Bank, and the U.S. representative on IDA are directly responsible to the Secretary of the Treasury.

Several recent incidents further illustrate the role of the international lending agencies (World Bank and IDB in particular) as implementers of U.S. policy. The case of Peru best illustrates this. After the Velasco government nationalized the International Petroleum Company, U.S. aid dropped from $60 million to $9 million in 1969 causing the Peruvian president to accuse the Inter-American Development Bank "of being used as a weapon of political pressure."[73]

Despite the obvious and continuing manipulation of International Banks to serve U.S. policy ends, Secretary Meyer still feels compelled to defend publicly the "objectiveness" of the Export-Import Bank's decision not to grant a Chilean request for a loan to purchase U.S.-made civilian aircraft:

Secretary Meyer: ". . . Despite allegations to the contrary, we have maintained an open position with respect to pending Chilean loan applications before the Export-Import Bank. I would add that this includes the LAN-Chile request for commercial aircraft which was subject to the normal criteria for such projects."[74]

However, even a staunch conservative Congressman, Representative Gross of Iowa, wondered why the Administration spokesmen made such a point of the "merits" of loan review decision making.[75]

Mr. Gross: ". . . Mr. Meyer, you spoke of dealing with this situation on merit. Can't I assume that you deal with all of these situations on merit? Why do you make a point of dealing with this on merit? I just don't understand. Both you gentlemen spoke of dealing with this situation on merit. I assumed that you deal with every situation with respect to the Export-Import Bank and with respect to any other phase of this on merit. What was the reason for the remark, anything in particular?"

Mr. Meyer: Mr. Gross, the reason for the emphasis, which is factual as you have endorsed, is because allegations always creep into a decision making

---

[73] Quoted by Mark L. Chadwin, p. 103, cited in footnote 40. Chadwin goes on to cite the case of the Export-Import Bank rejection of a loan to Chile—Boeing airplanes and the World Bank's rejection of loans to Guiana as other cases of what he delicately describes as "credit diplomacy."

[74] "Recent Developments in Chile, October 1971," p. 4, cited in footnote 7.

[75] Ibid., p. 12.

process or merit that that decision making process has been purely political, not merit. What Mr. Sauer and I both have stated priorly and today is that the decisions that are made in the banking relationship are on merit.

Mr. Gross: I don't want to quibble over rhetoric but it did strike me as being unusual to make such a point of it.

In terms of formal decision-making structure of the International Banks, overt U.S. control is not always manifested because, as one observer has pointed out, "to date the U.S. never has voted formally against a loan request either in the World Bank or the IDB but that is partly because the bank boards operate by consensus; issues on which there is disagreement are not brought to formal vote."[76]

Protestations to the contrary, the public and private statements of Administration officials illustrate the degree of control that the Secretary of the Treasury has over the Export-Import Bank. His willingness to *use* this control to retaliate against countries such as Chile merely underscores the fact that political values have first priority over banking criteria in shaping loan decisions.

It is clear from the record, then, that the "international" lending agencies are mere appendages of the U.S. government. Contrary to the preoccupation of conservative Congressmen, there is no danger that these institutions will deviate from the official, articulated, hard-line position taken by the Nixon Administration.

U.S. BUSINESS INTERESTS. The final institutional input to U.S. policy making in Latin America, and in many ways the most important, is that of U.S. business interests—a collage of private sector operations, major and minor, that have direct investments of between $10.4 and $11.7 billion in Latin America.[77] U.S. private investments are distributed in a variety of sectors roughly corresponding to overlapping historical periods. Investment and direct ownership in extractive industries (mining and petroleum) and related service industries (utilities such as electric, other power, and telephone) was characteristic of the period up through the 1950s. In the last 20 years U.S. investors have shifted toward manufacturing, trade and banking.

The pattern of U.S. investment for Latin America as a whole is maintained in Chile. Table 1 indicates the date of initial investment and the type of U.S.

---

[76] Chadwin, pp. 104 and 106, cited in footnote 40.

[77] Mark L. Chadwin, pp. 97–98, cited in fotnoote 40. U.S. private investment in Chile has declined from $850 million in 1970 to about $75 million in 1971—a decline of some 90 percent. See also, "Recent Developments in Chile, October 1971," p. 18, cited in footnote 7, and "U.S. Direct Investments in Latin America," (U.S. Department of State unclassified memorandum, June 9, 1971).

TABLE 1

Selected U.S. Firms with Majority Investment In Chile Prior to Copper Nationalization: Ranked by Date of Operation

Firm	Date of Operation in Chile	Principal activity
W. R. Grace	1881	Transportation
Bethlehem Steel	1913	Iron mining
Anaconda	Circa 1916	Copper mining
First National City Bank (NY)	1916	Banking and finance
Kennecott	Circa 1920s	Copper mining
Dupont	1920	Explosives
ITT	1927	Telephone
RCA	1942	Radio and television
ITT	1942	Radio and television
Kasier (Argentina)	1946	Iron and steel products
Oscar Kohorn & Co.	1948	Textiles and fibers
Englehard Minerals & Chemicals	1955	Iron mining
American Cyanamid	1955	Pharmaceuticals
Standard Oil (NJ)	1959	Oil distribution
Parke, Davis & Co.	Pre 1960	Pharmaceuticals
Chas Pfizer	Pre 1960	Pharmaceuticals
Sterling Drugs	1960	Pharmaceuticals
Armco Steel	1960	Iron and steel products
Mobil Oil	1961	Oil distribution
International Basic Economy Corp.	1961	Banking and finance
W. R. Grace	1961	Food manufacturing
CPC International	1961	Food manufacturing
General Motors	Pre 1962	Auto assembly
Simpson Timber Co.	1965	Pulp and paper
Sperry Rand Corp.	1966	Office equipment
Singer Sewing Machine	1966	Iron and steel products
General Mills	1967	Food manufacturing
Ralston Purina	1967	Food manufacturing
Dow Chemical	1967	Petro chemicals
Firestone Tire and Rubber	1967	Rubber tires
Northern Indiana Brass	1967	Copper fabricating
Bank of America	1967	Banking and finance
Ford Motor Co.	1968	Auto assembly
Monsanto Co.	1969	Petro chemicals
General Tire	1969	Rubber tires

TABLE 1—*Continued*

Selected U.S. Firms with Majority Investment In Chile Prior to Copper Nationalization: Ranked by Date of Operation

Firm	Date of Operation in Chile	Principal activity
IRECO Chemicals	1969	Explosives
Cerro	Late 1960s	Copper mining
General Telephone & Electronics	1970	Radio and television
Chemtex Inc.	1971	Textiles and fibers

Source. North American Congress on Latin America, *New Chile* (Berkeley, Calif.: NACLA, 1972), pp. 150–168; "Recent Developments in Chile, October 1971," p. 18, cited in footnote 7, and D. Lynne Kaltreider, "A Tale of Two Interventions and Other Related Actions," unpublished paper, November 1971.

investment and activity in selected major industries prior to copper nationalization. It is clearly discernible from this table that pre-World War II investments were basically those in extraction of raw materials or in basic utilities. With the end of World War II, the growth of a large internal consumer market and high tariff walls, U.S. private investment began to "diversify." The 1960s witnessed a rather wide variety of investments designed to tap and exploit the potential Chilean consumer market that had developed as a result of the boom in the copper industry during the Korean conflict. The "appetite" of the Chilean middle class for U.S.-type consumer goods is well known, and investments in the 1960s reflect the attempt of U.S. firms to cash in on this Chilean tendency to use precious foreign exchange to purchase middle class consumer items.

Despite the diversification of investment, the bulk of U.S. direct investment in Chile remained in the mining and smelting category (53.4 percent—Table 2). The balance of U.S. investment was in consumer-type activities (34.0 percent). The critical area of manufacturing accounted for only 7.7 percent with trade making up the remaining 4.8 percent.

Only Peru has a higher proportion of foreign investment concentrated in the mining sector, and Chile has the lowest percentage of foreign investment in manufacturing of any Latin American country. A nation-by-nation examination suggests that in each country foreign investment is concentrated in one sector rather than diversified throughout the economy. Taking Latin America as a whole there appears to be a greater dispersion. This sectoral specialization, the result of the profit-maximizing behavior of investors, leaves investors *isolated* and vulnerable to nationalist coalitions which embrace or cross socioeconomic sectors—as was the case in Chile.

Table 3 reveals that U.S. investments spread out throughout the industrial sector remained after the nationalization drive and disinvestment that

TABLE 2

U.S. Direct Foreign Investment in Latin American Republics and Other Western Hemisphere (Excluding Canada)
(Book Value at End of 1969 in Millions US$)

Country	Total	Mining and Smelting	Petroleum	Manufacturing	Transportation and Utilities	Trade	Other
					Percentage Breakdown by Sector		
Latin America	11,667	11.5	26.4	34.9	5.3	11.2	10.6
Mexico	1,631	8.3	2.1	67.9	1.7	11.7	8.2
Panama	1,071	1.8	22.3	8.4	5.2	32.2	30.1
Other Central America[a]	630	1.3	24.4	17.9	20.5	6.8	28.9
Argentina	1,244	x x	x x	63.4	x x	5.5	31.1
Brazil	1,633	6.1	6.1	68.1	1.5	11.5	6.6
Chile	846	53.4	x x	7.7	x x	4.8	34.0
Colombia	684	x x	50.0	23.2	4.2	9.2	4.4
Peru	704	62.9	x x	13.8	x x	8.4	15.1
Venezuela	2,668	x x	66.4	15.6	.7	10.3	7.0
Other[b]	554	9.0	34.3	12.1	9.9	5.9	28.7
Other western hemisphere[c]	2,144	26.9	30.0	12.6	3.5	4.6	22.6
TOTAL Latin American Republics and Other western hemisphere	13,811	13.9	26.9	31.5	5.0	10.2	12.5

Source. U.S. Department of Commerce, *Survey of Current Business*, October 1970.

xx—Combined in other industries.

[a] Includes Costa Rica, El Salvador, Guatemala, Honduras, and Nicaragua.

[b] Includes Bolivia, Dominican Republic, Ecuador, Haiti, Paraguay, and Uruguay.

[c] Includes all of the western hemisphere, except Canada and the 19 Latin American republics.

occurred since Allende's election. These firms represent, perhaps, the type of foreign investment that the Chilean government desires, will permit, and possibly encourage in the future. From the political standpoint, these firms are enmeshed in the sector of the economy most closely linked to the middle class and to the political opposition.

As a result of the long, private investment ties to Chile, U.S. business groups, particularly the large copper concerns (Anaconda and Kennecott), have staged rear guard legal action in Chile attempting to receive compensa-

TABLE 3

Remaining U.S. Investments in Chile, Not Nationalized, Bought Out, or in Process of Buyout

Firm	Principal Activity
Continental Cooper and Steel	Steel products
Crown Zellerbach	Manufacturing
Dow Chemical	Petro chemicals
Ensign Bickford	Manufacturing
Firestone Tire and Rubber	Rubber tires
General Cable	Copper fabricating
General Electric	Electrical equipment manufacturing
General Motors	Auto assembly
ITT	Hotels and electrical equipment manufacturing
IRECO	Chemicals
Xerox	Photo reproduction equipment

Source. "Recent Developments in Chile, October 1971," p. 18, cited in footnote 7. These firms own either a part or all of their Chilean operation—they account for $75 million direct, U.S. private investment in Chile.

tion for their investments. It is likely that the copper companies will seek compensation from the U.S. government and taxpayers and there are reports that they will receive some payments.

More important, U.S. copper companies may be acting to seize Chilean markets by increasing their sales from the United States, thus driving the Chileans out of their established markets. A trade journal recently reported:

Effective immediately, the Commerce Department has ended export licensing for refined and unrefined copper and copper based scrap commodities for most destinations. The action means that validated licenses no longer will be required for copper items for all destinations except the Asian communist countries, Cuba and South Rhodesia.[78]

In addition, AID loans have been extended to Yugoslavia to develop copper mines to be jointly owned with foreign investors. It is clear that the U.S. corporation will concentrate their struggle in the international commercial arena—an area where the Chileans may be at a disadvantage.[79]

The principal lobbyist for U.S. business interests in Latin America has been the Council of the Americas—an interest group with a membership of some 210 firms representing 90 percent of all U.S. investments in Latin

[78] International Trade Reporters Survey and Analysis of Current Developments, February 4, 1972.

[79] Theodore Moran, "Dependencia and the Future of Economic Nationalism in the Chilean Copper Industry," Journal of Andean Studies, Spring 1972.

America.[80] Through formal and informal meetings at regular intervals, the Council and key U.S. government officials work closely in shaping U.S. policy.[81] The Council's activities and the ability of its members to secure sensitive decision-making positions within the Executive Branch of the U.S. government assures corporate representation and decisive influence over major governmental decisions in areas which affect them.[82]

The Nixon administration's hostile policy toward economic nationalism in Chile and Latin America is substantially shaped by officials in government who are or were the representatives of U.S. firms in Latin America.

THE COUNCIL ON FOREIGN RELATIONS. The range of policy options open and under consideration to U.S. policy makers was discussed at a series of meetings held by the Council on Foreign Relations (CFR) during 1971. Corporation executives, international functionaries, State Department officials, as well as academics and others with an interest in Latin America, attended. The free and uninhibited discussion that occurred presents an unusual opportunity to examine the position of opinion leaders from influential segments of "public opinion."[83]

The general impression left after a reading of the CFR minutes is the lack of any innovative thinking and any coherent proposals to meet the key problems discussed but hardly explored in any depth. The participants did not pose any specific alternative policies to confront the problems of mass marginality, dictatorship, the growing gap between the United States and Latin America, and the failure of the Alliance for Progress, nor did most of the participants understand the dynamic forces underlying the growth of the nationalist challenge. The best that some of the participants could come up

[80] Originally, this organization was more accurately called the Business Group for Latin America. In 1965 it changed its name to Council for Latin America; in 1970, it adopted its present title because, according to its own propaganda, this was more "in keeping with the spirit of partnership." David Rockefeller (Chase Manhattan Bank of New York) was the first chairman. In 1970, Jose de Cubas (Westinghouse Electric International) assumed this position.

[81] The interchange of personnel between business organizations and government facilitates mutual understanding over major policy issues. For example, Charles A. Meyer was active in Council affairs before his selection as Assistant Secretary of State for Inter-American affairs; as were Council activist John R. Petty (now Assistant Secretary of the Treasury for International Affairs) and many others.

[82] This relationship raises questions of conflict of interest; how could Meyer and Petty "objectively" evaluate the "merits" of a Chilean loan request given their connection with U.S. business in Latin America? A study of thirty key U.S. policy makers who shaped U.S. policy during the first five years of the Alliance for Progress revealed that seventy percent were connected with the world of corporate business prior to taking office, Kraig Schwartz, "The Socio-Economic Career Patterns of 30 Persons Who Shaped U.S. Policy Toward Latin America" (unpublished).

[83] This discussion is based on the confidential minutes of four closed meetings of the Council on Foreign Relations which were sent to the North American Congress on Latin America (NACLA). These minutes were published in their entirety in NACLA *Newsletter, V* (7).

with was either a return to a revised version of dollar diplomacy or a policy of "disengagement."[84] The few participants with a relatively clear set of ideas around which to focus U.S. policy were mostly the executives from private corporations—they defined U.S. policy and interests in terms of promotion and protection of U.S. business and, more specifically, corporate investments in Latin America.

A spokesman for Standard Oil called for overt direct action: "The U.S. should frankly acknowledge the role of senior partner and should take some initiatives." He then went on to suggest the establishment of "international" machinery to defend private investments as well as a unilateral policy which would not tolerate "economic aggression." More specifically, he urged that "U.S. policy should aim at protecting and promoting U.S. interests [investments] in the region but within an international context." Underlying the corporate viewpoint was a general malaise and growing· discontent with the behavior of Nixon's foreign policy makers: U.S. policy was attacked as being the "antithesis of protector and promoter of U.S. interests;" the government was accused of being "passive" toward Chile and Peru; Nixon was attacked for not encouraging U.S. investment where it was not welcome (presumably the implication is that Nixon should make the proper political arrangements in Latin America *to make* investment welcome). Rather than using the inter-American councils as active instruments to promote and protect U.S. interests, the U.S. representatives are perceived as "passive." Rejecting the notion of a "low profile," the corporate spokesman characterized the behavior of the Nixon administration as "inadequate and harmful." Projecting current problems in Latin America into a global context, the corporate spokesman warned that failure to act against nationalization in Latin America could generate a "ripple effect" in other areas—a point of view taken up and supported by others during the discussion.[85] For example, a spokesman for American Smelting pointed out, "In Peru there may be a great deal of pressure on the government to take over existing major investments, especially if the United States makes no response to measures taken in Chile." He went on to attack U.S. policy makers because, "There is little evidence of concern for the future supply of raw materials in the formation and execution of U.S. foreign policy." Similarly, a spokesman for the State Department suggested sanctions against uncompensated expropriation, fearing the "demonstration effect of Peruvian and Chilean actions on the rest of Latin America." Most govern-

---

[84] John Plank and others argued that "on a benefit-cost analysis basis Latin America is not very important"—a view which he ascribed to Kissinger and through the latter to Nixon. He went on to argue that Kissinger convinced Nixon that "protection of U.S. private interests in Latin America must not be permitted to assume an overriding priority." In light of Nixon's recent policy declarations, it is obvious the investor arguments were more convincing than Plank's.

[85] It should be pointed out that this "ripple effect" concept was also picked up and developed by both Secretary of State Rogers and Assistant Secretary of State Meyer. See the sections on the State Department and Congress.

ment advisors—public and private—felt that the Latin Americans perceived the United States as "wavering as to whether it will take up the cause of private investors." John Campbell summed up this outlook when he noted that, "we will enter a period soon when choices will be necessary. Our attitude must be either for a strong action or for rolling with the punches and dealing with each situation as it arises." Feeling the nationalist threat most directly, private investor spokesmen called for preemptive action. An executive from Standard Oil called for the U.S. government to "make its position clear before incidents arise."

On January 19, 1972, Nixon announced the tough U.S. stand on expropriations, backing the strong position advocated by the overseas investors and their supporters in the Treasury and State Departments. The Nixon announcement terminated loans and aid to countries nationalizing U.S. property. The proviso calling for "prompt, adequate and effective compensation" is a euphemism for opposition to nationalization since few, if any, underdeveloped countries have large sums of hard currency available to divert from socioeconomic development to U.S. corporations.[86] The Nixon statement made clear that the United States would use its virtual veto power in the World Bank, the Inter-American Development Bank, and other international lending agencies to block loan requests from countries that expropriated U.S.-owned companies. The Nixon policy statement states that the United States could be expected to "withhold its support from loans under consideration in multilateral development banks."[87]

That the U.S. government should put the full weight of its economic and political power (as well as its international prestige) behind the overseas investor community belies the contention of some officials and academicians who claim that the "United States does not need Latin America" and therefore, that private investors should be left to their own devices. The post-Alliance for Progress discussions of democracy versus dictatorship, the "true" nature of "national security," the efficacy of bilateral and multilateral aid, the

---

[86] The key passage of Nixon's speech reads:

Under international law, the United States has a right to expect that the taking of American property will be nondiscriminatory, that it will be for a public purpose, and that its citizens will receive prompt, adequate, and effective compensation from the expropriating country.

Thus when a country expropriates a significant United States interest without making reasonable provision for such compensation to United States citizens, we will presume that the United State will not extend new bilateral economic benefits to the expropriating country unless and until it is determined that the country is taking reasonable steps to provide adequate compensation or that there are major factors affecting United States interests which require continuance of all or part of these benefits.

[87] In the case of the Inter-American Development Bank, U.S. influence allowed it to veto long-term, interest-free loans long before Nixon made his public policy speech. According to some bank officials interviewed in October of 1971 (three months prior to his January 21, 1971 speech), U.S. manipulation of bank policy was already a well-established practice. See the sections on the Treasury Department and the International Banks.

rationality or irrationality of nationalism, the "permanent" gap between the United States and Latin America, and the differences between Latin American countries, are all subsumed under the primary concern: maintaining U.S. interests. Latin American attitudes toward U.S. private investment shape the U.S. government's policy toward dictatorship or democracy and the other issues considered above. For example, while Nixon states that the United States counts on Brazil (governed by a stern military dictatorship for eight years) as the leading country in Latin America, the President's policy toward democratic Chile has been a composite of overt and covert threats.

Similarly, in their discussion of nationalism, policy makers, investors, and advisers are less concerned with the rhetoric than they are with the substantive policy toward investment. Comparing Brazil and Chile, Rodman Rockefeller noted that ". . . Brazil is large and successful enough not to have to resort to nationalistic and 'anti-colonialist' pressures in an effort at self-protection . . . The Brazilians express a confidence and a sense of latitude in their treatment of foreign investment." Regarding Chile, his company was trying to keep alive economically and meanwhile sell out. He noted that, "A U.S. firm has no leverage at all in Chile at this time." Commenting on recent political developments in Chile, Plank added that, ". . . Latin American societies . . . are not to be trusted at free political play." The problem of priorities in policy making then appears to be resolved largely in terms of the larger economic policies rather than in terms of specific policy measures directed at particular U.S. firms. As one of the participants in the CFR conference noted with regard to Peru:

> Peru's position in Latin America has changed and the U.S. has seen fit to act with restraint. U.S. policy is criticized from both sides. We have important interests in Peru that must be safeguarded, but it is difficult to know what reaction is best in each individual case in relation to the whole. The reaction in the IPC case is still generally regarded as the best we could have had. Messrs. Barber and Archibald [two participants at the CFR Conference], stated at the time they felt it would have been unwise to provoke a confrontation on this issue. The State Department is often accused of having no policy at all but this is an over-simplification. *It has to balance a number of different interests, political and economic;* there is no automatic formula to be applied in case of conflict between the Peruvian government and American companies.[88]

The same analysis applies in the case of Chile. The issue began to boil down to *when* and *how* the United States would launch its attack on the Chilean government's nationalization program. There was little doubt that a business oriented political leadership such as the Nixon Administration would act on behalf of *his* investor constituents, heeding the advice of their spokesmen and disregarding those who would preach a policy of benign neglect.

88 Our italics.

CONCLUSIONS: U.S. POLICY AND ITS IMPACT

Despite the low-profile policy promised by the Nixon Administration, and despite the claims that a wait-and-see attitude would be adopted toward the Chilean "experiment" with democratic socialism, it was not long before President Nixon announced a tough U.S. stand on expropriations. Aid, credits, and other financial agreements would not be forthcoming to countries that nationalized private U.S. holdings. This statement affected all international bank policies in addition to those of U.S. governmental agencies. Thus, in large part the debate between liberals and conservatives, hardliners and moderates has been resolved—in favor of the hardline conservatives. The implications of the antinationalist U.S. foreign policy are far-reaching: an increasingly close and vastly expanded relationship with the pro-U.S. military junta in Brazil, tacit support of rightist military coups such as occurred in Bolivia, and economic isolation and pressure on nationalist governments such as the Chilean.[89]

Despite the appearance of a pluralistic decision-making structure with competing viewpoints on particular aspects of policy, the overall thrust of U.S. foreign policy is largely in the direction of supporting U.S. business interests abroad. An analysis of the *discussion* of policy making presents a pluralistic image while the execution of policy largely follows the line of policy favored by a single interest—the U.S. investor community. United States economic interests appear to be the only concrete, specific, and visible reference point to which policy makers refer. United States corporation images of political reality appear to be a safe point from which policy makers begin to define general policy positions, taking account of the complexity and variety of overseas interests involved.

The Executive Branch agencies continue to exercise leadership in the making of foreign policy despite the increased hue and cry emanating from Congress in recent years. Congressmen continue to pressure for particularistic interests—individual firms or lines of industry that have had problems with Latin governments. Congress serves as a forum for airing dissident and critical opinions but has been of little importance *except where the position of Congress coincides with that of the Executive branch and the business community*, in which case Congressional opinion is perceived by Executive policy makers as a "pressure" to get things done quickly—in doing what they were already predisposed to do in any case. This was clearly the case in Nixon's announcement of a "hardline" on expropriations; his aides announced that it was intended to "head-off Congressional action." We have

[89] The examples substantiating this point of view are numerous. In February 1972, the *Alliance for Progress Newsletter* announced that IDB, IBRD, and EXIMBANK had loaned Brazil 398 million dollars for a steel mill. In the same issue an article mentioned that Chile was turning to European firms to help Chile build cars. *Alliance for Progress Weekly Newsletter*, X (8), pp. 2, 3.

seen, however, that Nixon's top appointees in State and Treasury had already adopted harsh policies opposed to expropriations long before Congress had taken a poll of its own members.

Long-term prospects for the development of a postimperial foreign policy appear dim in light of the current Administration's continuing commitment toward promoting the interests of U.S. investors and confronting Latin American economic nationalists. The best that can be said regarding foreign policy changes is that Dominican-style "gun-boat diplomacy" has been replaced by "credit-diplomacy" . . . for now. The low-profile approach suggests that U.S. policy makers will give increasing importance to indigenous military elites and oppositionists in dumping the economic nationalists; this has already occurred in Bolivia and more recently in Ecuador. By confining themselves to maintaining credit pressure from the outside, U.S. policy makers allow their national allies inside the country to mobilize on internal issues—a strategy that appears to be paying off in Chile.

The more immediate experiences concerning U.S. policy and overseas investment suggest that when a crisis situation emerges—when a major U.S. investor group in a Latin country is endangered—there is an increasing convergence of U.S. government and business responses. Once the crisis passes, the two major interests may diverge. The overlap in policy is largely a result of the career patterns and prior socialization of many of the leading policy makers; individuals who have come from corporate or corporate related careers and/or who may be headed for such a career, but who in any case share many of the key beliefs associated with business enterprise ("foreign private investment is essential for the development of underdeveloped countries"—and similar beliefs).

Whatever the value of any particular enterprise affected by economic nationalism, it has been shown how U.S. policy makers have a tendency to view the particular problem from the standpoint of the impact on the whole overseas investment community. Hence, the constant preoccupation not only of high administration officials but of seemingly "parochial" Congressmen with the so-called "ripple effect." In gauging U.S. responses to expropriation of a firm, U.S. policy makers have in mind the $86 billion[90] which U.S. corporations have invested throughout the world. The problematic situation that nationalization measures create, and the uncertainties *within* the U.S. as well as *outside,* have led U.S. policy makers to reject economic nationalism and to attempt to manipulate a variety of national and international institutions in order to safeguard overseas U.S. economic interests.

The gradual escalation of U.S. pressures against economic nationalism in Chile took a new turn when a U.S. court in New York blocked the bank accounts of 14 Chilean agencies. Despite Chile's agreement to pay over 90 percent of the Kennecott debt that had purportedly caused the attachments,

---

[90] Gabriel Kolko, *The Roots of American Foreign Policy* (Boston: Beacon Press, 1969), p. 74.

the federal judge refused to lift attachments against nine Chilean enterprises. Chile's agreement to pay the enormous debts incurred by past regimes has led to efforts to renegotiate the payments schedule. Once agreeing to renegotiation, Chile has become increasingly vulnerable to external pressure that may have adverse internal social, economic, and political effects on the Allende government. The Chilean government is being economically encircled in order to create the necessary and sufficient conditions for the internal opposition to take power.

United States policy makers perceive the real challenge to be neither the Soviet Union nor China, but economic nationalism and social revolution in Third World areas under U.S. hegemony. Thus, while the U.S. policy makers propose an opening to China they heighten pressures on Chile and the rest of Latin America. While the U.S. "opening" toward China is a new and major development in U.S. foreign policy, the objectives are not very different; recognition of a Great Power is the first step toward mutual agreement in defining traditional spheres of influence. It is within this framework that we can understand why the United States can open relations with the major Asian Communist power, China, but not with revolutionary Cuba. We can also understand why the U.S. plans to increase trade with an authoritarian communist regime in Asia while limiting credits and eliminating loans to a parliamentary, democratic socialist government such as Chile.

Despite the hostility of U.S. policy makers and private investors toward economic nationalism, there are important factors that should encourage some restraint on U.S. public activities. The large foreign debt which Latin nations (including Chile) owe to U.S. financial institutions is a double-edged sword; while it provides the creditor nation leverage to pressure for favorable policies, it also provides the debtor nation with a bargaining weapon which can be expressed in the form of a threat to repudiate the debt and thus influence important financial interest groups in the creditor country. Conservative but prudent bankers who still have hopes of recuperating their loans may wish to moderate the extremist demands of U.S. private investors whose properties have been nationalized. While the nonnationalized U.S. economic groups continue to have an economic stake in Chile and feel that there is some hope for partial or total recovery, it is to be expected that bargaining, negotiation, and some agreements can be reached regarding specific issue areas. More specifically, it is likely that Chile will be allowed to refinance the debt in exchange for guarantees that the Allende government will make prompt, complete payment. Thus, within a conflict framework which locks U.S. private interests and government in combat with Latin American economic nationalists, the possibilities of short-term arrangements are possible and probable, given the loss of U.S. omniscience in this hemisphere and the emergence of somewhat "durable" nationalist regimes in Latin America.

8

James Petras, H. Michael Erisman & Charles Mills | The Monroe Doctrine and U.S. Hegemony in Latin America[*]

U.S. expansion has passed through several phases corresponding to different periods in U.S. internal growth and varying according to the United States' capacity to involve itself abroad. In the first half of the nineteenth century, U.S. expansion was largely the product of an expanding capitalist plantation system that required territorial acquisition for its continued growth—hence the early period of U.S. imperialism was largely based on agrarian interests and followed a classical colonial pattern. The early application of the Monroe Doctrine was confined to the Caribbean rim, the major area in which the United States was heavily involved and capable of policing. The expansion of commercial and banking interests throughout the Caribbean area by the end of the nineteenth century was combined with an influx of U.S. capital and corresponded with the emergence of the now familiar pattern of neocolonial control. U.S. economic interests controlled the economy while U.S. policy makers nurtured and promoted client governments through military intervention, economic and diplomatic pressures, and electoral frauds. Throughout the first half of the twentieth century, U.S. economic interests began to diversify and to expand beyond the Caribbean rim into South America, taking the form of direct investments, initially in petroleum and mining, and, after

* We thank the State University of New York at Binghamton for financial support and the Department of Political Science and Institute of Public Administration at The Pennsylvania State University for secretarial assistance in the preparation of this chapter.

World War II, extending into the manufacturing sectors. The diversification of U.S. economic interests, the proliferation of diverse forms of interpenetration and association between Latin American and U.S. elites, and the complex activities and organizations that they generated made the Monroe Doctrine somewhat anachronistic and difficult to apply. Hence, beginning with the Good Neighbor Policy and later with the Alliance for Progress, a new policy approach was elaborated that allowed for consultation and collaboration between the client-states and the United States without challenging the latter's hegemonic position in the southern hemisphere. The proposals to "multi-lateralize" the Monroe Doctrine and to organize *regional* military and economic organizations were attempts to codify and incorporate the multiple relationships that now exist, and to allow the United States to act *on a variety of levels of decision making within Latin America*, thus offsetting the increasingly difficult task of reacting from the outside in crisis periods with military force in the classical Monroe Doctrine style. While Latin America is ruled by regimes "open" to the free flow of goods and capital, the United States is willing to negotiate and bargain over the terms of dependency and to allow "joint" participation in regional economic development organizations. When it appears that regimes will seek to increase their political autonomy and to diversify their economic outlets and inputs, the United States reverts back to the traditional policy of unilateral decision making and attempts to impose its monopoly over the political and economic relationships in the area. Thus while the Monroe Doctrine has been modified to accommodate changes and developments within Latin America, these modifications have been conditional and have not diminished—but perhaps they have augmented—U.S. control within the area. An historical account of the evolution of the Monroe Doctrine and of U.S. economic expansion can throw considerable light on the meaning of specific political formulas adopted to incorporate Latin America within the U.S. "informal" empire and on the dynamic process by which the relations *within* the empire have been modified.

U.S. HEGEMONY AND THE MONROE DOCTRINE

Simon Bolivar once observed that "[t]he United States appears to be destined by Providence to plague Latin America with misery in the name of liberty." What Bolivar was suggesting as a possibility has certainly become a reality— U.S. behavior toward Latin America, while often couched in idealistic terms, has indeed been oppressive. Almost from the moment of independence the United States looked upon Latin America as its particular sphere of influence and set out to establish its control over the area. The United States' hegemonic position, with its attendant exploitation, has contributed to and perpetuated underdevelopment and the inhuman conditions facing most Latin Americans. History has unfortunately shown Bolivar to be a prophet.

A variety of explanations have been offered to account for U.S. behavior.

Apologists of U.S. expansion defend the policies of Washington in terms of inevitability, security necessities, or altruism.[1] Conversely, critics of U.S. policy and development tend to stress internal dynamics of capitalist expansion as the primary factor influencing the U.S. relations with Latin American countries. This economic ingredient in U.S. imperialism was made graphically evident by Major General Smedley Butler of the U.S. Marine Corps, who stated:

> I helped make Mexico and especially Tampico safe for American oil interests in 1914. I helped to make Haiti and Cuba a decent place for the National City Bank boys to collect revenue in. I helped purify Nicaragua for the international banking house of Brown Brothers in 1909–12. I brought light to the Dominican Republic for American sugar interests in 1916. I helped make Honduras "right" for American fruit companies in 1903.
>
> (Gerassi, p. 231)

Butler's statement clearly reveals the interrelation between economic interests and military intervention—a linkage that has been obscured by latter-day defenders of U.S. policy. Our view is that economic expansion has been a major consideration in policy toward Latin America.

The justification for U.S. imperial behavior, particularly as advanced by Washington's power wielders, has generally been based on the Monroe Doctrine. The Monroe Doctrine, along with its various corollaries and interpretations, has been the policy vehicle that the United States has employed in pursuing its imperial designs on Latin America. By investigating the Monroe Doctrine's development, its usages, and its relationship to socioeconomic political forces both within and outside the United States, one can acquire some insights into the nature of the relationship between U.S. imperialism and Latin America.

The motivating force of U.S. expansion in Latin America is economic self-interest; the particular economic interests vary, however, shifting from commercial and agricultural to mineral and industrial. The Monroe Doctrine's significance as the basic policy vehicle also varies according to the world position of the United States. Up until World War II, the Monroe Doctrine

---

[1] The inevitability theme is perhaps best presented in the Manifest Destiny concept, which holds that U.S. expansion into Latin America is unavoidable since the natural law of social evolution inexorably leads higher civilizations (such as the United States) to rule primitive areas (such as Latin America). Those advocating a security explanation contend that self-defense necessities require the United States to control Latin America, especially the Caribbean, so that powers hostile to Washington will be excluded from the region and therefore cannot pose a threat to the North American mainland. Hence U.S. imperialism is justified as a defensive imperative. Finally, the altruistic position posits that the United States is imperialistic in order to bring the benefits of U.S. culture to Latin America; the United States is in effect shouldering the White Man's Burden. For a discussion of these explanations, see Edward J. Williams, *The Political Themes of Inter-American Relations* (Belmont: Duxbury Press, 1971), pp. 13–33.

functioned as a central element in U.S. imperial policies, but its importance has diminished as the United States assumed global dimensions. Throughout the 1960s, the Doctrine was deemphasized by Washington. This deemphasis of the Monroe Doctrine, historically the primary rationalization for U.S. imperialism in Latin America, is not indicative of a change in the nature of U.S. imperialism or its relationship with Latin America. Quite the contrary, the change has been in style not substance—that is, the new doctrinal approaches have been introduced and new programs such as the Alliance for Progress have been established to facilitate U.S. penetration of Latin American societies. Contemporary Latin America remains a prime target for U.S. expansion in the Third World and is still considered by Washington as its special sphere of influence.

THE MONROE DOCTRINE IN HISTORICAL PERSPECTIVE. The Monroe Doctrine emerged during a period that, from the U.S. perspective, was characterized by considerable instability and uncertainty in the western hemisphere. From 1810 to 1824, most of Spain's colonies fought successful wars to achieve their political independence. Washington considered these new governments unstable and had serious doubts about their ability to maintain their independence if seriously challenged by European powers; Czarist Russia was claiming sovereignty over large areas in the Pacific Northwest; the Holy Alliance, a coterie of reactionary European states led by Austria, Russia, and France, appeared inclined to aid Spain in regaining her lost colonies in the New World; and England was moving to establish her commercial primacy in Latin America. The United States viewed these events with uneasiness and anticipation. United States policy makers were concerned that attempts by powerful European countries to replace Spain would jeopardize U.S. security and, perhaps, its very existence as a newly independent democratic republic. United States policy makers also recognized that the evolving situation in Latin America also provided the United States with the opportunity for territorial and/or economic expansion into Latin America. The Monroe Doctrine was Washington's response to this dual situation— tying its "security" to overseas expansion.[2]

---

[2] The No-Transfer Resolution of 1811 served in many respects as a precursor to the Monroe Doctrine. The United States was concerned that Spain might cede its territory in Florida to the English, thereby making it much more difficult and perhaps impossible to incorporate the land into the United States. To forestall this possibility and to set the stage for U.S. acquisition of Florida, Congress in 1811 passed a resolution prohibiting one European nation from transferring its hemispheric territory to another. The No-Transfer principle itself was not included in the original Monroe Doctrine, but its spirit of unilateral U.S. action to limit and ideally to exclude activity by European states in the western hemisphere was certainly manifested in the Doctrine. In 1870, the Grant Corollary formally extended the Monroe Doctrine's scope to include the No-Transfer concept. For a discussion of the development of the No-Transfer Resolution of 1811, see J. Lloyd Mecham, *A Survey of United States-Latin American Relations* (Boston: Houghton Mifflin Company, 1965), pp. 26–29.

The Doctrine was a unilateral policy pronouncement set forth by President James Monroe on December 2, 1823 in a message to Congress. Prior to announcing the Doctrine the U.S. government had, at England's request, considered the possibility of a joint U.S.-British pledge to cooperate in preventing the Holy Alliance from intervening in Latin America to reestablish Spanish control. Monroe and most cabinet members at first favored a joint U.S.-British initiative, but Secretary of State John Adams was adamantly opposed (Perkins, pp. 35–50). Adams pointed out ". . . the object of [the English] appears to have been . . . really or especially against the acquisition to the United States themselves of any part of the Spanish American possessions. . . . By joining her, therefore . . . we give her a substantial and perhaps inconvenient pledge against ourselves and really obtain nothing in return. . . ." (Freeman and Nearing, p. 236). Adams wanted to frustrate only English, not Yankee, imperial pretensions. Ultimately, Adams prevailed and the United States forged ahead alone, ignoring the British and particularly the Latin Americans themselves in promulgating the Doctrine.

In the 15 years prior to Monroe's statement, the Spanish possessions and especially the Spanish Caribbean colonies had become of prime importance to the United States. A rapid rise of American trade with the Spanish colonies took place during the Napoleonic Wars. Decaying Spanish power, coupled with the emancipation of large portions of Latin America, underlined the hopes of the United States that gains made during the highly abnormal war years could be made permanent (Whitaker, p. 24). In the period of 1821 to 1825, 31 percent of U.S. exports were directed toward Latin America—25 percent in the Caribbean area alone (Taylor, p. 452). As an example, Cuba received most of its imports from New England; by far the greatest proportion of tonnage employed belonged to New England shipowners. Over 1000 U.S. ships entered Cuban ports in 1824 alone (Whitaker, pp. 129 and 133). John Quincy Adams declared in April 1823 (shortly before Monroe's declaration): "Cuba almost in sight of our shores, from a multitude of considerations has become an object of transcendent importance to the political and commercial interests of our Union" (Whitaker, p. 127). The commercial-capitalist forces unleashed by the national liberation struggle immediately began to shape U.S. foreign policy in the direction of overseas expansion. National independence was a condition for U.S. expansion, not a universal doctrine applicable to other areas. A bourgeois national liberation movement in the postindependence period can easily adopt an aggressive overseas expansionist policy, casting aside its own national-democratic rhetoric.

The creation of conditions favorable to U.S. commercial interests was of prime importance in the enunciation of the Monroe Doctrine. It was hoped that the emancipation of Latin America (coupled with Cuba's probable annexation), would open Latin American markets to U.S. manufacturing and commercial groups (Whitaker, 546). The anticolonial motives were secondary, and the Monroe policy was, in good measure, directed toward perpetuating existing U.S. advantages in the area and in laying down the foundations of U.S. hegemony on the continent (Aguilar, p. 25).

The essential ingredients in the Monroe Doctrine include the following points. It prohibited European states from further colonization in the western hemisphere; it called for nonintervention, enjoining European countries to forego involving themselves directly (generally viewed as using physical force) in the affairs of hemispheric nations and pledging the U.S. to refrain from so interfering into matters concerning the remaining European colonies in Latin America; and it rejected the extension or imposition of European political systems into the hemisphere, contending that European and American sociopolitical cultures were basically different and indeed incompatible. Monroe went on to point out that whenever the United States determined that the Doctrine had been breached, it would consider the violation a hostile act and would feel free to mount an appropriate response to defend itself. As originally enunciated, the Doctrine had a dual perspective encompassing U.S.-European and U.S.-Latin American relations. In regard to U.S.-European relations, the Monroe Doctrine adopted a tone of self-defense and cloaked its rivalry with European imperialism in the rhetoric of national independence. In the early nineteenth century as an *embryonic imperialist and newly independent* nation, the United States was more concerned with consolidating its hold on the North American continent and limiting European expansion than realizing its overseas ambitions vis-à-vis Latin America. As the nineteenth century progressed, however, the U.S.-Latin American component of the Monroe Doctrine had the greatest impact, particularly as agrarian and industrial growth exceeded the capacity of the internal U.S. market.

In both its intentions and its substance the Monroe Doctrine represented an attempt by the United States to incorporate Latin America within its sphere of influence. Washington used the Doctrine to exclude external powers from the hemisphere in order to have a free hand to impose its political-economic hegemony, including annexation of those adjoining Mexican territories such as California that offered the greatest economic promise. Nevertheless, the United in 1823 did not possess the *capability* to carry out a very vigorous expansionist policy; but this lack of physical means does not obviate the fact that the Doctrine's *ultimate goals* were imperialistic. Aside from the Doctrine's intended consequences as envisaged by U.S. policy makers, the manner in which it was proclaimed foreshadowed an imperial design: Washington assumed the right to regulate the relationships of Latin American states with extrahemispheric powers. Not only was this claim itself undertaken unilaterally by the United States, but Washington's leaders reserved for themselves the sole prerogative to interpret and enforce the Doctrine. It was such unilateralism that constituted the first clear signs of the Doctrine's imperialist content. To U.S. policy makers it was immaterial whether the Latin states concurred with Monroe's vision regarding relationships between the Old and New Worlds or whether they accepted U.S. guidance in their foreign affairs; the U.S. *on its own initiative,* infringing on the sovereignty of other hemispheric nations, sought to impose a political framework that served U.S. commercial interests and wedged Latin America within the U.S. sphere of influence.

Essentially the Monroe Doctrine was a formal decision by the United States to base its foreign policy on traditional spheres of influence politics. Washington was attempting to imitate the European imperial powers: the western hemisphere was to be Washington's private bailiwick just as the European states possessed their territorial preserves in Asia and Africa. The original statement of the Doctrine sought *specifically* to establish U.S. influence or control only over the Latin countries' *extrahemispheric* relationships. But in application, the spheres of influence thinking underlying the Doctrine represented an implicit claim to general socioeconomic-political hegemony. The dominance of the United States was to become much more explicit through various interpretations and modifications in the implementation of Monroe's 1823 message throughout the nineteenth and twentieth centuries.

Although there were several incidents after 1823 that apparently violated Monroe's dictum,[3] the United States did not see fit to invoke the Doctrine and as such it lay dormant until resurrected by President James Polk in 1845.

Spurred by domestic socioeconomic pressures, the United States in the late 1830s and 1840s became engrossed in a drive toward territorial expansion involving the Mexican territories of Texas and California.

Despite incipient industrialization, United States foreign trade in the period 1816 to 1860 increased at a faster rate than Great Britain's, the most industrialized nation of the age. In this period, the total value of U.S. foreign trade increased by 230 percent, while that of Great Britain increased by 205 percent (Taylor, p. 177). The driving force behind this trade boom was an expanding, vigorous, export-minded agricultural sector.

Wheat and cotton were the two primary commodity exports. Expanding Latin American markets were of prime importance to American wheat producers who could not compete effectively in European markets. Had it not been for the West Indies and South America, flour exports would have been seriously affected (Taylor, p. 187). Wheat, however, was of peripheral impor-

---

[3] Some of these violations were: (a) in 1825 the French fleet was sent to Haiti to exact indemnities in return for French recognition of its independence; England forcibly intervened in a dispute between Brazil and Argentina, setting up Uruguay as a buffer state between the two; (b) in 1833 Britain moved into the Falkland Islands off the Argentina coast and also took over the Bay Islands off Honduras; (c) in 1838 France seized the Martin Garcia Island in the La Plata River and also occupied Veracruz in Mexico; and (d) in 1841 England established a protectorate over the mouth of the San Juan River in Nicaragua, consolidating its control over the Mosquito Indians who lived in the region. Discussions regarding these and other violations of the Monroe Doctrine can be found in J. Lloyd Mecham, pp. 54–56, cited in footnote 2; Dexter Perkins, *A History of the Monroe Doctrine* (Boston: Little, Brown, and Co., 1963), pp. 68–75; and Edwin Lieuwen, *U.S. Policy in Latin America* (New York: Frederick A. Praeger, 1965), pp. 14–15.

tance in relation to cotton. For more than a generation, cotton carried the bulk of U.S. international payments loads (Williams, p. 7). By 1860, cotton constituted over half of the total value of U.S. domestic exports (Taylor, p. 185).

U.S. economic development required the opening of additional lands to cotton and slavery to increase U.S. export earnings. The annexation of Texas was a means of enhancing the growth of cotton that, in turn, pressured U.S. policy makers to seek new markets abroad.

The pressures for markets and land exerted by the agricultural interests, and most especially by the South's need for more slave territory, were complementary and reinforcing economic engines of expansion driving the United States toward territorial annexation (Williams, p. 8).

United States expansionism did not, however, proceed unopposed. France and especially England perceived the United States as an imperial competitor and threat to their Latin American interests and to the existing hemispheric power balance. Consequently, both European countries attempted through diplomatic measures to prevent the United States from annexing Texas. They implored the new state to maintain its independence and even considered jointly guaranteeing continued Texas autonomy. European intervention in California was, in reality, minimal but Washington was nevertheless very much alarmed by rumors that England was attempting to buy the region from Mexico. President Polk responded to these European maneuvers, whether real or imagined, by reviving and expanding the Monroe Doctrine.

In a message to Congress on December 2, 1845, Polk reasserted the Monroe Doctrine and then added two new elements to it which became known as the Polk Corollary. First, he expanded the concept of European nonintervention by forbidding external powers from interfering *diplomatically* into relations between American states. Second, he extended the noncolonization idea by stating that henceforth Latin nations could not *voluntarily* accept European dominion, and incorporated into the Monroe Doctrine a modified no-transfer principle that prohibited Latin countries from ceding any or all of their territory to an extrahemispheric state.[4]

The Polk Corollary made it abundantly clear that the United States intended to use the Monroe Doctrine as the policy vehicle for imposing U.S. hegemony over Latin America. Polk's basic thrust was to extend the regulatory prerogatives claimed by the United States regarding *all* relations between Latin nations and extrahemispheric states. In particular, Washington for the first time *openly* asserted the right to control Latin initiatives toward external nations. In the original Monroe Doctrine, the United States had limited itself,

---

[4] The No-Transfer Resolution of 1811 dealt only with territorial transactions between *European* states; it said nothing about such dealings between Latin American and extrahemispheric countries. Thus Polk did not bring the original No-Transfer principle, but rather a variation thereof, into the Monroe Doctrine.

at least in its explicit claims, to restricting the activities of European powers that attempted to intervene directly in Latin America. However, with the Polk Corollary the United States imposed a policy directly on the Latin nations, threatening them with U.S. intervention should they decide to undertake certain actions (such as ceding territory) toward outside powers. In the context of colonizing and annexing Mexican territory Washington was, through the Polk Corollary, justifying its own imperialism in Latin America by contending that it was simply trying to prevent European neocolonialism.

The Polk Corollary served as the policy basis for the Mexican-American War of 1846 to 1848. By insisting that extrahemispheric nations could not intervene in any way in relationships between American states, even when those relationships involved U.S. expansion, and by rejecting prior to the fact the legitimacy of any transfer of American territory to outside countries, Washington preserved such territory for possible U.S. takeover. The Polk Corollary provided a rationale for annexation when Washington deemed such action feasible. Having thus established a policy framework to facilitate U.S. imperialism, Polk embarked on the Mexican-American War and seized vast areas of Mexico, including the coveted territory of California.

Early on, U.S. expansionist policies, whether colonial or neocolonial, were always cloaked in the rhetoric of antiinterventionism; imperialist ideology was rarely explicitly embraced as the rationale for expansion. On the contrary, during the latter half of the nineteenth century U.S. expansion was usually posed in antiimperialistic terms—U.S. expansion was always presented in terms of "security" or of "self-defense" against European expansion. Thus the myth grew in the United States of the virtuous self-made continent opposed to the decadent imperial Europe—a myth that allowed the United States to impose its policies and establish client-states in the Caribbean while posing as an upholder of national self-determination to its people and the world.

After the Civil War the United States entered an era of rapid industrialization. The absence of a deep-rooted feudal structure, vast natural resources, a growing population, and rapid technical progress combined to transform the U.S. economy within a few decades. Toward the end of the nineteenth century, American farmers and manufacturers reached a stage when a production surplus had been created that could not be disposed of in the home markets. In its need for markets the United States turned to Latin America (Freeman and Nearing, p. 242). The emergence of the United States as a modern industrial state marked the transition of American policy in the hemisphere from one of direct annexation to one of indirect control and commercial hegemony. Because of U.S. economic power it was no longer necessary to militarily subdue nations except when popular revolts occurred. The Monroe Doctrine would play a major role in the establishment of this "informal empire."

American commercial activity rose precipitously in the late nineteenth century. In 1880 the foreign commerce of the United States had reached a value of $93 million; by 1898 it had risen to $223 million (Freeman and Nearing, p. 242). Increasingly the United States wished to displace European (and especially British) industrial, financial, and commercial competition in the hemisphere. In 1889 Secretary of States James G. Blaine tried to secure, through the sponsorship of Pan Americanism, supremacy for the United States in Latin America through the formation of a customs union in which "the United States, supplanting Europe, should become the industrial provider of the agricultural nations in Latin America" (Freeman and Nearing, p. 244). The Blaine plan was ambitious for its day, considering the United States itself was still dependent on Europe for the capital necessary for the exploitation of its own vast resources. Blaine did, however, set forth the primary design of U.S.-Latin American policy for the next 50 years, a design echoed in the words of Senator Beveridge: "The trade of the world must and shall be ours. . . . We will cover the ocean with our merchant marine. We will build a navy to the measure of our greatness. . . . Our institutions will follow our flag on the wings of our commerce." (Aguilar, p. 41.)

The grandiose imperial pretensions that the United States attributed to the Monroe Doctrine were vividly demonstrated by the Olney Declaration of 1895. The Declaration arose from a long-simmering boundary dispute between Venezuela and British-controlled Guiana that intensified when England, spurred by the discovery of gold in the contested area, moved decisively into Venezuelan-claimed territory. London rejected Washington's demand that the controversy be submitted to arbitration and a direct confrontation ensued, the United States insisting that the English categorically rejected the Doctrine's validity. It was within this context that Secretary of State Richard Olney announced in 1895 that:

Today the United States is practically sovereign on this continent, and its fiat is law upon the subjects to which it confines its interposition. Why? . . . It is because, in addition to all other grounds, its infinite resources combined with its isolated position render it master of the situation and practically invulnerable as against any and all other powers.

All the advantages of this superiority are at once imperiled if the principle be admitted that European powers may convert American states into colonies or provinces of their own.

(Mecham, p. 64)

Ultimately the British capitulated, agreed to arbitration, and thereby informally recognized the Monroe Doctrine's relevance to such controversies.

In many eyes Olney's proclamation greatly extended the Monroe Doctrine's scope since it linked the Doctrine with an assertion of U.S. hemispheric hegemony, especially with respect to relations between Latin states and outside powers as well as internal policies. In essence Olney was stating that U.S. interests, as defined solely by Washington, were legitimately the paramount interests in the western hemisphere and that any action to protect them was fully justified under the Monroe Doctrine. Subsequently, the United States did not hesitate to exercise its self-proclaimed fiat and satisfy its imperialist interests. In 1898, the U.S. militarily intervened against the Cuban rebels' wishes[5] in the war between Cuba and Spain and proceeded, after Spain's defeat, to occupy the island from 1898 to 1902, exacting territorial and economic concessions from the Cubans, and then forcing the Cubans to accept a constitution that contained the Platt Amendment giving Washington, in effect, an unlimited right (one that was later exercised frequently) to unilaterally intervene in the island's affairs. From 1900 to 1903, Washington organized activities leading to a revolt in northern Colombia, resulting in the Republic of Panama, which proceeded by granting the United States rights on the Panamanian Isthmus for a canal.

While his proclamation's general tone was certainly sweeping, it would appear that Olney himself viewed it in a more limited light since he seemed to consider it applicable only to situations such as the Venzuelan-British dispute where extrahemispheric powers were directly involved. Seen from this perspective, the Olney Declaration did not drastically expand the Monroe Doctrine because concrete outside involvement in Latin affairs remained a prerequisite for the United States to exercise its fiat. According to this particular interpretation, then, the United States did not have or even claim a free hand to do whatever it pleased in the hemisphere; U.S. activity was to a certain extent circumscribed because a clear and present external intrusion had to exist before Washington could invoke and move under the Monroe Doctrine. But Olney's arrogance and his obvious desire to enlarge the U.S. imperium in Latin America paved the way for Theodore Roosevelt to undertake the Monroe Doctrine's most drastic extension.

In the late nineteenth and early twentieth century, the Caribbean, because of the proximity of its markets and raw materials and its strategic position in relation to the Panama Canal, became the primary area of U.S. activity in Latin America. United States investments in the Caribbean rose from $270 million in 1897 to $1,282 million by 1914. By 1914 the Caribbean absorbed almost four times the total investment of all South America ($365 million) (Faulkner, p. 74).

In 1904 Theodore Roosevelt, acting in accordance with the demands of powerful industrial, mining, railroad and banking interests, invoked the

---

[5] The Cubans rejected U.S. intervention for the very good reason that it was unnecessary. By 1898, the rebels had, for all practical purposes, defeated the Spanish forces and were on the verge of achieving their independence. The only activities remaining undone were final mopping up operations and formal Spanish capitulation. Thus the claim that the United States was rendering invaluable assistance to the Cubans was patently absurd —the Cubans didn't need such help. Rather the U.S. incursion was undertaken for self-aggrandizement, as later events demonstrated when Washington occupied the island and imposed its political-economic hegemony. The Cubans themselves recognized the motives underlying U.S. activities and rightfully resisted.

Roosevelt Corollary as the basis for U.S. military intervention in order to firmly incorporate the Caribbean area in the U.S. sphere of influence. Under heavy competition from European imperialists who were intervening in Caribbean countries to collect their debts, Roosevelt declared in a message to Congress that:

> If a nation shows that it knows how to act with reasonable efficiency and decency in social and political matters; if it keeps order and pays its obligations, it need fear no interference from the United States. Chronic wrongdoing, or an impotence which results in a general loosening of the ties of civilized society, may in America, as elsewhere, ultimately require intervention by some civilized nation, and in the Western Hemisphere the adherence of the United States to the Monroe Doctrine may force the United States, however reluctantly, in flagrant cases of such wrongdoing or impotence, to the exercise of an international police power. . . . It is a mere truism to say that every nation, whether in America or anywhere else, which desires to maintain its freedom, its independence, must ultimately realize that the right of such independence cannot be separated from the responsibility of making good use of it.
>
> (Gil, p. 70)

The Roosevelt Corollary incorporated the concept of preventive intervention into the Monroe Doctrine to undercut European expansion in favor of U.S. expansionist interests. Washington contended that anytime it determined that a situation existed that might conceivably lead an extrahemispheric power to intrude into Latin America, the United States had the right and indeed the duty to execute its own interventionary action. Under this doctrine it was not necessary for a foreign or Latin American government to do anything concrete to trigger a U.S. intervention; all that was required was Washington's unilateral decision that U.S. action was appropriate. In effect, the United States was claiming that it could intervene in Latin America anytime it felt so inclined. Accordingly the United States assumed the role of hemispheric policeman, imposing its hegemony under the guise of keeping the peace, preserving stability, and thereby forestalling foreign intrusions. More to the point, the U.S. military posture in the Caribbean greatly enhanced the expansion of American commercial interests in the area—and U.S. investment completely eclipsed European interests in the area. The Roosevelt Corollary represents the apogee in the Monroe Doctrine's development as a policy vehicle for U.S. imperialism; its promulgation unequivocally designated Latin America a sphere of U.S. influence and removed once and for all any doubt that Washington considered Latin sovereignty subordinate to U.S. interests.

The intensification of U.S. military intervention in the Caribbean, justified under the Roosevelt Corollary, came in the wake of William Howard Taft's "Dollar Diplomacy" and extended and deepened U.S. economic penetration of the area. U.S. investments in agriculture, mining and petroleum represented an extension of the activities of existing U.S. enterprises producing the same commodities at home or seeking a source of materials for processing in the United States (Bernstein, p. 39). In its early stages the migration of U.S. capital was without political implications; this rapidly changed as U.S. investors acquired extensive economic interests in foreign countries. United States investors, backed by diplomatic pressure from the U.S. government, began to make demands on host governments for concessions and privileges. Diplomatic pressure was superseded by more active interference as in the subsidizing of the Panama revolt. In much of the Caribbean the supremacy of U.S. capital was ultimately to be insured by armed intervention (Freeman and Nearing, p. 18). United States marines would enter a country "to protect American lives and property," and would, after a time, supervise national elections. Invariably the new president would be favorably disposed toward the United States, granting profitable concessions to U.S. firms (Poetker, p. 74).

The pattern of U.S. penetration and intervention is best illustrated in the cases of Haiti and Santo Domingo. American capital moved quietly into Haiti and Santo Domingo through government sponsored loans, and through purchase of bank shares and investments in plantations of various kinds (Faulkner, p. 79). In 1904, to settle the Dominican debt, Dominican officials, after much diplomatic pressure was exerted by the United States, allowed the United States to take control of the national customs, agreeing that the Republic's foreign debt was not to be increased without the consent of the United States. Political interference reached a peak in 1912 when President Taft forced the resignation of a Dominican President who was hostile to U.S. interests. Ultimately, pressed by the demands of the National City Bank and Equitable Trust Co. of New York, the United States established direct military rule in Santo Domingo in order to assure U.S. investors complete control over the finances and administration of the republic (Freeman and Nearing, pp. 130 and 129).

A similar pattern emerges in Haiti. U.S. investors (primarily large commercial banking groups) eliminated European creditors, consolidated the public debt and secured control of the national bank, and then pressed the State Department to insure their investment, whenever necessary, through political pressure and armed intervention (Freeman and Nearing, p. 135).

The classic fusion of military intervention and commercial interests occurred in Cuba. The American-dictated Platt Amendment to the Cuban constitution allowed U.S. intervention in Cuba, thus guaranteeing the political hegemony of the United States, which in turn allowed American business to secure valuable economic concessions. American investments in Cuba, guaranteed by periodic armed interventions, rose from $50 million in 1896 to $265 million in 1915. Similarly, U.S. exports to Cuba rose from $27 million in 1897 to $200 million in 1914, making Cuba the sixth largest customer for U.S. exports (Bernstein, p. 148).

The heavy influx of U.S. capital and exports into Cuba may be attributed equally to the rich natural resources of the island and to the policies of U.S. military occupation forces that periodically granted valuable concessions such as public utilities and paving and sewage to U.S. firms and ensured tariff agreements favorable to American business interests. Having granted concessions during the periods of military rule, the United States felt "morally responsible" for upholding these after the occupation was terminated (Freeman and Nearing, p. 180). By the mid-1920s, the ownership of Cuba lay almost completely in the hands of New York commercial interests—specifically, the National City Bank. The National City Bank directly controlled (1) the General Sugar Co. (the largest in Cuba); (2) its directors controlled the Consolidated Railways and had immense sugar holdings in the gigantic Cuba Co.; and (3) its 24 branches controlled the financial life of the island— lending money to native planters on sugar security at 10 percent interest.

U.S. exports prospered as a result of the Reciprocal Trade Agreement of 1903 that guaranteed the United States preferential tariffs in its trade with Cuba (20 to 40 percent reduction in the Cuban tariff) and greatly contributed to Cuba's underdevelopment (Bernstein, p. 147).

It was the U.S. monopolization of Cuban markets and domination of virtually every phase of Cuban economic life for the benefit of American investors that ultimately led to the reassertion of Cuban economic nationalism in the late 1950s.

By facilitating massive private U.S. investment, extending loans, and/or manipulating foreign trade, Washington created patterns of economic dependence which firmly established U.S. economic hegemony over the nations of the Caribbean and doomed them to perpetual underdevelopment and exploitation. The Roosevelt Corollary did yeoman duty as a policy vehicle for extending U.S. imperialism in the Caribbean, fastening these countries to the U.S. economy and contributing to U.S. development and Caribbean underdevelopment.

A further elaboration of the Monroe Doctrine was the Lodge Corollary of 1912 which complemented the Roosevelt Corollary and filled some gaps not covered in previous interpretations. The Lodge Corollary's formulation marked the Monroe Doctrine's full maturation as a policy vehicle for U.S. imperialism.

The Lodge Corollary, embodied in a Senate resolution sponsored by Senator Henry Cabot Lodge, arose from U.S. concern over rumors that a Japanese corporation was attempting to purchase Magdalena Bay, an important harbor on Mexico's California coast, from a U.S. company that controlled the area. Whether such a transaction constituted a threat to U.S. security, as some said, or not, the situation nevertheless provided a golden opportunity to further clarify the Monroe Doctrine. The Senate resolution declared:

> When any harbor or other place in the American continents is so situated that the occupation thereof for naval or military purposes might threaten the communications or safety of the United States, the govern-

ment of the United States could not see without grave concern the possession of such harbor or other place by any corporation or association which has such a relation to another government, not American, as to give that government practical power of control for national purposes.

(Mecham, p. 70)

The Lodge Corollary expanded the Doctrine's exclusionary noncolonization principle by asserting that foreign *economic interests* as well as foreign governments were now prohibited from acquiring land in the Americas. Furthermore, it extended the no-transfer concept's restrictions on Latin sovereignty to include a U.S. veto over *all* territorial exchanges between Latins and outsiders; Washington now claimed the prerogative to regulate not only such relations between Latin states and external powers, but also transactions which both hemispheric officials and private actors carried on with foreign nongovernmental economic interests. A violation of these U.S. pronouncements was, from Washington's viewpoint, a sufficient cause for U.S. intervention.

The Lodge Corollary, although seldom invoked formally, well exemplified the general thrust and nature of U.S. imperialism in Latin America up to this time. Washington, using the Monroe Doctrine and its various corollaries as the policy vehicle, sought to impose strict guidelines, backed by the threat and often the reality of U.S. military intervention, on the extrahemispheric relations pursued by the Latin states. Ideally all foreign influence in Latin America was to be dislodged and excluded. Thus the hemisphere would be open only to U.S. domination. The Colossus of the North could then employ its great economic power, supplemented when necessary by military action, to make recalcitrant states amenable to U.S. influence, to penetrate and control Latin economies and ultimately the countries' entire sociopolitical structures.

There are three points which summarize this discussion of the Monroe Doctrine as a policy vehicle for U.S. imperialism prior to World War II. First, the Doctrine as enunciated, interpreted, and applied was an instrument for *regional dominaion*—it was directed solely at Latin America and for most of the nineteenth and early twentieth century a subregional doctrine affecting the Caribbean but later extended to the rest of South America. The Monroe Doctrine provided a rationale for unilateral action to *establish* and then preserve Latin America as a sphere of U.S. influence within which Washington could pursue economic expansion. Initially U.S. imperial activities were centered primarily in geographically contiguous areas (such as Florida, Texas, and Californi) and in the Caribbean region (such as Central America, northern South America, and the island nations). Concentration on the Caribbean subregion resulted from short-term choices made by U.S. decision makers and available power capabilities rather than any restrictions inherent in the Doctrine. The Monroe Doctrine was intended to and later did serve as the basis for more extensive U.S. efforts to impose its hegemony throughout the hemisphere.

Second, the Monroe Doctrine was essentially a *reactive* policy vehicle. The physical presence or a clear threat of competing imperial countries was generally considered necessary before the United States could take action under the Doctrine. Consequently the initiative was not held by Washington (except to the extent that the Doctrine deterred interaction between outsiders and Latins) but rather by hemispheric and competing imperial countries. The Doctrine's deterrent function backed by growing U.S. economic and military power was usually sufficient. The policy was designed to, and indeed in some cases probably did, forestall external competition for control over Latin American resources and Latin overtures to foreign governments by creating a fear that the United States would invoke the Doctrine to intervene. The idea of an "external threat" was systematically used to permit U.S. intervention (for example, the Roosevelt and Lodge corollaries), thereby giving rise in due time to an offensive policy couched in "defensive" doctrinal terms.

Third, the Monroe Doctrine served to rationalize and facilitate one particular type of activity—actual or threatened direct unilateral military intervention. Thus interpreted and applied, the Doctrine was a rather restrictive policy vehicle for U.S. imperialism. Its utility as an instrument of control was confined to small, permeable, neighboring countries easily dominated. Alternative forms of hegemonic control, such as economic support for client rulers or assistance to friendly governments in repressing domestic political opponents were not easily fit into the "unilateral" framework worked out in the Monroe Doctrine and in the corollaries. Insofar, then, as the United States employed military action to establish and preserve Latin America as its sphere of influence, the Doctrine was quite useful. But the range of countries and situations to which it could be applied was quite limited. As an imperialist policy vehicle intended to motivate or justify U.S. hegemony on a continent-wide basis, the Monroe Doctrine left a good deal to be desired.

THE GOOD NEIGHBOR POLICY AND THE MONROE DOCTRINE

For better than 100 years after its promulgation in 1823 the Monroe Doctrine stood as the touchstone for Washington's policy toward Latin America. U.S. statesmen ostentatiously extolled the Doctrine, interpreting and expanding it so that it could be used to justify their particular activities; Congress, the press, and the public all looked upon it as something akin to a holy writ that deserved undying reverence and respect. Indeed the Monroe Doctrine during this period became in many respects the sacred cow of U.S. foreign policy. But in the late 1920s and 1930s changes occurred—the Doctrine was deemphasized and began to fade into the background as the Good Neighbor Policy was developed.

When the Great Depression struck, the U.S. economy contracted dramatically. There was a 46 percent decline in industrial production, while coal and steel production regressed 28 and 31 percent respectively. National income dropped from $81 billion to $40 billion between 1929 and 1932, while the total value of exports and imports fell from $9.6 billion to $2.9 billion (Aguilar, p. 67). The Depression forced the Latins to fall back on their own resources and encouraged national efforts at manufacturing products they could no longer import. U.S. policy toward Latin America began to undergo a change as a result of the depression situation. The emergence of Latin American economic nationalism forced the United States to strike a balance between the necessity of making some concessions to Latin America while at the same time advancing the long-term interests of the U.S. free enterprise system (Green, p. 35). Franklin Roosevelt's Good Neighbor Policy was U.S. imperialism's answer to the Depression and Latin American nationalism. The Good Neighbor Policy was a change in the form of U.S. Latin American policy rather than its content. That is . . . although the United States continued efforts to further its economic hegemony over Latin America, these efforts were now couched in terms of multilateralism and cooperation (Aguilar, p. 70).

Quantity about concerning unilateral intervention plagued U.S. policy makers

The Good Neighbor Policy represented an effort to soften the Doctrine's more blatant interventionist aspects. The first movement in this direction was the 1928 Clark Memorandum repudiating the Roosevelt Corollary. Basically the Memorandum argued that the Doctrine was designed to deal with external, especially European, incursions into the hemisphere; its purpose was not to regulate inter-American relations. Therefore Clark concluded that the Roosevelt Corollary, which allowed and indeed encouraged unilateral U.S. interventions in Latin America even when no plausible foreign threat existed, was incompatible with and should be separated from the Doctrine. In short the Clark Memorandum took the position that unilateral initiatives by Washington were not justifiable under the Doctrine, although a caveat was added stating that such activities were permissible when necessitated by self-defense. Thus the United States had not renounced self-initiated unilateral intervention per se, but had simply indicated that the Monroe Doctrine was not the proper policy vehicle for such actions.

Questions concerning unilateral intervention plagued U.S. policy makers and especially the Roosevelt administration throughout the 1930s. The Latins were insisting that *all* intervention—military, economic, and diplomatic— by one state into another's domestic or foreign affairs be renounced; Washington equivocated, not wanting to completely abandon the Monroe Doctrine in order not to hamstring itself in intervening to protect or even extend U.S. economic interests in Latin America. At the Montevideo Conference in 1933 the United States rejected "in principle" the right to unilateral intervention, although it narrowly defined intervention to include only military activities, and even then insisted that in those instances where international law permitted initiatives the United States would exercise those prerogatives. Hence Washington's renunciation in principle meant little; the United States still claimed the right to economic-diplomatic intervention (as it acted in overthrowing the nationalist Grau government in Cuba in 1933) and indeed even military intervention since international law was manipulated to justify such actions. At President Roosevelt's behest the United States did moderate its position somewhat at the 1936 Buenos Aires Conference, accepting without formal reservation a strong nonintervention resolution that prohibited for any reason, direct or indirect, unilateral intervention into a country's internal or external affairs. However, Washington continued to define intervention in purely military terms. More important, the United States indicated that it would abide by the proposed nonintervention principle only if the Latins reciprocated by accepting the concept of collective responsibility, which meant that multilateral military interventions when sanctioned by inter-American organizations were permissible. Reciprocity and collective responsibility were key elements in Roosevelt's Good Neighbor Policy. In stressing collective responsibility, Roosevelt underplayed unilateral policies such as the Monroe Doctrine and instead sought to develop multilateral agreements and institutions that Washington could use to maintain hemispheric stability and thereby protect its varied interests. But according to the reciprocity doctrine, if the Latin states shunned their duties by refusing to support collective initiatives, the United States was then free to undertake unilateral action under the Monroe Doctrine or some other rationale (for example, "self-defense").

Two basic factors converged to produce the Good Neighbor Policy. First, by 1930 U.S. hegemony in Latin America was rather well-established. Washington's many pre-1930 interventions, especially those based on the Roosevelt Corollary, had made the United States the dominant hemispheric power. The previous period of intervention and economic penetration created a series of regimes that followed the U.S. lead on most critical issues. Possessing client regimes, the United States was in a position to discuss "multilateral" organizations since the new mode of decision making would not challenge U.S. hegemony in the area.

Prior to 1914, despite the upsurge of American economic activity in the Caribbean, European powers, especially Great Britain, remained the primary sources of capital for Latin America (Bernstein, p. 32). British investments in Latin America are estimated to have grown from $330 million in 1870 to about $3,000 million in 1914. In 1914 British investments in Latin America comprised 20 percent of all British overseas investments and 43 percent of total foreign investments in Latin America. Latin America constituted 13 percent of French and 16 percent of German overseas investments (Bernstein, pp. 36, 38, and 40). By 1914, U.S. investments dominated the Caribbean, but equaled only about 20 percent of total foreign investments in Latin America and only about half of the total British investments in Latin America (Bernstein, p. 39). World War I greatly expedited the transformation of the United States into a chief creditor nation in the hemisphere (Freeman and Nearing, p. 12). During World War I, American investments rose 50 percent while European capital remained at former levels or declined (Bernstein, p. 10).

By 1914 the United States had started a concerted attack on British "laissez faire" imperialism in Latin America. The concept of "laissez faire" imperialism centers on the notion that the control of key enterprises and the domination of foreign trade can securely attach the recipient country to the investing nation's financial control and direction, thus making it into a sphere of influence. The central pivot of U.S. policy in Latin America became the displacement of British "laissez faire" imperialism and the subsequent accession of the United States to that position (Bernstein, p. 119).

After World War I the relative value of British trade and investment in Latin America remained static. France and Germany ceased to be important sources of competition (Bernstein, pp. 46 and 48). Only U.S. trade and investment continued to grow. The flow of capital from the United States into Latin America during World War I paved the way for a major expansion of U.S. influence in the region during the 1920s. In Argentina, the traditional bastion of British economic power in Latin America, for example, U.S. trade nearly doubled its 1913 level by 1927. The U.S. share of the Argentine market increased from 14.7 percent in 1913 to 24.7 percent in 1925, while Great Britain's share fell from 31 percent to 19 percent. U.S. capital invested in Argentina rose from $40 million in 1912 to $600 million in 1928, while British investment levels remained static (Tulchin, pp. 80 and 81). In the 10 years after 1914, U.S. exports in Latin America increased nearly 350 percent while Britain's increased only 18 percent (Tulchin, p. 40). This relative decline of European and particularly English economic influence in Latin America meant that the United States enjoyed almost free reign to consolidate its primacy without any real threat of outside interference. Roosevelt did not have to worry about building a U.S. sphere of influence in Latin America— that task had to a great extent already been accomplished by economic penetration. Rather, he moved to legitimize Washington's existing control, choosing multilateralism and the Good Neighbor Policy as the means to this end.

The second basic impetus behind the Good Neighbor Policy was the fact that as the 1930s progressed, the United States became increasingly concerned about the impending war in Europe and sought to tie the strategic economic resources of the Latin states to the U.S. war effort. Roosevelt therefore backed away from the "big stick" approach to inter-American relations and began trumpeting the need for hemispheric cooperation.

Economic interests continued to expand their control over the strategic sectors of the economy and hence U.S. economic interests dominated the key decisions affecting Latin American development. In fact, the Good Neighbor Policy and World War II cut Latin America off from alternative sources of financing and trade, thus deepening Latin American dependence on the United States. As Green has pointed out, the Good Neighbor Policy deliberately encouraged economic ties between the United States and the Latin

American elites to overcome political and economic nationalism in Latin America.

During the Roosevelt years the United States initiated an economic offensive in Latin America. The initiative consisted of the expansion of potential markets in Latin America in order to stimulate the sagging U.S. economy. In 1934, to spur trade, Congress approved the Reciprocal Trade Agreements Act and the creation of the Export-Import Bank. Between June 1934 and January 1940 the United States concluded 11 bilateral agreements with Latin American governments under the provisions of the Reciprocal Trade Agreements (Connell-Smith, p. 93). These agreements, coupled with the influx of American capital through the bilateral promotion loans of the Export-Import Bank, were designed to stimulate trade within existing lines of U.S. production in order to buoy up sagging U.S. business interests, while only incidentally helping Latin American development (Green, p. 44). The major criticism by Latin Americans of American loans was the lack of an American commitment to buy any new Latin American goods that the loans might produce (Green, p. 65). Also, U.S. insistence on low Latin American tariffs as necessary for economic cooperation made impossible the realization of any significant expansion of new Latin American industries that would have required, in addition to substantial U.S. loans, policies of tariff protection for their successful growth and development (Green, p. 76). Another creation of the Good Neighbor Policy was the Inter-American Development Commission. The IADC was to stimulate diversification of Latin American production in the expectation that the Latin American producers would find ready markets in the hemisphere. Such diversification was, however, to be limited to products not competitive with existing lines of production in already established western hemisphere markets (Green, p. 75). The basic assumption of the IADC was that in the long run Latin America's major industries should be complementary to, not competitive with, the major export industries of the United States (Green, p. 125). Under the expansionist impetus of the Good Neighbor Policy, U.S. investors found manifold opportunities for investment in Latin America. By the beginning of World War II, U.S. direct investments had spread throughout Latin America, and accounted for about 40 percent of direct U.S. investments abroad (Olden, p. 31).

Another major concern of U.S. imperialism during the Good Neighbor era was elimination of fascist penetration of the hemisphere. Roosevelt, anxious to displace the influence of German military missions in Latin America (which intermingled fascist propaganda with military training), initiated a program of military assistance to Latin America that successfully displaced the Axis powers prior to the outbreak of World War II. The success of the United States' efforts centered on Washington's willingness to underbid its competition and offer supplies and quality technical assistance at bargain prices (Grayson, p. 332). By acquiring a supply monopoly on military goods, the United States, in addition to benefiting its own industries, gained a significant degree of economic and political leverage over Latin American military establishments, thus helping to prevent the rise of anti-imperialist nationalism in the armed forces. Such leverage was a potent instrument in the defense of U.S. economic interests in Latin America (Green, p. 181). The roots of massive U.S. military involvement in Latin America in the 1950s and 1960s were established during the Good Neighbor period (Grayson, p. 332).

By the late 1930s, defense of U.S. hegemony indicated that the proper course for the United States was to ward off German influence in Latin America by tying the Latin American economies as closely as possible to its own (Green, p. 93). With the onslaught of hostilities the Latin American economies were more than ever dependent on the economy of the United States; there was nowhere else to turn for needed goods and markets (Green, p. 111). The United States geared the economies of Latin America to meet its own military needs. In particular, the strategic materials production programs were responsible for drastic and sometimes costly rearrangements of Latin American economies (Green, p. 101). In Bolivia, for example, labor scarcity plus power and transportation scarcities meant that the "all out" effort for tin production required by the U.S. war effort might seriously damage other important areas of Bolivia's economic activity (Green, p. 102). Similarly, in Brazil, massive labor relocation was required to meet U.S. demands for rubber—a product which the United States obtained from Brazil at about one-fifth of its true worth (Green, p. 106). Latin America did not reap benefits commensurate with its sacrifices. The U.S. government bought strategic materials from firms controlled largely by American capital, so that the profits from these purchases were largely returned to the United States itself (Green, p. 100). Additionally, the expanded purchasing power that accrued to Latin America was drastically undercut by inflation because of the inability of the United States to deliver goods that would soak up expanded Latin American purchasing power (Green, p. 111).

The Good Neighbor Policy represented a shift from purely military to economic instruments of power and penetration. Latin America remained within the sphere of U.S. influence, the good neighbor rhetoric notwithstanding. Washington's basic objective in Latin America—U.S. economic and political control—was unaltered. The change in policy was based on previous legal and military measures that eliminated rival imperialist competitors. In the post-World War II period U.S. policy based on the economic penetration and political collaboration evidenced in the Good Neighbor era would continue to hold sway and the Monroe Doctrine's deemphasis continues.

In the final analysis, the Good Neighbor Policy represented a shift in style rather than substance vis-à-vis U.S. relations with Latin America. Unilateral intervention and the Monroe Doctrine were not abandoned as available policy vehicles for U.S. expansion but were relegated into the background in favor of multilateralism. Roosevelt's multilateralism was in many respects little more than a symbolic gesture since Washington maintained tight control, often through economic pressure, over various inter-American organizations, allowing no action to be taken that would be detrimental to U.S. interests or to its hemispheric hegemony. The Good Neighbor Policy was a facade, a means to disguise the fact that Latin America remained a sphere of U.S. influence. After World War II the new expansionist components in U.S. policy toward Latin America, first apparent in the Good Neighbor era, would come into full bloom.

THE EVOLVING U.S. ECONOMIC INTEREST IN LATIN AMERICA AFTER 1945

POSTWAR PERIOD. World War II provided the opportunity for the final displacement of British economic power in the western hemisphere and the consolidation of U.S. hegemony. By 1941 Great Britain was unable to provide loans to Latin America, its flow of investments decreased drastically, and Latin American raw materials were closed to European markets. The United States replaced European goods and markets and by 1941 had become the primary source of loans and investment in Latin America. The United States successfully supplanted the unavailable European markets by the purchase of Latin American raw materials (Green, p. 95).

During World War II Britain was forced to liquidate an important part of its private investment and government bond holdings, especially in Argentina, Brazil, and Uruguay (Olden, p. 32). The scaling down of British investments in Latin America resulted from constant wartime U.S. pressure that forced the British to give up a long-term lease on Brazil's Itabira iron ore deposits (Olden, p. 32). By the war's end the United States surpassed Britain in total private investment in Latin America, controlling some $3,672 million compared to the $3,575 million controlled by Great Britain (Bailey, p. 50). By 1948 there was a drastic decline in British influence. British investments in Latin America were halved between 1946 and 1948 while those of the United States nearly doubled (Olden, p. 33). The decline of British economic competition after World War II assured the consolidation and the preeminence of U.S. imperialism in Latin America (Green, p. 267).

Economic hegemony in Latin America became of even greater importance to the United States after World War II as the United States shifted from a position of relative self-sufficiency to one of increasing dependence upon foreign sources of supply. The United States shifted from the position of a net exporter of metals and minerals to that of a net importer (Magdoff, p. 49). In 1951 the President's Commission on Foreign Economic Policy noted the importance of Latin America when it stated ". . . it is to (the underdeveloped) countries that we must look for the bulk of any possible increase in (strategic materials). The loss of any of these materials . . . would be the equivalent of a grave military set back" (Magdoff, p. 51). New industries, new technology, and the reemergence of a powerful European economic community gave a new importance to raw materials (Magdoff, p. 32).

U.S. investment continued to expand in Latin America. Having saturated the Caribbean, U.S. investments made significant inroads into South America. Venezuela, Brazil, and Chile experienced the largest increases in direct U.S. investment (*Survey of Current Business*). In the early postwar period the largest U.S. investments in Latin America were in agriculture, petroleum, and mining and smelting, all of which were tightly integrated with the U.S. economy, their levels of production being determined by the demands of U.S. markets. By the mid-1960s, the pattern of U.S. economic penetration in the hemisphere had taken on new forms. While extractive industries continued as an important feature of U.S. investment in Latin America, U.S. business began to make significant inroads in the industrial sector.

Percent Total of Some U.S. Direct Investments
in Latin America by Sector

	Mining and Smelting	Petroleum	Manu-facturing	Trans-portation and Utility	Trade
1950	13	29	16	22	5
1960	15	36	17	—	7
1970	11.5	26.4	34.9	5.3	11.2

The replacement of exclusively extractive-oriented investments by a more pervasive and eclectic pattern of U.S. investment in Latin America coincided with the emergence of the Alliance for Progress. The Alliance for Progress was designed to promote the interests of the U.S. investors involved in the manufacturing sectors and the modernizing enterprises, hoping to consolidate a new "alliance" between the multinational corporations and the Latin American middle class—excluding both European and Asian competitors as well as indigenous Latin nationalists. This new alliance was to replace the old pact between the landed oligarchy and U.S. investors in mineral industries. The diversification of U.S. projects and loan programs through the Alliance paralleled the growing diversity of U.S. investments, away from the traditional primary sector toward industry and services. The notion of "partnership" that underlay the Alliance was at the heart of the new approach being promoted by U.S. business abroad: joint ventures with Latin capital in industry as well as service and management contracts in the petroleum and mining industry.

For U.S. policy makers, Latin American nationalism remained the greatest threat to U.S. economic interests in the hemisphere. Nevertheless, the emergence of strong economic competitors in Western Europe and Japan marks

Latin America: Origin of Imports (Percent)

	1950	1955	1960	1965	1967	1969
United States	51.1	46.7	44.7	40.0	38.5	36.7
Western Europe	27.9	28.3	32.6	29.0	30.4	31.6
(EEC)	12.8	17.1	19.6	17.5	18.6	18.7
Japan	.8	2.5	3.5	4.4	4.7	6.1

Latin America: Destination of Exports (Percent)

	1950	1955	1960	1965	1967	1969
United States	45.9	44.0	42.1	31.9	32.2	30.2
Western Europe	29.8	28.7	31.9	32.8	33.9	34.3
(EEC)	13.2	15.6	18.5	20.0	20.8	20.8
Japan	1.3	2.9	2.8	4.3	4.8	6.4

Source. UN Yearbook of International Trade, June to December 1969.

a new challenge to U.S. economic primacy in the area. U.S. competitors are capturing Latin American markets and displacing North American buyers.

The threat to U.S. markets in Latin America is bolstered by a substantial influx of capital investment. By the mid-1960s, over 35 percent of Japanese investment was concentrated in Latin America in such various concerns as the Usimanas Co. (Steel-Brazil), the Ishikawajima Harima Co. (Shipbuilding-Brazil) and Nissan Motors (Mexico). West German investments, too, are rising in Latin America with a substantial stake in Brazil already emerging (*Business International,* July 21, 1967, p. 225). Both West Germany and Japan increased overseas foreign investment by 400 percent within the last five years. Thus foreign investments are growing rapidly while U.S. investments seem to have levelled off at an annual growth rate of 8 percent (*Survey of Current Business*). The uncontested economic primacy enjoyed by the United States after World War II in Latin America is being challenged from the outside as well as from the inside.

THE MONROE DOCTRINE AND POSTWAR U.S. POLICY TOWARD LATIN AMERICA

The United States was forced to neglect hemispheric affairs in the immediate postwar period in favor of bolstering European capitalism's struggle against social revolution. In the immediate post-World War II period Washington directed its attention toward consolidating its informal economic ties with formal features and regional organizations. In 1947, after having achieved economic supremacy in the hemisphere, the United States abandoned its traditional aversion to formal alliances and signed the Rio Treaty.[6] In 1948 the United States was instrumental in creating the Organization of American States (OAS). The Rio Treaty was descibed by its signatories as a collective defense agreement that provided for cooperation between hemispheric nations in meeting aggression and threats to the peace. The OAS, which emerged from the 1948 Bogata Conference, provided an institutional framework for the previously unstructured inter-American system—it sought to facilitate periodic conferences and to bring together under one organizational roof various hemispheric agencies. With the OAS the U.S. sought a regional umbrella under which it could initiate policies that in other periods it would have pursued unilaterally. More specifically, U.S. policy makers thought that a regional organization like the OAS could provide the rubber stamp of legitimacy on U.S. actions, thus evading the onus of being accused of arbitrary aggression. Instead of being accused of being the aggressive expansionist power within the hemisphere U.S. policy makers could argue in terms of "measures adopted by a regional organization for self-defense from a foreign threat."

Essentially, the Rio Treaty and the OAS formalized or institutionalized the "collective responsibility" rhetoric that Franklin Roosevelt had introduced. But as was the case with the Good Neighbor Policy, these new initiatives did not mean that the Monroe Doctrine had been either abandoned by the United States or multilateralized in the sense that U.S. action was subject to decisions made by the OAS. The United States continued to claim the right to take unilateral steps under the Monroe Doctrine to handle any situation in which "multilateral" OAS responses were not forthcoming.

The Monroe Doctrine was, however, deemphasized by Washington during 1947 to 1948 in favor of anti-Communism as the linchpin for U.S.-Latin American relations. At the Bogota Conference a resolution strongly supported by the United States was passed condemning international Communism as incompatible with American concepts of "freedom" and urged OAS members to take measures to resist it. This anti-Communist theme became popular as a policy vehicle for U.S. imperialism in the years to come. Washington justified its hegemonic activities in terms of "protecting" the hemisphere from the international Communist movement. The anti-Communist appeal also allowed the United States to mobilize Latin American votes in the United Nations against the U.S.S.R. and the revolutionary currents in the Third World. The basic strategy, especially during the 1950s, was to get the OAS to adopt reso-

---

[6] Basically, the Rio Treaty commits its signers to assist individually any member(s) suffering armed attack and also provides formal mechanisms for consultation among the hemispheric states to decide what collective action (such as diplomatic sanctions, economic reprisals, use of force) the organization will take to counter aggression or threats to the peace. However, member countries cannot be required to take any armed action against their consent. For a good concise discussion of the Rio Treaty's provisions, see Ibid., pp. 190–196.

lutions labeling Communism as an "alien ideology" and its presence in the hemisphere as the functional equivalent of foreign aggression. Action could then be taken, ideally in concert with OAS members or unilaterally if necessary, to root out social revolutionaries wherever the United States decided it to be expedient. Washington tended to include in its definition of Communism any activity that threatened U.S. economic interests or the maintenance of Latin America within the U.S. sphere of influence.

The first important application of Washington's postwar Latin American policy came in Guatemala. In 1944 General Jorge Ubico, Guatemala's dictator since 1931, was overthrown and Juan Arevalo was elected President the following year. Arevalo was a moderate reformer who, among other things, abolished forced labor, enacted a labor code, and attempted to upgrade the educational system. In 1951 Colonel Jacabo Arbenz legally succeeded Arevalo and began to pursue national-populist policies. Specifically, he moved against United Fruit, a U.S.-owned company that had a stranglehold on Guatemala's economy.[7] Arbenz nationalized some United Fruit land that was not being cultivated and insisted that the company begin to pay taxes on its profits, allow its workers to unionize, and pay its employees government-set minimum wages. These domestic programs, combined with the fact that Arbenz was trying to normalize relations with Eastern Bloc countries, infuriated the Eisenhower administration which began to insist that Guatemala was being taken over by subversives who were functioning as agents for international Communism. Thus the stage was being set for U.S. intervention.

At the 1954 OAS conference in Caracas, Secretary of State John Foster Dulles focused attention on the Guatemalan question. At the outset, Dulles wanted the conference to authorize immediate action against Guatemala, but he ultimately settled for a general declaration (without specifically mentioning Guatemala) that stated:

> The domination or control of the political institutions of any American state by the international Communist movement, extending to this hemisphere the political system of an extra-Continental power, would constitute a threat to the sovereignty and political independence of the American States, endangering the peace of America, and would call for a meeting of consultation to consider the adoption of appropriate action in accordance with existing treaties.
>
> (Gil, pp. 211–212)

[7] United Fruit's penetration of Guatemala's economy almost boggles one's imagination. It was the country's largest landowner; its profits were generally exempt from taxes; it received a 72 percent *annual* return on its total investment; it owned 43 percent of the country's railways; and it controlled the main port as well as Guatemala's entire maritime shipping business. See Carleton Beals, *Latin America: World in Revolution* (London: Abelard-Schuman, 1963), pp. 260–261; John Gerassi, "Violence, Revolution, and Structural Change in Latin America" in Irving L. Horowitz, Josue deCastro, and John Gerassi (eds.), *Latin American Radicalism* (New York: Random House, 1969), p. 462; and Adolfo Gilly, "The Guerrilla Movement in Guatemala," *Monthly Review*, 17:9–40 (May 1965), pp. 39–40.

Dulles' efforts to protect U.S. economic interests and hemispheric hegemony were reminiscent of Theodore Roosevelt's "big stick" approach to Latin relations. However, in 1954 Washington's rationale for domination was not the Roosevelt Corollary, but rather a combination of OAS policy declarations and the Monroe Doctrine. Anti-Communism was the dominant theme that the United States used to rationalize its interventionist activities. Washington's approach proceeded first along "legalistic" and then "military" lines as follows: the Caracas Resolution established anti-Communism as the principal criterion for legitimizing or delegitimizing governments and judging their hemispheric policies and positions; similarly, the Resolution gave prior OAS approval to anti-Communist initiatives by its members. Arbenz' domestic programs and his foreign policy were described by the United States as pro-Communist; therefore, the U.S. was "justified" taking action to oust him. Although the Monroe Doctrine was never mentioned by name, the section in the Caracas Resolution dealing with the intrusion of foreign political systems as a threat to the hemisphere is pure 1823-vintage Monroe Doctrine. Indeed Dulles' statements at the time indicated that he certainly looked upon the resolution as an OAS blessing for unilateral U.S. action under the Doctrine. It is this complex fusion of anti-Communism and the Monroe Doctrine that makes the Guatemalan episode an excellent example of the policy approach the U.S. would utilize during the 1950s to maintain its hegemony in Latin America.

The main target for U.S. imperialism in the early 1960s was Cuba. Fidel Castro, who came to power in 1959 determined to assert Cuba's economic independence and bring about a thoroughgoing social revolution, incurred Eisenhower's wrath by nationalizing the massive Cuban assets held by U.S. companies.[8] Washington closed U.S. markets to Cuban sugar, cut off all trade relations, and organized an economic blockade, hoping thereby to cause economic chaos leading to Castro's downfall. Castro weathered this attack by reorienting Cuba's trade toward the Eastern Bloc and obtaining economic and technical assistance from the Soviet Union. Castro's successful nationalization programs and support of social revolution in Latin America was viewed by the United States as a challenge to its hemispheric hegemony. Throughout the 1960s the U.S. policy toward Latin America was influenced by, and in response to, the Cuban events.

[8] U.S. interests had penetrated the Cuban economy to the point where they for all practical purposes controlled it. In 1956, the U.S. Chamber of Commerce bragged that "The only foreign investment of importance [in Cuba] are those of the United States. American participation exceeds 90 percent in the telephone and electric industries, about 50 percent in public service railways, and roughly 40 percent in raw sugar production. The Cuban branches of United States banks are entrusted with almost one-fourth of all bank deposits . . ." Quoted in Leo Huberman and Paul M. Sweezy, *Cuba: Anatomy of a Revolution*, 2nd ed. (New York: Monthly Review Press, 1960), p. 22. In addition, Cuba's overall economic health was heavily dependent upon selling its main agricultural export—sugar—in the U.S. market. Consequently, Cuba's pre-Castro economic dependence on the United States was almost total and Washington had never hesitated to exploit this vulnerability, using economic pressure to get Cuban governments to follow pro-U.S. policies.

Having failed to get the OAS to take a strong anti-Castro action, the United States moved unilaterally in 1961, sponsoring the Bay of Pigs invasion. President Kennedy readily admitted U.S. complicity, but refused to concede that such involvement constituted intervention into Cuba's affairs. Echoing Franklin Roosevelt, he insisted that Washington had not intervened because U.S. armed forces did not actually participate in the invasion. But Kennedy went on to warn:

> But let the record show that our restraint is not inexhaustible. Should it ever appear the inter-American doctrine of non-interference merely conceals or excuses a policy of inaction—if the nations of this hemisphere should fail to meet their commitments against outside Communist penetration—then I want it clearly understood that this government will not hesitate in meeting its primary obligations, which are the security of our nation.
>
> (Mecham, p. 227)

Although this quote contains Monroeist overtones in the sense that the United States claimed the right to undertake unilateral intervention, the rhetoric was borrowed essentially from the Dulles Cold War era with its emphasis on Communist threats to U.S. security. The influence of Franklin Roosevelt's rhetoric regarding collective responsibility and reciprocity is also present in Kennedy's statement. Like Roosevelt, Kennedy insisted that the United States would adhere to nonintervention only as long as the Latin states reciprocated by agreeing to follow U.S. policy, that is, multilateral anti-Communist actions. If such reciprocity was not extended, Kennedy argued, Washington would feel free to take whatever steps were needed to protect its security and promote its interests. Kennedy was saying, then, that it was not the Monroe Doctrine, but the right to defend U.S. hegemony and economic interests in foreign countries (self-defense) that justified the Bay of Pigs and indeed any future anti-Communist interventions the United States might decide to unleash.

Having failed to overthrow Castro by force, the Kennedy administration decided to expel Cuba from the OAS. At a Punta del Este meeting in January 1962, the United States pushed through resolutions that held that:

> . . . adherence by any member of the Organization of American States to Marxism-Leninism is incompatible with the inter-American system and the alignment of such a government with the communist bloc breaks the unity and solidarity of the hemisphere. . . .
>
> . . . the present government of Cuba, which has officially identified itself as a Marxist-Leninist government, is incompatible with the principles and objectives of the inter-American system. . . .
>
> . . . this incompatibility excludes the present government of Cuba from participation in the inter-American system. . . .
>
> (Connell-Smith, p. 252)

Cuba, expelled from the OAS by Washington's rabid anti-Communism, was also subjected to diplomatic-economic sanctions (most OAS members, in response to U.S. pressure, broke diplomatic relations and suspended trade with Castro's government). Subsequently, U.S. policy was geared to *isolating* Cuba from Latin America; having failed to overthrow Castro, the United States sought to preserve the rest of Latin America within its sphere of influence.

In October 1962 came the U.S. naval blockade of Cuba. Castro, alarmed by the Bay of Pigs invasion, moved to bolster his defense capabilities by accepting Soviet military equipment (including bombers and medium-range missiles) and advisors. Cuba's security measures served as a pretext for Washington to launch a global confrontation to limit Cuban influence in the hemisphere. The United States proclaimed that the Russian missiles represented an offensive threat to U.S. security. Kennedy then imposed a naval blockade on Cuba and after U.S.-Soviet consultations the missiles were finally withdrawn. Kennedy justified his actions on two grounds: (1) the United States was exercising its right of "self-defense" in responding to the "offensive" threat posed by the Russian missiles, and (2) the OAS had unanimously passed a resolution authorizing the blockade. This rationale, through which Washington claimed the right to impose its will on Cuba, served to freeze the status quo in Latin America; Cuba would remain, although isolated, and the United States was given the green light to proceed in Latin America unhindered by Soviet support to revolutionary forces.

The Bay of Pigs, the 1962 Punta del Este expulsion, and the missile crisis all represented attempts by the United States to regain total control. In the first instance, Washington unilaterally intervened with force to restore Cuba to U.S. client status. In the second, the United States resorted to diplomatic pressure and an economic blockade designed to limit Cuba's capacity to support social revolution while the United States mobilized its resources for massive political-military penetration. Finally, Kennedy's interference with Cuba's sovereign right to carry on foreign relations, including military agreements, with any country it chose was directed at convincing the Soviet Union that postwar spheres of influence patterns were still operative. United States aggression toward Cuba was not novel. Unlike the past, however, the Monroe Doctrine was not in evidence as the U.S. policy rationale. Instead, the Eisenhower-Kennedy administrations justified their attempts to preserve their hemispheric influence by relying on anti-Communism (Punta del Este), "self-defense" (the missile crisis), or a synthesis of both (the Bay of Pigs).

The Cuban experience, demonstrating that *indigenous* Latin revolutionaries operating without significant external support could successfully seize power, challenge U.S. hegemony, and especially take actions against major U.S. economic interests, shook Washington to its very roots. The United States publicly admitted that the most serious threat to its hemispheric domination would not involve exogenous penetrations, but rather would be mounted by indigenous revolutionary forces. Consequently, Washington increased its allocation of manpower and resources toward controlling domestic events in Latin America, choosing as its means the Alliance for Progress and counter-insurgency programs.

The Alliance For Progress was launched in 1961. According to the Kennedy team the Alliance was to be a "partnership" between North and South Americans that would set the Latin states on the road to material affluence and social justice. The operational mechanics, briefly stated, included the following steps. The United States would contribute money and expertise, and the Latins would respond with additional funds, reforms, and a willingness to follow Washington's advice on all major issues affecting development policy. The official reason given for the program was the U.S. desire to assist Latin America in achieving meaningful socioeconomic development. In reality Washington was motivated by a number of considerations, including the fear of another social revolution. The Alliance's basic thrust was not *for progress,* but *against revolution* (Morray, pp. 99-119). By instituting symbolic reforms, promoting elite modernization, and providing the Latin masses with a few socioeconomic services, it was thought that popular discontent could be reduced, thereby lessening the possibility of "new Cubas."

If the core was counterrevolutionary restoration, the Alliance was also designed to benefit U.S. economic interests by opening Latin America to further penetration by U.S. capital. The Alliance Charter clearly stated that its signatories were committed to promoting conditions that would encourage the flow of foreign investment. Kennedy officials were quite open in acknowledging that massive U.S. private investment in Latin America not only would be encouraged but indeed facilitated with the Alliance's framework. In addition the Alliance often functioned to subsidize North American companies by requiring that Latin states spend the money they received under the program for U.S. goods and services. Consequently Washington's verbal benevolence was transformed in practice into crass economic self-interest.

The Alliance functioned as a socioeconomic prophylactic to prevent Latin revolutions, thereby helping to preserve the U.S. sphere of influence. It involved comprehensive participation by U.S. advisers in the day-to-day decisions and affairs of hemispheric states to protect and enhance U.S. economic and political interests. The Alliance differed from the Monroe Doctrine as a policy vehicle for U.S. imperialism since the Alliance was basically preventive in nature—it sought through socioeconomic programs to *forestall* any domestic upheavals that might conceivably threaten U.S. domination. Conversely the Monroe Doctrine was essentially reactive—it was geared to meet, generally with military means, actual or very imminent challenges to Washington's hegemony coming primarily from outside the hemisphere. These differences meant that during the Alliance's heyday in the early 1960s one heard very little talk in Washington about the Monroe Doctrine.

The broad scope of activities that the Alliance for Progress included gave the U.S. unlimited opportunities for penetrating Latin America's administrative decision-making structure: planning agencies, urban, industrial and rural development projects, health, education and welfare ministries all had programs and ideas largely shaped by U.S. advisers financed by AID or private foundations. The comprehensive issues raised and the collaborative (partnership) formulas espoused by the Alliance were ideal vehicles for enabling the United States to penetrate several layers of Latin American decision-making structure, deal with problem areas that might affect U.S. interests, design "solutions," and avoid "crises" situations that might necessitate the overt use of U.S. force.

During the 1960s, the United States attempted to control domestic events in Latin America through the Alliance for Progress and a more elaborate and complex military assistance program; both military and economic programs were perceived as complementary. Secretary of Defense Robert McNamara made this point quite clear when he commented in June 1963 that:

> Until about 1960 military assistance programs for Latin America were oriented toward hemispheric defense. As it became clear that there was no threat of significant overt external aggression against Latin America, emphasis shifted to internal security. . . .
>
> (Petras, pp. 350–351)

McNamara reasserted this position in 1967 when he said that:

> the primary objective [of the U.S. military assistance program] in Latin America is to aid, where necessary, in the continued development of indigenous military and paramilitary forces capable of providing, in conjunction with police and other security forces, the needed domestic security.
>
> (*Foreign Assistance Act*)

The emphasis on "internal security" was manifested in the counterinsurgency activities that President Kennedy (who was particularly enamored with the Green Berets) instituted to function as the military counterpart to the Alliance. Counterinsurgency entailed cooperation between the United States and Latin governments to eradicate indigenous revolutionary forces throughout the hemisphere. These programs did not envision massive direct intervention by U.S. military forces, but instead called on Washington to supply equipment, logistical support, training, and advisors so that the Latin regimes themselves could develop an effective capacity to suppress popular insurgents in their countries (Barber and Ronning). As the Alliance faltered because of the unwillingness of Latin oligarchies to implement socioeconomic reforms and Washington's reluctance to support changes that might affect U.S. corporate interests, counterinsurgency became the main element in the United States' counterrevolutionary policy during the Johnson and Nixon administrations. Certainly by 1970, primary emphasis in U.S. hemispheric policy was not on using the Alliance to mitigate popular discontent that might produce instability, but instead stressed the buildup of formal and informal coercive bodies to repress nationalist and socialist threats to the status quo—a status quo that, in Washington's eyes, entailed maintaining Latin America in the U.S. sphere of influence.

An important consequence of this military cooperation has been the increased political role played by the armed forces in Latin America during the 1960s and 1970s. U.S. assistance (such as arms, training, and advisors) has greatly strengthened the Latin military and, in effect, has underwritten its capacity to intervene in the political process. With some important exceptions (Peru and Bolivia under Torres) the armed forces have functioned to suppress any elements they consider radical, whether inside or outside the government. Washington not only has encouraged such takeovers, but also has been lavish in its aid to these military dictatorships to help them consolidate their power (for example, Brazil and Argentina) (*Rockefeller Report*). The pro-U.S. generals, realizing that their position is to a great extent dependent on continued U.S. aid, have been hesitant to adopt measures which might displease U.S. investors and provoke U.S. policy makers into rescinding support. The military has acted as Washington's agent in the Latin political process, assuring stability maintenance and loyalty to global U.S. policy goals. By building up and indoctrinating the Latin armed forces to the point where they exercise a policy and personnel veto and then using them to protect U.S. economic interests, Washington's military penetration has gone straight to the heart of hemispheric political systems (Wolpin). Working through its military allies, the United States has substantial leverage in determining who can occupy the main decision-making posts and what basic policies they can follow.

The U.S. invasion of the Dominican Republic demonstrated that the United States was still willing to intervene unilaterally to suppress insurgencies in Latin America when its military clients are unable to handle the situation. The crisis actually began when Juan Bosch was elected President in 1963 and set about instituting various socioeconomic reforms. Both the Dominican oligarchy and U.S. corporations were opposed to Bosch's constitution, especially Article 19 demanding profit-sharing plans for industrial and agricultural workers, Article 23 setting limits on landholdings, Article 25 regulating land ownership by foreigners, and Article 28 calling for land redistribution. Also, the new President's effort to diversify the sources of external funding for development did not particulary please Washington. For example, Bosch cancelled an oil refinery contract with U.S. companies because he felt that its terms would lead to the flight of excessive profits. In 1963, conservative military elements ousted Bosch, setting up a civilian junta that backed away from socioeconomic reform and catered instead to big-business interests. Initially, Washington remained formally aloof from the new regime, but finally the Johnson administration extended strong support. In April 1965, a pro-Bosch faction in the army attempted to seize power. The rebels called for a mass uprising, began to distribute arms to the people, and invited the exiled Bosch to return to assume the Presidency. President Johnson, recognizing that there were serious cleavages in the Dominican military and that the armed forces that were acting as Washington's agents might not be able to put down the uprising, ordered 20,000 U.S. troops to intercede. Later, the OAS, under heavy U.S. pressure, sanctioned the intervention.[9] Johnson justified his move in anti-Communist terms, declaring:

> The evidence we have on the revolutionary movement (in the Dominican Republic) indicates that it took a very tragic turn. Many of them trained in Cuba, seeing a chance to increase disorder and to gain a foothold, joined the revolution. They took increasing control. What began as a popular democratic revolution that was committed to democracy and social justice moved into the hands of a band of Communist conspirators. . . . Our goal, in keeping with the great principles of the inter-American system, is to help prevent another Communist state in this Hemisphere.
>
> (Goff and Locker, p. 278)

This statement set the basis for the Johnson Doctrine, that claims for the United States the right to take unilateral military action anytime the United States determines that a situation might lead to a Communist government. In effect, this policy means that when Washington's military clients in Latin America cannot successfully carry out a counterinsurgency program against indigenous revolutionaries, U.S. armed forces will intervene to restore a client regime.

In 1966, Joaquin Balaguer, Washington's handpicked candidate, won the tightly controlled Presidential election while U.S. troops were still occupying the nation. Balaguer, a conservative whose policies have favored the Dominican oligarchy and U.S. corporate interests, received heavy military-economic assistance from the Johnson administration to help him solidify his hold on the country. From Washington's viewpoint, its counterinsurgency

---

[9] The OAS passed a U.S.-sponsored resolution creating an OAS peace-keeping mission commanded by a Brazilian general that was to police the Dominican situation. United States troops already in the Dominican Republic constituted the great bulk of this force, although five Latin nations (Brazil, Honduras, Nicaragua, Costa Rica, and Paraguay) contributed some personnel. But this surface multilateralism notwithstanding, the operation remained basically a U.S. venture.

Immediately after the Dominican crisis, the Johnson Administration began pushing the OAS, albeit unsuccessfully, to form an Inter-American Army to deal with similar problems which might subsequently arise. This represented an attempt to get the OAS, which was originally designed to counter external aggression, into the internal security area. Essentially Washington was seeking to institutionalize collective intervention and to obtain OAS legitimacy for future counterinsurgency action which the U.S. may wish to undertake to repress domestic Latin revolutionary movements that threaten hemispheric stability and U.S. political-economic interests. For a discussion regarding the Inter-American Army concept, see James Petras, "The United States and the New Equilibrium . . .", *op. cit.*, pp. 115–118.

intervention had been a resounding triumph—it had subdued the revolutionary populace on the island, led to a staunchly pro-U.S. regime, and served as a warning to other Latin movements that might be tempted to challenge U.S. hemispheric hegemony.

Obviously, counterinsurgency as an instrument of neocolonial control depends upon Washington's capacity to create effective administrative and military units while atomizing and manipulating the underlying population. The counterinsurgency strategy emerges in a time of declining neocolonial regimes, a last stage prior to direct U.S. military involvement. These counterinsurgency activities have not been based on the Monroe Doctrine. Rather the rationalizations have varied; they have included anti-Communism, U.S. "security" requirements, protecting established governments from "illegal subversion," and the necessity for "stability" in order for the Alliance to work, for economic development to occur, and for democracy to develop. Implicit in all this, policy rhetoric is a basic theme of hostility toward large scale social change from below that challenges Washington's hemispheric hegemony. In short, the unspoken premise underlying U.S. relationships with Latin America is blanket counterrevolution to defend the status quo.

CONCLUSION

Since World War II, the Monroe Doctrine, as a general rule, has not been the primary policy vehicle for U.S. imperialism, although Washington has not repudiated the Doctrine, keeping it available for possible use in *particular* crisis situations when the United States needs a rationale for unilateral intervention. Two interrelated reasons can be cited for the Monroe Doctrine's deemphasis: (1) basic changes (three to be exact) in the overall context within which the United States pursues its foreign policy, and (2) alterations in the modes employed by Washington to maintain and exert its hegemonic hemispheric control.

The first contextual transformation involved a U.S. shift from an essentially regional to a global economic-military power. Prior to World War II, U.S. imperialism was generally restricted to a limited area—specifically, territory contiguous to the United States, Central America, and the Caribbean. The Monroe Doctrine actually operated within these narrow geographical confines. The limited application of the Doctrine can be graphically seen in its application: the United States usually ignored "violations" in southern Latin America until World War II; it was not committed to continentwide enforcement of the Doctrine. In practice, then, the Monroe Doctrine was a policy vehicle for selective regional imperialism.

After World War II, Washington embarked on a policy of global imperialism involving worldwide military-economic expansion as epitomized in the Truman Doctrine, the Marshall Plan, the Containment Policy, foreign aid and loan programs, and large-scale movement by U.S. investors into Europe,

Africa, Asia, and the Middle East. But in implemening this globalism, the United States was confronted with the problem of nationalism. The rebellions that had destroyed the European colonial empires created many new states determined to defend and assert their newly won sovereignty. Indeed, this independent spirit even affected Latin America, manifesting itself in calls by indigenous economic nationalists for Latins to reestablish control over their domestic markets and resources. These nationalistic Third World nations looked justifiably with suspicion on almost any international activity by Western countries and, in particular, rejected sphere of influence concepts (such as the Monroe Doctrine) as neocolonialistic. Faced with the necessity of finding an innovative idea to act as a viable policy vehicle that would rationalize its expanded imperialist pretensions, Washington ultimately chose global anti-Communism. U.S. expansion was justified as a response to an "international Communist conspiracy" led by the Soviet Union intent on conquering the world to impose its "slavery" on innocent, unwilling people. Apologists for United States imperialism argued that, as the leader of the "free world," the United States had a duty to combat Communism wherever Washington decided that it represented a threat. As a result, it was argued, the United States was not being imperialistic in playing an interventionist international role, but instead was simply fulfilling its moral or legal obligations to help others defend themselves against direct or indirect Communist aggression. Washington's imperial activities in Latin America, which in the postwar period extended well beyond the Caribbean to encompass the whole continent, were an integral part of global empire-building and, as such, the policy vehicle of global anti-Communism was applied to the hemisphere. Latin America was, in other words, incorporated into the Cold War. Consequently, the Monroe Doctrine, whose use had historically been limited to the Caribbean and which was somewhat in disrepute because of its sphere of influence connotations, tended to be underplayed in favor of global anti-Communism as the policy vehicle for U.S. expansion in Latin America.

One important aspect of anti-Communism is that it provides a much broader basis for U.S. imperialism than does the Monroe Doctrine. The Doctrine, as mentioned previously, was essentially a reactive policy designed primarily to counter explicit attempts by extrahemispheric countries to gain political, economic, or military influence in Latin America that might menace Washington's hegemony. Anti-Communism, however, opens the way for a multifaceted and especially more aggressive U.S. policy since it does not require a clear threat from a specific external power as an excuse to take action. The mere presence of revolutionary forces suffices. This means that the United States, using the rhetoric of global anti-Communism, can move directly against Latin Americans who resist or challenge U.S. domination, a procedure that is difficult to justify under the Monroe Doctrine. "Recalcitrants" are simply labelled Communists and thus become enemies of the United States and the West in the world power struggle; therefore they qualify as targets for Washington's repression. The ease with which one can designate a group or even a government as Communist or as agents of international Communism (generally any nationalist or antiimperialist position is equated with Communism) confers on Washington almost unlimited opportunities to pursue its imperialist policies, establishing and preserving its exploitive empire on the grounds that it is protecting Latin America from an "alien ideology" incompatible with the inter-American system. The United States uses its economic-military influence to force the OAS to pass anti-Communist resolutions, facilitating U.S. control by giving it a veneer of hemispheric legitimacy.

During 1945 to 1960, the OAS acquiesced to Washington's demands that the mere existence of Marxist *ideology* in the hemisphere be considered tantamount to foreign (Russian or Chinese) aggression, thereby laying the groundwork for U.S. initiatives under the Doctrine if necessary. Thus the Monroe Doctrine was not totally discarded. Instead, what emerged from 1945 to 1960 was a complex and often vague combination of global anti-Communism and the Monroe Doctrine as the rationale for U.S. intervention. The stress placed on anti-Communism was intended to bring Washington's Latin American policy in line with the global policy approach.

The second contextual change centers on U.S.-Latin economic relations. Immediately after World War II, the United States became progressively more dependent on Latin America's vast natural resources as its own domestic supplies proved inadequate to meet demands. The internal growth of the United States required that the Hemisphere's riches be exploited. In addition, Washington relied on the area for strategic raw materials to help fuel its military-industrial complex and thereby give the United States the capacity to pursue its global expansion. U.S. private capital poured into Latin America displacing the Europeans who were forced to liquidate many of their remaining hemispheric holdings to finance their war efforts and postwar reconstruction. In addition to moving beyond their traditional Caribbean bailiwick into southern Latin America, U.S. investments also became more diverse as they penetrated economic sectors that previously had not attracted much attention (services and industry). The U.S. economic stake in Latin America took on increasing scope, complexity, and strategic importance in the postwar years. These developments meant that a rather sophisticated approach was required to protect U.S. interests, especially after 1960 when Western Germany, Japan and the Communist countries began to mount challenges to U.S. economic primacy in the hemisphere. The Monroe Doctrine does not possess the necessary sophistication—its orientation toward crude gunboat diplomacy and short-term military intervention makes it useful primarily for dealing with crisis situations in small countries rather than an instrument for exercising control on a routinized basis in larger societies. Consequently, it has been deemphasized as a policy vehicle for U.S. economic hegemony, being largely replaced by the Alliance For Progress. Joint "aid" programs give Washington great influence in practically all important political-economic decisions in the Latin nations and provide well-established channels through which the U.S. can protect its manifold interests.

The third and final contextual change relates to Washington's changing perceptions regarding challenges to its hemispheric empire. In the pre-World War II era, the United States tended to view threats to its Latin sphere of influence primarily in terms of intrusions by extrahemispheric nations (such as England, France, Germany). Indeed, the original Monroe Doctrine, as well as many of its corollaries, was motivated in part by a desire to eliminate all foreign competition in the area, thereby giving Washington a free hand to establish and/or extend its primacy. Even today the United States has not renounced the Doctrine, preferring to keep it available as a possible rationale for preventing external powers from achieving significant influence in Latin America.

But in the 1950s and especially since 1960, the most serious challenge to the United States was seen as coming from inside rather than outside the hemisphere. Within Latin America strong revolutionary nationalist and socialist movements, epitomized by the Cuban Revolution, emerged which were dedicated to liberating their countries from U.S. control. Neither the Monroe Doctrine, with its accent on meeting exogenous threats, nor simplistic global anti-Communism, premised on an "international conspiracy," were adequate policy guides for responding to indigenous revolutionary movements. Beginning with the Kennedy Administration they were deemphasized.

The Monroe Doctrine in particular was made a shambles by the success of the Cuban Revolution and its ramifications, and the United States was forced to alter the ideological basis for its military-political-economic hegemony. Washington deemphasized the Doctrine in favor of hemispheric "partnership." This new approach manifesting itself in the Alliance and in counterinsurgency was based on a closer working relationship between the United States and its client elites in the Latin countries. Such ideological adaptation provided Washington not only with policy vehicles allowing it to respond to *indigenous* challenges to its hemispheric domination, but also with a facade behind which it could continue to manipulate and exploit the region.

These three contextual changes have led the United States to modify its mode of imperial control in Latin America. The Monroe Doctrine, because it is not compatible with the new approaches and context, has been pushed into the background. Historically the Doctrine has served best as a rationale for direct, often large-scale unilateral military intervention. But the United States uses such methods only as a last resort. Today, the United States asserts its domination primarily through economic penetration and military support for client regimes or special groups such as the Latin armed forces. In short, *indirect control* utilizing indigenous elites economically and militarily dependent on the United States has generally been substituted for the unilateral direct action implied in the Monroe Doctrine. This approach to building and maintaining empires has been operationalized in the Alliance and in the various internal security programs that serve as Washington's contemporary imperial rationales. It has been camouflaged in the writings describing the process as "externally induced" modernization or "nation building." The partnership notion embodied in the Alliance and counter-insurgency extends the scope of U.S. imperialism and makes it more dynamic, since Washington achieves regularized, day-to-day entry into and involvement in many different levels of Latin American society and decision making from economic/social planning to political/military indoctrination and internal security activities.

It should be noted that the success of previous interventions under the Monroe Doctrine aided in setting the stage for these current modes of imperial control. The Doctrine, especially as applied in the Caribbean, assisted in creating open access for foreign capital, and the United States was then able to acquire its present massive economic influence. The Doctrine also facilitated the establishment of client governments that the United States supports today and that act as Washington's local agents by encouraging additional U.S. investment, suppressing domestic radicals, protecting existing United States economic interests, and backing U.S. positions in the OAS. Paradoxically, then, the Monroe Doctrine's contributions in furthering U.S. empire-building may have helped engender a situation where the Doctrine itself is generally no longer needed to maintain or extend Washington's domain. It is, of course, conceivable that the Doctrine may be useful as a policy vehicle for future unilateral United States interventions and for this reason has not been repudiated.

It is the convergence of the above factors—the shift from regional to global imperialism, increasingly extensive and complex economic interests, altered perceptions regarding threats to the empire, and new modes of control—that have resulted in the Monroe Doctrine's deemphasis as the policy vehicle for U.S. hegemony in the western hemisphere. While the rationale has changed, Washington continues to look upon Latin America as its special sphere of influence and exploitation.

The Latin American experience has made the United States the neo-colonialist power par excellence in the world. Washington has used the western hemisphere as a laboratory for its relations with Third World countries. It has taken those policies and practices that worked in building an informal empire and applied them in building a global empire that today includes clients in Europe, Asia, Africa, and the Middle East. United States' success in this endeavor has not gone unnoticed by other nations aspiring to a neocolonial role. For example, Western European states such as France and England are trying to structure their postcolonial relations with many Afro-Asian countries on the contemporary U.S.-Latin American model. They have, in effect, become students of U.S. imperialism. Because Washington's evolving hemispheric policy has worldwide implications, it merits close scrutiny by everyone committed to combatting neocolonialism.

APPENDIX

TABLE 1
U.S. Investments in the Third World 1960 to 1967 (in Millions of Dollars)

	1960	1961	1962	1963	1964	1965	1966	1967
Asia	2,291	2,482	2,495	2,784	3,062	3,611	3,891	4,282
Africa	925	1,070	1,246	1,423	1,629	1,904	2,078	2,277
Latin America	8,387	8,166	8,472	8,657	8,932	9,371	9,854	10,213

Source. *The Rockefeller Report on the Americas,* New York Times Edition (Chicago, Ill.: Quadrangle Books, 1969), pp. 90–91.

In the Third World, Latin America continues to be the major area for U.S. investment. Total U.S. investments in Latin America are almost double those for both Africa and Asia.

TABLE 2
Private Investments in Latin America 1897 to 1958 (in Millions of Dollars)

	1897	1914	1929	1946	1958
United States	308	1,700	5,429	3,672	9,769
England	2,060	3,700	4,500[a]	3,575	2,547[a]
France	628	1,200	454[a]	307	—
Germany	—	900	700[a]	—	160

Source. United States Senate, United States Business and Labor in Latin America (A study Prepared at the Request of the Sub-Committee on American Republics Affairs of the Committee on Foreign Relations by the University of Chicago Research Center on Economic Development and Cultural Change), January 22, 1960.

[a] Approximate. European investment reigned supreme in Latin America until World War I. With the forced liquidation of European assets during the war years, the United States was able to expand its own investments and gain predominance for the first time in the postwar period. The depression set back all investment in the area, but the relative superiority of U.S. investment continued and was dramatically accentuated after World War II.

TABLE 3

Geographic Distribution of U.S. Investments in Latin America 1897 to 1969 (in Millions of Dollars)

	West Indies and Central America	South America
1897	270.4	37.9
1914	1283.2	365.7
1929	2415.4	3013.8
1943	1176.7	1544.5
1950	1488.0	2957.0
1960	2515.0	5702.0
1969	3080.0[a]	7952.0

Source. Survey of Current Business, U.S. Department of Commerce, September 1960, (*40* (9), p. 20) and October 1970, (*50*, (10), p. 28) and Cleona Lewis, *America's Stake in International Investment* (Washington: The Brookings Institution, 1938).

[a] Approximate. Early U.S. overseas investments were concentrated in the nearby Caribbean. As the Caribbean became saturated and European influence elsewhere in the hemisphere declined, the United States moved into South America with considerable investments. The post-World War I shift from the Caribbean to South America continued into the World War II period. After World War II, the trend experienced a dramatic upturn, South American investments being nearly twice those of the Caribbean at the end of the 1950s.

TABLE 4

Industrial and Export Growth Rates of Leading Nations 1953 to 1959

Country	Export Growth Rate (Percent)	Industrial Growth Rate (Percent)
Japan	19.5	12.7
West Germany	14.5	3.7
Italy	11.8	7.4
France	5.5	9.1
Sweden	7.2	3.7
United Kingdom	3.7	2.5
United States	3.4	1.3

Source. Shinohara, *Growth and Cycles*, p. 46 as cited in K. Beida, *The Structure and Operation of the Japanese Economy* (Sydney, Australia: Wiley & Sons Australasia Pty. Ltd., 1970), p. 12.

While the United States enjoyed an undisputed economic superiority in the early post-World War II era both Europe and Japan reemerged in the 1950s as significant economic rivals.

TABLE 5

Japan's Foreign Investments by Region and Industry 1951 to 1967 (in Millions of Dollars)

		Amount, Millions of U.S. Dollars	Percent
Region	North America	348.5	29.6
	Europe	27.2	2.3
	Oceania	11.4	1.0
	Latin America	329.3	27.9
	Asia	226.6	19.2
	Middle and Near East	220.5	18.7
	Africa	15.0	1.3
	Total	1178.4	100.0
Economic Sector	Natural resource development	504.4	42.8
	Trade	187.9	15.9
	Finance and Transportation	41.8	3.5
	Manufacturing and others	444.3	37.7

Source. The Economic White Paper, Government, Tokyo, 1968, as cited in K. Beida, *The Structure and Operation of the Japanese Economy* (Sydney, Australia: Wiley & Sons Australasia Pty. Ltd., 1970), p. 35.

Note. 1. The source of regional breakdown is the Ministry of Finance.

2. Analysis by industry was made by the Economic Planning Agency. Investments in natural resource development are those made with the purpose of importing the commodity exploited thereby. Investments in trade are those made in relation to overseas activities of trading firms or their sales agencies.

Japan has become an important economic force in Latin America. Japanese investments in Latin America are second only to its investments in North America, and far outrun its investments in Asia.

TABLE 6

Geographic Distribution of Japanese Subsidiaries and Joint Ventures Abroad, at the End of March 1966

Area	Amount, Millions of U.S. Dollars
North America	134.3
Central and South America	156.2
Asia	80.5
Europe	19.9
Germany	(4.36)
Belgium	(3.33)
France	(2.92)
Italy	(2.62)
Portugal	(1.59)
United Kingdom	(1.29)
Luxembourg	(1.00)
Switzerland	(0.83)
Ireland	(0.71)
Spain	(0.41)
Netherlands	(0.35)
Greece	(.020)
Lichtenstein	(0.04)
Malta	(0.22)
Africa	8.2
Oceania	5.5
Total	404.6

Source. O.E.C.D., Liberalisation of International Capital Movements: Japan, Paris, 1968, pp. 20–21 as cited in K. Beida, *The Structure and Operation of the Japanese Economy* (Sydney, Australia: Wiley & Sons Australasia Pty. Ltd., 1970), p. 228.

Subsidiaries and joint ventures, where Japan controls the major decision-making power are the chief modes of Japanese economic penetration in Latin America. Japan has more dollars in subsidiaries in Latin America than other area including North America.

BIBLIOGRAPHY

Aguilar, Alonso. *Pan Americanism: From Monroe to the Present* (New York: Monthly Review Press, 1968).

Bailey, Norman A. *Latin America in World Politics* (New York: Walker and Company, 1967).

Barber, Willard F. and C. Neale Ronning. *Internal Security and Military Power: Counterinsurgency and Civic Action in Latin America* (Columbus, Ohio: Ohio State University Press, 1966).

Bemis, Samuel F. *The Latin American Policy of the United States* (New York: Harcourt Brace and World, 1943).

Bernstein, Marvin D. *Foreign Investment in Latin America* (New York: Alfred A. Knopf, 1966).

Connell-Smith, Gordon. *The Inter-American System* (New York: Oxford University Press, 1966).

Faulkner, Harold V. *The Decline of Laissez Faire: The Economic History of the United States*, Vol. VII (New York: Holt, Rinehart and Winston, 1962).

Foreign Assistance Act For 1967, hearings before the House Foreign Affairs Committee, April 11, 1967 statement.

Freeman, J. and S. Nearing. *Dollar Diplomacy* (New York: Monthly Review Press, 1966).

Gerassi, John. *The Great Fear in Latin America* revised ed. (New York: Collier Books, 1965).

Gil, Federico. *Latin American-United States Relations* (New York: Harcourt Brace Jovanovich, 1971).

Goff, Fred and Michael Locker. "The Violence of Domination: U.S. Power and the Dominican Republic" in Irving L. Horowitz, Josue de Castro, and John Gerassi, eds. *Latin American Radicalism* (New York: Random House, 1969), pp. 249–291.

Grayson, George W. "The Era of the Good Neighbor," *Current History*, 56 (June, 1969), 327–332.

Green, David. *The Containment of Latin America* (Chicago: Quadrangle Books, 1971).

Magdoff, Harry. *The Age of Imperialism* (New York: Monthly Review Press, 1969).

Mecham, J. Lloyd. *A Survey of United States-Latin American Relations* (Boston: Houghton Mifflin Company, 1965).

Morray, J. P. "The United States and Latin America" in James Petras and Maurice Zeitlin, eds. *Latin America: Reform or Revolution* (Greenwich, Conn.: Fawcett Publications, 1968), pp. 99–119.

Olden, Herman. *U.S. Over Latin America* (New York: International Publishers, 1955).

Perkins, Dexter. *A History of the Monroe Doctrine* (Boston: Little, Brown, and Company, 1963).

Petras, James. "Revolution and Guerrilla Movements in Latin America: Venezuela, Colombia, Guatemala, and Peru" in James Petras and Maurice Zeitlin, eds. *Latin America: Reform or Revolution* (Greenwich, Conn.: Fawcett Publications, 1968), pp. 329–369.

Poetker, Joel S. *The Monroe Doctrine* (Columbus, Ohio: Merrill Books, 1967).

The Rockefeller Report on the Americas (Chicago: Quadrangle Books, 1969).

Survey of Current Business (Washington: U.S. Department of Commerce, 1969-1970).

Taylor, George Rogers. *The Transportation Revolution, 1815-1860; The Economic History of the United States,* Vol. IV (New York: Holt, Rinehart and Winston, 1951).

Tulchin, Joseph S. *The Aftermath of War* (New York: New York University Press, 1971).

Whitaker, Arthur P. *The United States and the Independence of Latin America, 1800-1830* (New York: Russell and Russell, 1962).

Williams, William Appleman. *The Roots of the Modern American Empire* (New York: Random House, 1969).

Wolpin, Miles, "External Political Socialization as a Source of Conservative Military Behavior in the 'Third World' " (Unpublished manuscript) (Antigonish, Nova Scotia: St. Francis Xavier University, Department of Political Science).